Neil Hanson is the author of several acclaimed works of narrative history: *The Custom of the Sea*, *The Dreadful Judgement*, *The Confident Hope of a Miracle*, *The Unknown Soldier* and *First Blitz*. He lives in Yorkshire with his family.

For more information on Neil Hanson and his books, see his website at www.neilhanson.co.uk

Praise for *First Blitz*:

'The 1940s bombing raids over London have taken such a powerful grip upon our imagination that the existence of an earlier Blitz, in World War I, will come to many readers as a complete surprise. Yet as Neil Hanson . . . demonstrates in this gripping and well-researched book, it was in many ways more terrifying'
Daily Mail

'Neil Hanson is that rare beast – a popular historian who never talks down to his readers. Clearly and engagingly written, his book puts more academic historians to shame by discovering a big subject, investigating it thoroughly and drawing bold but far-reaching conclusions from it'   *Sunday Telegraph*

'Using first-hand witnesses plus government war records, Hanson draws a powerful picture of the impact of these first air raids'
Time Out

'History invariably falls into two categories: academic and narrative . . . To marry the two is a rare art – and it is an art Neil Hanson has mastered . . . This is a compelling story compellingly told . . . Gripping'   *Navy News*

Praise for *The Unknown Soldier*:

'In Neil Hanson's prose, the dark ceremonial of Remembrance Sunday (has) an almost unbearable poignancy . . . A beautifully illustrated book that has all the sombre grandeur of the Beethoven funeral march'   John Crossland, *Sunday Times*

'Neil Hanson had the imaginative idea of combining the story of the Unknown Soldier – the symbolic body buried in Westminster Abbey to represent all the myriad legions of Britain's missing – with the individual stories of three of those missing. His researches in four countries – the homelands of his subjects, plus France, the land where all three fought and died – have yielded an astonishing mine of information, which Hanson, a non-academic historian and an excellent writer, skilfully blends into an absorbing and consistently moving narrative framework . . . The story of the Unknown Soldier is itself a fascinating one, revealing the enormous impact the losses of the Great War had on the fabric of Britain . . . Hanson tells the story fully and well (and) puts flesh on the bones of the unknown soldier in the life-and-death stories of his three protagonists' *Literary Review*

'One of the best books I've read on the insanity of life in the trenches' *Daily Mail*

'The books that are read most widely are . . . the ones that allow families to see the way the war invaded every household and left traces and wounds palpable to this day. This is the register of *The Unknown Soldier*, Neil Hanson's account of British and German families trying to cope with the loss of sons who had no known grave' *Times Literary Supplement*

Praise for *The Confident Hope of a Miracle:*

'The launching of the Spanish Armada was one of the most extraordinary episodes of the Elizabethan age. Neil Hanson has written a truly gripping account of the armada's progress – from triumphant departure to doom on the high seas. His narrative is epic in scope and meticulous in detail – a vividly conjured tale of intrigue and heroism, tempest and shipwreck'
Giles Milton, author of *Nathaniel's Nutmeg*

'This year's greatest triumph of sheer driving narrative and a masterpiece of popular history . . . There are passages that can stand comparison with the finest historical prose but what is just as attractive is Hanson's originality (and) impeccable scholarship'
Glasgow Herald

'An exceptionally vivid account . . . Hanson is essentially a narrative historian with all the talents required of that genre: a gimlet eye for interesting detail, an ability to convey atmosphere and a story-teller's instinct for pace. He has written a marvellous book'
Daily Telegraph

'Hanson's narrative is brilliant – melding deep research and page-turning writing. When he deals with the disaster of the Armada's homeward passage, battling monstrous seas and shipwreck, he reaches dramatic heights that make him the equal of Parkman or Prescott' *Sunday Express*

Praise for *The Dreadful Judgement:*

'Conjures up the vanished city . . . Hanson writes with knowledge and verve, as if making a television documentary on a natural disaster . . . informative and lively account' *Sunday Times*

'Hanson's prose is animated by the ferocious energy of the fire and seems to be guided by its inexorable movement. He creates the literary equivalent of the special effects in a disaster movie . . . compelling' *Daily Telegraph*

'Popular narrative history at its best, well researched, imaginatively and dramatically written . . . the author marshals his story and his mass of contemporary quotation with great skill' *The Times Literary Supplement*

Praise for *The Custom of the Sea:*

'An engrossing account' *Sunday Times*

'A terrific story . . . a riveting read' *Spectator*

'Neil Hanson has done an excellent job of reconstructing the true story of captain Tim Dudley and his doomed crew' *Maxim*

Also by Neil Hanson

THE CUSTOM OF THE SEA
THE DREADFUL JUDGEMENT
THE CONFIDENT HOPE OF A MIRACLE
THE UNKNOWN SOLDIER
FIRST BLITZ

and published by Corgi Books

ESCAPE FROM GERMANY

The Greatest PoW Break-out of the First World War

NEIL HANSON

CORGI BOOKS

TRANSWORLD PUBLISHERS
61–63 Uxbridge Road, London W5 5SA
A Random House Group Company
www.transworldbooks.co.uk

ESCAPE FROM GERMANY
A CORGI BOOK: 9780552155496

First published in Great Britain
in 2011 by Doubleday
an imprint of Transworld Publishers
Corgi edition published 2012

Addresses for Random House Group Ltd companies outside the UK
can be found at: www.randomhouse.co.uk
The Random House Group Ltd Reg. No. 954009

The Random House Group Limited supports the Forest Stewardship Council
(FSC®), the leading international forest-certification organization. Our books
carrying the FSC label are printed on FSC®-certified paper. FSC is the only forest-
certification scheme endorsed by the leading environmental organizations,
including Greenpeace. Our paper-procurement policy can be found at
www.randomhouse.co.uk/environment.

Typeset in 11/14pt Minion by Falcon Oast Graphic Art Lts.
Printed and bound by CPI Group (UK) Ltd, Croydon, CR0 4YY.

1 3 5 7 9 10 8 6 4 2

To Lynn, Jack and Drew, for whom there is no escape

CONTENTS

INTRODUCTION

Many years ago, while I was off school with some childhood ailment, I was rummaging through my father's bookshelves and chanced upon Eric Williams's *The Wooden Horse* – the story of a daring escape from a German prisoner-of-war camp, Stalag Luft III, during the Second World War. Gripped by the ingenuity and bravery of those prisoners in their sealed world behind the wire, I finished the book in a single sitting and went on to read several other such stories, including *Colditz* and *The Great Escape*. If it puzzled me then that there didn't appear to be any stories of First World War escapes, I didn't pursue the thought.

Years later, when I began to carry out research on the First World War, I soon discovered that there were many escape stories of equal, and even greater, resourcefulness and daring than those I'd read in my youth. Almost all were long out of print and largely forgotten. The accounts of those escapes were fascinating enough in their own right, but they also offered compelling insights into an era that was almost within my own compass – my grandfather had fought in the Great War and my father was born during it – yet, in its beliefs and attitudes, seemed impossibly remote from the society in which we now live.

It was a world in which a gentleman's honour – and by definition all officers were gentlemen, at least until the murderous attrition of the war began to allow a few others to rise from the ranks – was his most prized possession, and in which an officer had only to give his word that he would return and he would be allowed out of his prison camp for a country stroll.

Even stranger, imprisoned officers were allowed to communicate not just with their families but with their banks, their tailors and the shops with which they held accounts. While their less fortunate peers often endured misery, cruelty and semi-starvation, men of means held in the more benign camps could live in relative comfort, even luxury. The rigidities of the class system were also maintained behind the wire. So powerful was the Englishman's belief in the natural order of things that, even when he was subjected to deprivation, near-starvation and random or systemic brutality, it remained inconceivable that an officer would clean his room or make his bed. An orderly – a working-class other-ranks prisoner – was incarcerated alongside him purely to do the manual work for him.

So entrenched were such attitudes that it was a wonder the officers didn't make the orderlies dig their escape tunnels for them as well. It was one task they performed for themselves, even though the orderlies were much more accustomed to such work and, numbering a few ex-miners among them, would probably have taken far less time to complete it.

Class and rank also dictated whether a prisoner had to carry out forced labour for his captors, and whether he was expected to make the effort to escape. Break-outs by other-ranks prisoners were comparatively rare, partly because they usually lacked the financial and other resources available to officers, including the time in which to plan and carry out escapes: they had to work, either labouring for their captors or as orderlies for their officers. The patronizing official attitudes that regarded 'common soldiers' as mere sheep – followers of orders, incapable of acting on their own initiative – also led to the assumption that, once captured, they would show little inclination to attempt escape.

By contrast, officers were expected to resist capture at all costs – unlike their men, returning officer prisoners of war were required to provide a signed statement about the manner of and reasons for their capture that, if deemed unsatisfactory, might lead to disciplinary action. If captured, it was the stated duty of every officer to attempt to escape. If successful, they could again return to active service in the battle against 'the Hun', but even if their efforts failed, the extra men and resources required to contain them within their PoW camps, and to search for and apprehend them if they broke out, would have a demonstrable effect on the German war machine.

Whatever army regulations might have said about their duty, not all British officers were made of such stern stuff. Many – the majority – opted for the line of least resistance and made little if any attempt to escape, perhaps reasoning that it was better to live on their knees than die on their feet, dangling from the barbed wire or being shot at in the trenches. Yet while some chose self-preservation and a quiet life behind the wire, others were determined to break free and made repeated attempts to do so. Some individuals made as many as twenty separate escape attempts from up to a dozen different camps – and there were some 180 PoW camps in Germany alone, in addition to scores of forced-labour work *Kommandos* set up near mines, quarries, factories and so on. The Germans retaliated by concentrating these persistent escapees into special camps under stricter discipline and closer guard. The three most notorious were Fort Zorndorf in East Prussia, Fort 9 at Ingolstadt, and Holzminden, which was claimed to be the most closely guarded and escape-proof of them all. Yet, despite barbed wire, arc lights, attack dogs, sentries and patrolling guards armed with rifles and machine guns, escapes continued to be made.

Reading the stories of these habitual escapees, I was struck again and again by their daring, resourcefulness and persistence. These were men who allowed no obstacles, however huge, to deter them, and who, with quick wit and apparently inexhaustible good humour, performed miracles of improvisation, adaptation, courage and endurance that I suspect would be beyond most of us, their descendants, today.

During my research, I read scores of astonishing accounts of escapes and attempted escapes from Great War prisoner-of-war camps in Germany, France, England, Russia, Italy and

Turkey, but one stood out: the mass break-out from Holzminden in July 1918. In terms of the number of men who got out of the camp and the number who subsequently completed successful 'home runs' by crossing the border into neutral Holland, this one surpassed all others. This is the story of that break-out, a 'Great Escape' that rivals and indeed eclipses any of those far more celebrated Second World War escapes.

Neil Hanson, May 2011

CHAPTER 1

NO MERCY WILL BE SHOWN

The Maltreatment of Prisoners of War

'The Exodus' – when Holzminden opened in September 1917, other PoW camp commandants seized the chance to unload some of their most troublesome prisoners.

THE TAKING OF prisoners has always formed a significant part of wartime military operations, not only because every man captured was a potential soldier denied to the enemy, but also because, under interrogation, he might divulge invaluable intelligence about troop dispositions and deployments, strengths and weaknesses, strategy and tactics. Head counts of prisoners could be useful in calculating the extent of a battlefield military success and assessing the morale of enemy forces, and a few modest economic benefits might also be accrued by the captors, including the acquisition of weapons, equipment and the personal property of prisoners, and the diversion of any relief supplies sent to them from abroad. However, only in exceptional circumstances were such benefits likely to exceed the costs: holding prisoners required a considerable commitment of often scarce resources, such as foodstuffs, medicines, clothing, bedding and other supplies, facilities to house them and, above all, manpower to guard them.

The number of prisoners captured in the First World War was staggering – hundreds of times higher than in any previous war. Between 7 and 8.5 million men of all nations were captured by the combatants and incarcerated in prisoner-of-war camps. In 1916–17, Austria-Hungary alone held 1.8 million prisoners, the majority Russian, at a cost of 2.5 per cent of its total war expenditure – more, even, than it spent on explosives, motor vehicles or aircraft.

The combatant nations might have hoped to recoup at least part of the cost through 'some *ad hoc* transfer of funds' or from reparations in the event that they won the war, but in the short term, all the expense had to be borne by the captors. If that was a problem for all of the combatants in the First World War, it was particularly so for Germany. After four years of war, including fighting on two fronts for the first three years, Germany held 2.5 million prisoners, almost four times as many as Britain and France combined. The majority of German prisoners were Russian – 92,000 Russian soldiers had surrendered at the battle of Tannenberg alone – but by the end of the war, the total of British Empire servicemen who were or had been prisoners of war in German hands had reached 191,652. Of those, around 177,000 were still held captive at the Armistice, the remainder having died, been released on medical grounds, escaped or been transferred to internment in the Netherlands or Switzerland, as a result of an agreement between the warring powers.

Even in the middle of the most bloody and ferocious wars, combatant nations had almost always maintained some form of diplomatic contact, albeit often through a third party, and even when 'practically all human and material resources were being directed by both sides towards the war effort, and restraint in the conduct of war was progressively abandoned, there remained a national interest in the heart of enemy territory which, in most cases, seemed to necessitate some form of contact and negotiation: civilian internees and prisoners of war'.

That also held true for the First World War, and one of its more bizarre paradoxes was that, at the same time as the various national political leaders and generals were committing themselves to the disruption and destruction of not just the enemy's forces but the infrastructure of its state and the starvation of its population, they were simultaneously forced to dispatch money and supplies to feed their own soldiers being held captive. They continued to do so even though they knew that much of what they sent would be seized and diverted to other uses. It defied all logic: it would have been far more efficient and far less expensive for both sides to arrange the rapid exchange of prisoners so that, instead of being held captive at a prodigious cost in food, facilities and manpower, they could be returned to their own nation. Of course, returned prisoners would then have been free to take up arms once more, but the relative numbers would have been unchanged on both sides. However, no general or politician on either side was willing even to entertain such a radical notion and, as a result, captive soldiers in their hundreds of thousands continued to languish in PoW camps.

Two distinguished jurists lamented the woeful inefficiency and injustice of such a situation: 'In view of the cumbersomeness and expense of the whole machinery of prisons [for PoWs] and the cost of maintaining prisoners and providing them with the treatment they have a right to expect, is it impracticable to suggest that on capture, they should definitely lose their combatant status and be either sent home on parole or interned in a neutral country?' Evidently it was, for no such arrangement was made until the closing stages of the war. Even then it was restricted to those so badly wounded or ill that they were no longer fit for active service, and the very long-term prisoners who formed a tiny proportion of the whole.

Other than the fact that every PoW was one less enemy soldier to face on the battlefield, the only significant advantage that the warring nations could derive from holding prisoners was by using them as forced labour, and most authorities acknowledged that such labour could confer considerable financial and other benefits on the captors. The scale of recruitment into the armed forces had caused labour crises in all the belligerent nations. Sixty million men of all nations had taken up arms – between one-third and two-thirds of the entire labour force of each combatant country.

Yet while stripping the manufacturing industry of much of its labour, the belligerent governments were also demanding huge increases of production in all kinds of war matériel: munitions, tanks, trucks, aircraft, barbed wire, steel helmets, uniforms and boots, and myriad other manufactured goods.

The resultant void was only partly filled by recruiting previously unemployed men, women, old and unfit men, relatively young boys and girls, and foreign workers, where they were available. Prisoners of war provided another substantial and ever-growing pool of labour on which to draw.

In the early stages of the war, prisoners of all sides had been largely either left idle in their camps or put to work on land-improvement schemes that had little direct impact on agricultural or industrial production. However, as the hopes of an early victory nurtured by both sides were seen to be chimerical, and the numbers of prisoners steadily increased in parallel with the shortages of labour caused by mass conscription, PoWs on both sides were put to productive work. By 1916, 80 per cent of enlisted men and NCOs held in Germany were at work, though officers remained idle.

All authorities acknowledged that 'purposeful and regular employment' was beneficial to the prisoners' morale and physical health, 'and labour, whether voluntary or coerced', was also permitted under the Hague Rules – The Regulations Respecting the Laws and Customs of War – that had been agreed by all the combatants at The Hague Convention for the Pacific Settlement of International Disputes in 1899, and confirmed with some further amendments in 1907. The Hague Rules allowed the captors of prisoners of war to 'utilize their labour, except in the case of officers, according to their ranks and capacities', with NCOs filling supervisory roles over the enlisted men who were required to perform manual work. Under the Hague Rules, PoWs were not supposed to be employed within thirty kilometres of the front line, and their work was not to be humiliating, or excessive, or have anything to do with 'the operations of the war'. Interpretations of the latter prohibition varied greatly – some prisoners were employed in digging trenches, clearing minefields, loading ammunition and doing other war work – but even where they were used in industry or agriculture, which had no direct impact on the war effort, they were freeing others to fight or carry out war work.

Trade unions and civilian workers were often bitterly opposed to the employment of PoWs, suspecting that they were being used to depress wages and 'de-skill' previously specialized occupations. Some even believed that the use of PoW labour would foster the growth of 'vested interests dependent on the continuation of the war'. In theory, any work carried out by prisoners was required to be paid at rates commensurate with 'the tariff in force for soldiers of the national army employed on similar tasks . . . or at rates proportional to the work to be executed'. Some labour organizations actually demanded that PoWs be rewarded at above the standard local rate, in order to ensure that they were only taken on if no civilians were available. The balance of what prisoners had earned, less the cost of their board and lodging, was supposed to be held in escrow for them and paid to them on release.

Unions had reason to be concerned: the scale of PoW employment was staggering. In 1917–18, nine hundred thousand Russian captives were employed in Germany and another million in Austria-Hungary, the majority working in agriculture in an attempt to alleviate food shortages. Britain and France also made use of German PoWs in this way, with a few thousand prisoners in Britain set to work to bring marginal lands into production, and another fifty thousand employed on the farms of France, where 1.5 million boys and old men and at least 3 million women were already at work: they were filling the void left by the recruitment of more than 5 million agricultural workers into the army. The economic value of the employment of prisoners varied greatly from nation to nation, but Germany's *de facto* leader in the latter years of the war, General Erich Ludendorff, was in no doubt about their crucial role in the German war effort, claiming that prisoners of war were 'of the utmost importance in all fields of war activity'.

The principle governing the act of taking prisoners and sparing the lives of antagonists had evolved over the centuries from 'an act of grace' to a recognition of the rights of 'the helpless'. In earlier conflicts, what was deemed to be hopeless resistance was held to justify a refusal to give quarter. On several occasions during the Napoleonic Wars, while laying siege to fortified towns like Almeida, Ciudad Rodrigo and Badajoz, the Duke of Wellington declared 'the strict rule' that if the defenders declined the opportunity to surrender when offered the chance to do so, 'their lives were forfeited on the place being taken by storm'. Even as late as

1898, a US commander in the Spanish–American War was permitted to give no quarter if in dire straits and when his own position 'made it impossible for him to cumber himself with prisoners'. This dispensation applied not merely to 'men falling into the hands of the captor, either fighting or wounded on the field' but also to those 'in hospital, by individual surrender or capitulation, all disabled men or officers in the field or elsewhere, if captured, and all enemies who have thrown away their arms and ask for quarter'.

However, in the following year, 1899, the US became a signatory to the Hague Rules governing the conduct of war. They stipulated that prisoners were 'in the power of the hostile Government, but not of the individuals or corps who capture[d] them', and imposed a blanket prohibition on the killing or wounding of enemies who had 'surrendered at discretion, having thrown down their arms, or possessing no longer the means of defending themselves, and also against the declaration that no quarter will be given'. In all, nine of the articles in the Rules were relevant to the treatment of a prisoner of war:

Article 4

Prisoners of war are in the power of the hostile Government, but not of the individuals or corps who capture them. They must be humanely treated. All their personal belongings, except arms, horses, and military papers, remain their property.

Article 5

Prisoners of war may be interned in a town, fortress, camp, or other place, and bound not to go beyond certain fixed limits, but they cannot be confined except as an indispensable measure of safety and only while the circumstances which necessitate the measure continue to exist.

Article 6

The State may utilize the labour of prisoners of war according to their rank and aptitude, officers excepted. The tasks shall not be excessive and shall have no connection with the operations of the war. Prisoners may be authorized to work for the public service, for private persons, or on their own account. Work done for the State is paid for at the rates in force for work of a similar kind done by soldiers of the national army, or, if there are none in force, at a rate according to the work executed. When the work is for other branches of the public service or for private persons the conditions are settled in agreement with the military authorities. The wages of the prisoners shall go towards improving their position, and the balance shall be paid them on their release, after deducting the cost of their maintenance.

Article 7

The Government into whose hands prisoners of war have fallen is charged with their maintenance. In the absence of a special agreement between the belligerents, prisoners of war shall be treated as regards board, lodging, and clothing on the same footing as the troops of the Government who captured them.

Article 8

Prisoners of war shall be subject to the laws, regulations, and orders in force in the army of the State in whose power they are. Any act of insubordination justifies the adoption towards them of such measures of severity as may be considered necessary. Escaped prisoners who are retaken before being able to rejoin their own army or before leaving the territory occupied by the army which captured them are liable to disciplinary punishment. Prisoners who, after succeeding in escaping, are again taken prisoners, are not liable to any punishment on account of the previous flight.

Article 9

Every prisoner of war is bound to give, if he is questioned on the subject, his true name and rank, and if he infringes this rule, he is liable to have the advantages given to prisoners of his class curtailed.

Article 10

Prisoners of war may be set at liberty on parole if the laws of their country allow, and, in such cases, they are bound, on their personal honour, scrupulously to fulfil, both towards their own Government and the Government by whom they were made prisoners, the engagements they have contracted. In such cases their own Government is bound neither to require of nor accept from them any service incompatible with the parole given.

Article 11
A prisoner of war cannot be compelled to accept his liberty on parole; similarly the hostile Government is not obliged to accede to the request of the prisoner to be set at liberty on parole.

Article 12
Prisoners of war liberated on parole and recaptured bearing arms against the Government to whom they had pledged their honour, or against the allies of that Government, forfeit their right to be treated as prisoners of war, and can be brought before the courts.

At the start of the war, the Hague Rules had been written into *The British Manual of Military Law* and the German equivalent, the *Kriegsbrauch* (Customs of War). *The War Book of the German General Staff* acknowledged that the

complete change in the conception of war introduced in recent times has in consequence changed all previous ideas as to the position and treatment of prisoners of war. Starting from the principle that only States and not private persons are in the position of enemies in time of war, and that an enemy who is disarmed and taken prisoner is no longer an object of attack, the doctrine of war captivity is entirely altered and the position of prisoners has become assimilated to that of the sick and wounded . . . they are the captives not of private individuals, that is to say of Commanders, Soldiers or Detachments of Troops, but . . . the captives of the State. But the State regards them as persons who have simply done their duty and obeyed the commands of their superiors, and in consequence regards their captivity not as penal but merely as precautionary. It therefore follows that the object of war captivity is simply to prevent the captives from taking any further part in the war, and that the State can, in fact, do everything which appears necessary for securing the captives, but nothing beyond that.

Whatever the Hague Rules and *The War Book of the German General Staff* might say, the Kaiser had articulated a very different policy in relation to prisoners of war when addressing troops embarking at Bremerhaven for the German colonies in China: 'As soon as you come to blows with the enemy, he will be beaten. No mercy will be shown. No prisoners will be taken.' That statement was later repudiated, and claims by the British government in October 1917 that the Kaiser had been forced to issue a special order requiring British prisoners of war in Germany to be properly treated led to a furious denial: 'The German Government repudiate most emphatically the insinuation . . . that a special order by the Emperor was needed before British prisoners could be assured of proper treatment.

Enemy prisoners in German hands have always been treated humanely and in a proper manner.'

However strenuously such allegations were denied, British propagandists continued to make claims about brutality to Allied prisoners in German PoW camps and German atrocities against civilians. They were brilliantly successful in swinging international opinion against Germany – so much so that Dr Josef Goebbels used the campaign as a model for Nazi propaganda during the Second World War. Allegations about ill-treatment of prisoners of war had to be rather more accurate after 1915, when the prison camps of all combatants in the war were opened to inspection, first by American representatives and then, after the US declaration of war in March 1917, by the Dutch or Swiss, who, in theory at least, could expose any demonstrable falsehoods. Nonetheless, both sides continued to issue propaganda claiming that their prisoners of war were being maltreated by the enemy, not merely in an attempt to influence international opinion but also to encourage their own soldiers to fight to the death rather than risk being captured.

While it was a simple matter to agree in principle the Laws of War on Land, governing *inter alia* the fair treatment of prisoners of war, in actual battlefield conditions it was a rather more complex task to decide the point at which fighting should be deemed to have ceased and the right to surrender commenced. Wounded men were often still capable of bearing arms, and during the First World War there were reported cases on both sides of men who signalled their surrender only to draw their enemies out of cover, then took up their arms and attacked them again.

All the combatant nations in the First World War had committed themselves to adhere to the Hague Rules, but in the event, the regulations proved inadequate in some circumstances and were further modified in 1917 and again in 1918, after negotiations between the British and German governments, presided over by representatives of the Dutch government.

The moment of greatest danger for any prisoner was the actual moment of surrender, and many men on both sides were undoubtedly killed in the act of attempting it. Whatever the Hague Rules might say, soldiers on the battle-field who had seen their comrades blown apart or gunned down were not always disposed to feel merciful towards those enemies they captured, an attitude summed up by the cynical aside of one senior officer that 'No man in this war has ever been killed with the bayonet unless he had his hands up first.'

Two prominent international jurists even gave apparent endorsement to the right of soldiers to carry out what amounted to executions of unarmed men, when they argued that 'It is not reasonable to expect men who are attacking a fortified position held by the enemy and who suffer inevitably far heavier casualties than the defenders, from avenging their losses . . . merely because [the enemy] cease to resist when they are on terms of equality with the assailant.'

If they survived the moment of capture, prisoners remained in lesser, but still significant, jeopardy and often suffered harsh treatment as they were moved back through the lines: 'Between the place of capture and the prison, especially in early days, the conditions were barbarous and abominable, the civilian population showing greater brutality than the military guards.' Many wounded prisoners died within a few days of being taken captive and many British soldiers believed that medical care was deliberately withheld from their comrades to reduce the number of prisoners that the Germans had to house and feed: 'It was not an uncommon sight to see an English soldier looking like death, holding up an arm which was a mass of blood, straw, dirt and raw flesh. I heard that the reason given for this was that all minor wounds were left for three days, because at the end of that time, they (the Hun doctors) would know whether the wound was a dirty one or not!'

There were some glaring exceptions, but conditions for prisoners of war usually improved once they reached the prison camp where they were to be incarcerated. Once there, the overall survival rate of British prisoners of war was much better than that of the soldiers in the trenches, though mortality was shockingly high in comparison to that of interned civilians. The annual mortality rate of Belgian civilians held in captivity by the Germans and used as forced labourers was twenty-two per thousand, whereas among the British prisoners of war held in Germany, even excluding those who died from wounds sustained on the battlefield, the annual death rate was more than 5 per cent – fifty-two per thousand. Given that the UK civilian death rate for men aged twenty to forty in the years immediately preceding the First World War had only been five per thousand, and that the belligerents had instituted a programme of exchange for prisoners who fell seriously ill, the death rate of British soldiers in German captivity was appalling. Malnutrition and maltreatment must have been significant factors in that. The figures concealed even higher death rates for enlisted men than for officers. Almost one in fourteen – 11,978 out of 177,553 – of the British and Commonwealth other-ranks prisoners held in German prisoner-of-war camps died during the course of the war.

The conditions under which prisoners were held and their survival rates varied greatly from country to country. The chaos and anarchy into which Russia descended during the war, the revolution and civil war that followed, resulted in the death of around 40 per cent of PoWs held there. Such statistics masked even more shocking losses: three-quarters of the half million Austro-Hungarian prisoners held in Siberia died of malnutrition, exposure and disease.

The death toll among prisoners held by the combatants on the Western Front was far less extreme, though PoWs of all sides suffered privations and a high mortality rate during the first year of the war, because none of the warring nations had devoted any significant resources to preparing facilities to house the tens and then hundreds of thousands of men they had captured. There were inevitable problems – shortages of food and outbreaks of disease, including typhus and dysentery – which claimed many lives. The German High Command in particular had been so confident of sweeping through to Paris and claiming victory in short order that very few arrangements had been put in place to deal with prisoners. They were also taken aback by the sheer numbers of enemy soldiers surrendering to them, and the alacrity with which many did so. As one German officer later remarked, 'We were surprised that the Allies had so many troops to surrender and that they surrendered so readily.'

At least a thousand British prisoners of war were in German hands before August 1914 – the month in which the war began – was out and by the end of 1916, forty thousand Britons were held captive. The numbers increased throughout the remainder of the war, with an avalanche of almost a hundred thousand British soldiers taken prisoner during the last great German offensive, beginning on 21 March 1918.

The fatality rates among British PoWs would probably have been even worse, had it not been for the regime of inspection established in 1915 by the Red Cross and representatives of the neutral nations, particularly the Netherlands and Switzerland. By prior appointment, inspectors were able to examine any PoW camp, interview the inmates and report on the conditions under which they were being held. Nonetheless, soldiers on both sides and their relatives waiting at home were far from sanguine about the likely fate of men captured by the enemy. As one German woman wrote in August 1914, after being informed that her husband had been taken prisoner, 'Should I consider myself a widow?'

Yet, with some significant exceptions, both Britain and Germany 'played by the rules' to an astonishing degree in the care of prisoners – at least where officers were concerned. Officers, whether British or German, prided themselves on being gentlemen and, even in the midst of the most ferocious and brutal conflict in human history – in which the techniques of mass production were directed towards mass slaughter on an industrial scale – they still sometimes conducted themselves as if war were merely an extension of team sports on public-school playing fields or ritual combat from the golden age of chivalry.

There were elaborate courtesies, like the old-fashioned gentlemen's agreements that allowed officers of both sides to give their 'parole' – their word – to their captors that, if allowed to leave their prison camp on country walks, they would not try to escape, or in any way facilitate a future escape, or damage any property. Officers simply handed in a signed card agreeing to these conditions and were allowed out of camp, in batches of up to forty. 'No guard is sent with them but only one man as a guide.' No one ever availed himself of the chance to escape, for a gentleman's word really was his bond. Some prisoners refused to give their parole on principle, and others because they were convinced that were they to escape and be recaptured, the Germans would accuse them of 'having gleaned information while outside the camp on parole' and use it as an excuse to increase the term of solitary confinement they imposed for the escape attempt.

Even those British prisoners who refused to give their parole were allowed to correspond with their tailors in London to order replacement uniforms, since German Army regulations required every prisoner of war to salute the German officers in charge of him and to be correctly dressed when doing so. In this way would-be escapees were able to order from various British regiments military coats and hats that were not the standard khaki, or exotic dress uniforms. They could then be cut down and modified to resemble German Army uniforms or civilian suits and Homburg hats, which became part of escape kits. One British officer wrote to his tailor saying that he had been transferred from his former regiment to the Grenadier Guards, and ordered a blue-grey regimental greatcoat and two of the Grenadiers' blue and red 'undress caps', which, 'with a little cardboard stuffing, could be made to look exactly like the German home-service cap'. Civilian clothes were also sent to them, but the Germans either confiscated these or, if the British officer preferred, broad yellow-brown stripes would be sewn into them to identify the wearer as a PoW. However, what one tailor could do, another could undo, and such remodelled civilian clothes also formed part of some men's escape kits.

The Hague Rules did not specify precisely what should constitute the humane treatment of prisoners, but it was implicit in their provisions that the government into whose hands prisoners had fallen was bound to provide adequate food, clothing and shelter, and not subject them to prolonged solitary confinement, excessive punishment or brutality. Yet, despite the Hague Rules and the regime of neutral inspection of PoW camps, atrocities were undoubtedly perpetrated, particularly against enlisted men.

Among five hundred ex-prisoners reaching London at the end of November 1918 there was a soldier who claimed that a third of the 1,500 men imprisoned at his last PoW camp had 'died from starvation and exhaustion'. Another eye-witness testified that he had seen an English prisoner, suffering from dysentery, buried alive by German soldiers. They 'afterwards informed me that they had nailed the coffin lid down with four- and six-inch nails'. An Irish soldier who collapsed from exhaustion and malnutrition in a German stone quarry was immediately stabbed with bayonets by the guards. 'The German soldiers then placed the unconscious Irish soldier on the railway line and allowed a train to run over him.' An RAMC captain at a German camp hospital spoke of prisoners used as forced labour behind German lines, who had only torn cotton shirts to wear and were so emaciated that they could scarcely walk without aid. The thighs of men five feet ten inches tall were 'as thick as a normal man's wrist. They usually died within five days of arrival. Some had been stabbed, all had been starved.'

There were instances of brutality and maltreatment of officers as well, though on nothing like the scale inflicted on common soldiers, and it was certainly true – as the voluntary post-war statements of some inmates attested – that certain German prisoner-of-war camps were models of humane treatment. One officer, who spent time in three different camps, noted that 'When I got back home, I heard about all these frightful things going on in German camps [but] I never saw a single rotten incident.' At other camps, though, whether at the whim of their commandants or as part of a deliberate policy imposed by the officer commanding a particular army district, treatment of captives was anything but humane. The four camps operated by General Kommandierende (Commanding General) von Hanisch's Tenth Army Corps – Holzminden, Clausthal, Ströhen and Schwarmstedt – were exemplars of the latter approach, and among them, Holzminden soon became the most notorious. General von Hanisch, described by one British prisoner as 'a Prussian of the old school', gave the commandants 'a free hand to do as they liked with us. They did.'

CHAPTER 2

THE GERMAN BLACK HOLE

The Most Escape-proof Prison in Germany

'Agony!' – Escaped British prisoners, safe in neutral Holland, were unable to revenge themselves on Holzminden's hated commandant, Hauptmann Karl Niemeyer.

I N EARLY SEPTEMBER 1917, the first British captives were arriving at a new prison camp at Holzminden, sixty miles south-west of Hannover, in Lower Saxony. It had been built in 1913 as a cavalry barracks, but by September 1917, as modern industrialized warfare had rendered cavalry virtually obsolete, and as the numbers of Allied prisoners in German hands steadily increased, it was converted to a prisoner-of-war camp.

The *Offizier Gefangenenlager* (prison camp for officers) lay just over a mile outside the sleepy provincial market town of Holzminden, in 'a most lovely part of the country, set in a basin of wooded hills'. The majority of the area's population were small farmers, though Holzminden was also the site of a factory producing essential oils and synthetic flavourings for the perfume and food industries.

The *Lager Poldhu* (*Lager* being German for 'prison' and Poldhu the Cornish site of Marconi's pioneering wireless transmitting station in Cornwall) – the PoW grapevine that, by some quasi-mystical means, allowed war news, rumours, gossip and speculation to circulate between all the camps in

Germany – had suggested that Holzminden was a dream prison, with brand-new light and airy buildings set in spacious grounds and surrounded by beautiful scenery. The reality did not live up to that billing. What lay outside the wire was pleasant enough but the accommodation was spartan, the camp guards corrupt or hostile, and the facilities pitifully inadequate. All the prisoners and the hundred German staff had to be fed from three large boilers; the only other cooking facilities were tiny stoves for the private use of the prisoners, and there was just one for every 125 men.

Holzminden was then the largest British officers' camp in Germany, housing up to seven hundred men in two four-storey stone-built *Kasernen* – barrack blocks – with cellars beneath and steeply pitched roofs to shed the winter snows. Half of *Kaserne* A, separated from the prisoners' quarters by permanently locked doors reinforced with heavy wooden barricades, was occupied by the *Kommandantur*, the area reserved for German officers and camp personnel, including the commandant. The inner and outer gates of the camp stood at either end of the *Kommandantur* and anyone entering or leaving the camp had to pass between it and the guardroom that faced it. The remainder of *Kaserne* A and all of *Kaserne* B, apart from the cellars, were occupied by prisoners.

Each of the two barrack blocks was about fifty yards long by twenty deep, and they were separated from each other by a gap of seventy yards. In front of the prison blocks was the *Spielplatz* – a part-cobbled, part-gravelled area that doubled as a parade-ground and exercise yard, where the prisoners assembled for the twice-daily *Appel* – roll-call.

The prison yard also contained a series of troughs where the cavalry horses had been watered; two single-storeyed, wood-boarded cookhouses, one for each barrack block, set apart from the main building; a potato patch; a woodshed; the bath house for the prisoners; and the parcel room where parcels from prisoners' families and the Red Cross were to be stored and issued.

A cinder path ran around the edge of the *Spielplatz*. Beyond it was a plain wire fence, fixed to low wooden posts, that also sealed off the area behind and to the sides of the barrack blocks. It marked the start of the 'neutral ground' or no man's land, introduced after a flurry of early escapes. Patrolled by armed guards stationed thirty or forty yards apart, it was off-limits to all prisoners, and anyone straying into the area was liable to be shot without warning. Ferocious dogs 'trained to attack' – 'the things now called Alsatians' – were also used, and prowled the whole of the prison compound at night, 'keeping many awake with their howling and actually attacking officers'.

Beyond the no man's land to the rear and sides of the barrack blocks, the boundary was a low wall topped with steel palisades that were six feet high and set at five- or six-inch intervals. From the top of each one, a three-foot steel rail was inclined inwards at an angle of about 120 degrees and strung with four strands of barbed wire. The wall continued right around the site, broken only by a locked steel postern gate near the end of *Kaserne* B, through which the camp commandant would sometimes make an unexpected appearance; but to the front of the barrack blocks, the perimeter was set thirty yards inside the wall and formed by an eight-foot chain-link and barbed-wire fence 'of considerable thickness'. Immediately beyond the fence was a row of widely spaced sentry boxes where the guards huddled in bad weather, and beyond them, but still inside the wall of the camp, were the married quarters for the camp guards, a store shed and a gymnasium. The whole of the perimeter fence and the camp area was brilliantly illuminated by powerful electric arc lights, giving the armed guards stationed at intervals outside the fence a clear view of the exercise yard and the barrack blocks by night and day.

A road, Bodenstrasse, ran just outside the perimeter fence along the north and west sides of the camp; the other two sides were flanked by open fields. Other than a few wisps of trampled grass and the weeds between the cobbles, the only vegetation growing inside the wire was the crop in the potato patch and the row of half a dozen skeletal, malnourished saplings on the edge of the *Spielplatz*, but from the upper windows of the barrack blocks the prisoners could look out over a plain of crops and allotments, broken only by a row of well-spaced trees lining the far bank of a stream among the fields. 'The country is quite pretty,' one prisoner wrote, though the view in one direction was marred a little by the sight of another large prison camp for interned civilians in the middle-distance. The railway line also ran close enough to the southern perimeter of the prisoner-of-war camp for the inmates to be able to see the passing trains. That gave at least one prisoner immense pleasure: 'This sounds very childish, but small things please small minds, and one's mind gets very small after a bit of this.'

The red roofs of the town of Holzminden were also visible a mile away, its skyline dominated by a factory with a high chimney, the needle-sharp spire of the Lutheran church and the tall granary that stood on the quay alongside the River Weser. In the distance, dense forests of pine and fir cloaked the lower slopes of a range of high grey hills, rising to a craggy peak. To the west, just beyond the town, there were glimpses of the river, glinting silver against the deep shadows of the steep far bank. Running roughly north–south, it formed an additional natural barrier barring the way to any escaping prisoners making for the frontier with the neutral Netherlands more than a hundred and fifty miles away.

The prison facilities were unfinished. The bath house had not even been started and the parcel room and the canteen, from one or both of which the inmates might have hoped to augment their prison rations, were closed. In any event, the disruption caused by moving so many prisoners meant that parcels did not start arriving until several weeks had passed. In the meantime, they ate black bread so hard and stale that it could have been used to drive in nails, and watery gruel containing turnip and little else. All lost weight dramatically and those who were already thin became dangerously emaciated.

Most of the prisoners found themselves sharing rooms that were only twenty-two feet by fourteen, but had to accommodate ten to fourteen closely packed men. At the ends of the building on each floor, next to the stairs, there were small rooms only large enough for three or four. Although they were even more cramped, the greater privacy they afforded meant that they were eagerly sought after by the prisoners. There were also a number of smaller rooms in the attic, but they were bitterly cold in winter. In each room there was 'a washstand with three pipes attached', but, except on rare occasions, none produced hot water, and there were two lavatories on each floor; when the camp was full, that equated roughly to one for every fifty men. The prisoners' beds were 'abominable'. They had to lie on mattresses stuffed with wood shavings or 'parcel room packings', because the use of hay or straw had been expressly forbidden by General von Hanisch, whose responsibilities included the control of four prison camps, including Holzminden. 'The pillows were also filled with shavings and we only had one dirty sheet with two filthy blankets apiece.' The sheets were changed once a month and often less frequently than that, sometimes at intervals that exceeded two months, and the blankets were never changed at all.

Prisoners were not allowed to hang pictures or anything else on the walls of the rooms, and shelves were not permitted. Each room looked like 'a big, bare barn, with no comfort at all'. The inmates were shut in every night at six p.m. when the doors of both barrack blocks were locked; from then until seven a.m. they were confined to their quarters. They were also forced to keep their windows shut, 'with the exception of a small pane at the top'; in high summer temperatures, the heat in the crowded rooms was almost unbearable. Prisoners were not only forbidden to open the windows, they were also given the stark warning that anyone looking out during the hours of darkness 'will be shot at'.

Although Holzminden was a prison for officers, enlisted men worked as orderlies. Their duties were to wait on the officers and do the cleaning and maintenance work. They were dressed in the distinctive uniform that other-ranks prisoners of war were required to wear in Germany: a black cap with vivid yellow band, a black coat 'resembling a badly-cut shell-jacket', with yellow-brown sleeves, and black trousers with two-inch yellow-brown stripes. The pieces of yellow-brown fabric were not sewn on to the cloth of the uniform but inserted into it, preventing prisoners from removing the telltale coloured armlets and stripes in the event of an escape attempt. Some escapers painted out the stripes with watercolours or ink, which was sufficient sometimes to evade detection when the light was poor. The uniform also had 'KG' – which stood for *Kriegsgefangener* (Prisoner of War) – in red letters on the back of the tunic and the inmate's PoW number in red on the front. When a scarcity of suitable cloth in blockaded Germany dried up the supply of those uniforms, the enlisted men were dressed in even more distinctive clothing, pieced together from 'old pieces of coloured cloth, like patchwork quilts'.

Each orderly looked after between half a dozen and a dozen officers, and his working day began before seven a.m., at which time he had to take early-morning tea to his charges. The teapot, complete with tea-leaves, cups and saucers, was carried up on a tray and after placing the cups of tea 'within easy reach of the appropriate officers' right hands', he had to collect their boots, shoes, tunics and hats, clean and polish them as required, and then 'replace them in the designated position as expounded by each individual officer'. After the morning *Appel*, the orderly had to make the beds of all his officers and clean their quarters, dusting the chairs and the table, shaking the tablecloth, emptying the ashtrays, tidying and dusting the books, filling the water jug, rinsing and cleaning the sink, and emptying the dirty water in the waste bucket down the drain. The next job was to give the rugs and carpets, in those camps furnished with such luxuries, a thorough shaking and beating against the wall in the corridor and replace them in the room. When they'd finished their individual tasks, the orderlies were also collectively responsible for sweeping, cleaning and dusting the communal stairs and corridors. By this time the morning was well advanced or over. Immediately after lunch, the orderlies were put on general fatigues for the camp and there would then be the officers' afternoon-tea things to clear up and wash, and their rooms to straighten once more. 'Most officers seemed to indulge in afternoon tea, and they had it in their rooms, preparing it themselves, but the orderlies were expected to go along and clear up when the officers were in the dining room at dinner.'

In this more egalitarian age it is jarring to note how it was taken for granted that officers and gentlemen would see out their confinement in relative comfort, supplementing the prison food with a constant stream of parcels from home, waited on by rank-and-file orderlies and indulging in organized games, theatrical performances, classes and even tea and dinner parties. Meanwhile, the enlisted men once under their command would often find themselves housed in squalor, subsisting on food that was only at one remove from pig-swill and carrying out forced labour, 'a Via Dolorosa which only the toughest were to survive'.

Working as orderlies in an officers' prison camp at least meant that enlisted men were relatively comfortably housed and well fed – if only in comparison to the near-starvation diet of their less fortunate comrades still in the enlisted men's camps. Waiting on the officers was also far less arduous and hazardous to an orderly's health than forced labour. Most decent officers were also generous with 'perks', both in payment and kind, though there were others who were far less pleasant to their 'inferiors'. 'So far as I was concerned,' one orderly said, 'if an officer treated me as a human being, I responded to him; if he treated me like dirt, there were ways of getting back at him.' The martinets who made Private Norman Dykes's life a misery soon discovered that he had many ways of 'making these autocratic bullies pay for their complete lack of consideration ... Crockery breaks very easily. Food sometimes gets cold, or can be insufficiently cooked, or indeed burned, time can pass unnoticed and meals brought late, and many other trivial yet irritating methods of reprisal are open, providing one does not indulge too freely in them and thus lay oneself open to the charge of studied insolence.'

Even though, under the arbitrary rule of Hauptmann Karl Niemeyer, officers at Holzminden did not have the privileges that their peers at other camps enjoyed, they and the orderlies who waited on them still fared far better than those imprisoned in camps for enlisted men, where conditions were often grim. Large numbers of enlisted men held in Germany were used as forced labour in coal and salt mines, and death rates from a combination of brutal treatment, exhaustion, starvation and disease were high. 'Our treatment was only a pinprick compared to the men,' one officer said. 'They are slowly being done to death. I mean, they are in the mines, salt mines in particular, worked in an under-fed state until they are quite broken down and only then allowed to go back to the camps to die. The Trade Unions insist on German prisoners being paid good wages for work done in England whilst our men are in far worse than slavery.' One smuggled letter told of a salt mine where the prisoners were kept at work below ground on sixteen-hour shifts, and 'when we fall down exhausted, they beat us with rifles and bayonets'.

There were widespread atrocities. 'Private Barry, Scots Guards, was deliberately shot in a Barrack Room at Sennelager Block 2 on 17 January 1918 . . . So cold-blooded was it that the German not being able to take comfortable aim with his greatcoat on, unbuttoned it and cleared his right shoulder [before firing].' At the camp at Bohmte several prisoners were bayoneted for no more serious a crime than being slow to respond to the whistle summoning them to fall in for roll-call, and a Canadian private who refused to make munitions at Osnabrück – such war work was a clear breach of the Hague Rules – was 'lashed to a furnace for two hours and was burned all down one side. He fainted after the first half-hour.' At Güstrow in Mecklenburg, the cemetery held hundreds of men 'beaten to death, died of starvation and other cruel means, which would break the hearts of many if only the true story was told'. A prisoner at another camp for enlisted men saw the remnants of a working party who had been made to labour near the front lines – another breach of the Hague Rules. 'Their condition was terrible. There were about thirty of them left, I was told, from a party that was taken away about 120 strong, two months before.' Little wonder, then, that the orderlies at Holzminden, while giving every assistance they could to the officers, did not attempt to escape: had they been caught, at best they would have faced an immediate transfer to an enlisted men's or forced-labour camp, and in some cases that was close to a death sentence.

The orderlies were housed in a segregated part of Kaserne B and were even more tightly packed than the officers, crammed twenty to a room in double-decker bunks ranged around the walls. Their quarters were off-limits to all officers, as were the cellars, which housed the punishment cells and the storerooms for coal, potatoes and the prisoners' tinned food – a vital supplement to their dismal rations – sent in parcels from their families in England or by the Red Cross in Switzerland.

Those prisoners who were deemed to have breached the myriad camp regulations were given three days' solitary confinement in the basement cells of *Kaserne* B. There was no proper sanitation in the punishment cells – the prisoners used buckets at night – and their food was 'served out on the floor of the space on which were placed the makeshift latrines'. The cells were also 'teeming with rats'. As one prisoner sarcastically noted, 'If one felt lonely, there were always the rats. It was amusing, killing the rats, and reminded one of the dear old days on the Somme.'

Holzminden had been established as a *Strafe* (punishment) camp that was claimed to be 'utterly impregnable' and 'the most closely guarded and escape-proof prison in Germany'. It also rapidly established a reputation as the most brutal, renamed 'Hellminden' by its unwilling inhabitants, 'the worst camp in Germany' and 'the German black hole' by British newspapers. Sub-lieutenant Murdock Rose of the Royal Naval Reserve, who had been serving on HMS *Newmarket* when he was captured after his ship was sunk, spoke for most prisoners when he described Holzminden as 'this hole', and prayed, 'God spare me from ever seeing it again.'

Almost all of the inmates at Holzminden were what the Germans termed 'dangerous cases': inveterate escapees from other camps, including one man who had attempted to escape on twenty separate occasions. However, the German policy of concentrating them at supposedly impregnable camps like Holzminden and two other notorious camps – Fort 9 at Ingolstadt and Fort Zorndorf in East Prussia, a grim fortress surrounded by a moat and almost completely underground – proved counterproductive, since they simply became 'Escapers' Universities'. Just like old lags in prison, those incarcerated there pooled their knowledge, swapped ideas and techniques and, if they did not succeed in escaping from Holzminden, spread their knowledge even further when they were sent on to other prisons.

CHAPTER 3

MILWAUKEE BILL

The Most Brutal Camp Commandant

'Milwaukee Bill' – Niemeyer spent some years in America before the war and learned to speak what one British prisoner described as 'bartender Yank'. Niemeyer's dog showed little affection for its master and seemed to prefer the company of the prisoners under his control.

DURING THE AUTUMN of 1917, more and more prisoners arrived at Holzminden, and by the end of the year, there were 560 officers at the camp, and between 140 and 160 orderlies. Some prisoners were 'nineteen-seventeeners' captured in that year's fighting, but the majority were captives of one, two or three years' standing, transferred to Holzminden from Schwarmstedt, Ströhen, Clausthal, Freiburg, Krefeld and a number of other over-crowded camps, where the commandants were not slow to seize the opportunity to unload some of their most trouble-some inmates.

Before being sent to a prison camp, all newly taken prisoners were first interrogated in the hope of extracting useful military intelligence, although even those who were persuaded to talk often had little of real value to impart. As Norman Insoll, an officer at Holzminden, recalled, for about three weeks after he was shot down and taken prisoner he and other new captives were taken into an office every day and interrogated by various officers from the German war ministry. 'It was rather stupid, really. I mean they wanted to know where the British Fleet was. How was I, a boy of eighteen in the Flying Corps, to know? And then they wanted to know the number of my squadron. Of course, we weren't allowed to say and I told them I couldn't reply. Next day they got a major in, a very fierce-looking man, and they said, "You must tell the major what your squadron number is." I just laughed – and they laughed, and offered me a cigarette.' On 26 September 1917 a large group of British officer prisoners boarded a train for Holzminden from Schwarmstedt. After a roll-call at five a.m., they began the seven-kilometre march to the station two hours later. They made a 'quite comfortable' journey in second-class compartments during which Captain Douglas Lyall Grant amused himself and 'caused the Hun officers considerable annoyance by wearing a black-rimmed eyeglass attached to a huge piece of black tape and fixing them with a glassy stare' whenever they addressed him. As they approached Holzminden at four thirty p.m., the train passed close enough to the prison camp for Lyall Grant and his comrades to see the inmates who had already been installed, waving to them from the barrack blocks inside the camp.

> Subsequently we rejoined all our old friends, who, like the poor, are still with us ... From the train the barracks had looked very good but our hopes were dashed when, after a two-kilometre walk, dragging our hand luggage with us or leaving it on the road if it proved too heavy, we were greeted by many people shouting from the windows that it was the

worst camp they had struck and telling us to look out for a personal search of the most rigorous nature.

As they straggled through the gates, the new arrivals were greeted with stentorian shouts from a prisoner known as 'Irish Mick', who leaned out of an upper window in the barracks to shout, 'Bury your notes, bury your notes. They shtrip ye mother naked.' Although holding German currency was strictly prohibited, many prisoners had German marks as well as items of escape equipment, like compasses, wire-cutters and maps, secreted about them. There was no possibility of discreetly slipping them through the fence to the existing camp inmates because they had all been confined to their barracks before the new arrivals appeared. The commandant, Hauptmann Karl Niemeyer, 'who spoke good English', greeted them, confirmed Irish Mick's warning that they would all be body-searched and advised them to hand over any 'real money', maps, compasses and other contraband that they were holding.

'Whether this was a clever dodge or not, I don't know,' one prisoner said, 'but it naturally led to everyone surreptitiously burying all illicit goods' – money, maps and other escape equipment. As they stood in the dusty *Spielplatz*, waiting to be processed, they crouched and tried to dig discreet holes with their hands or penknives and buried their wads of notes and other contraband, planning to retrieve them later. However, instead of being searched, they were then marched straight off to an empty building and locked in for the night.

There was no opportunity to retrieve their hidden money

and escape kit before nightfall and most were to be disappointed in their hopes of recovering it: the next morning, before the barrack blocks were unlocked, they saw 'a band of "Landworms"', as they always called the *Landsturm* men – a militia composed of former reservists and men who, because of age or infirmity, had not been called up for regular military service – 'very busy on their hands and knees, searching for contraband on the grass plot where the prisoners had been standing the night before. It was a ludicrous sight to see all these men with their noses on the ground, scratching in the turf.' Ludicrous or not, they were successful in digging up almost all 'the hidden treasure'. One German NCO, who had either observed them hiding the money or whose curiosity was piqued by the freshly turned earth in the *Spielplatz*, had found no less than two thousand marks by the time the barrack-block doors were unlocked.

That morning, in line with Irish Mick's warning, the new inmates were taken into a room where they had to strip naked. They went through to another room where they were medically examined, then into a third, where their clothes were handed back to them, 'presumably after they had been searched'. During the search, Lyall Grant and one of his comrades 'managed to pull the Hun's leg pretty satisfactorily. A cordon was drawn around the building to prevent those who had already arrived from communicating with us. G and I made wild signs to some fellows to catch a parcel, which we waved about before we threw it out of the window, letting it fall well <u>inside</u> the cordon. Immediately two smart under-officers threw themselves upon it, tore off the paper and found a piece of mouldy bully [corned] beef.'

As their clothes were returned to them, each of the new arrivals was also 'handed a metal disc, the size of a penny, which bore the name of the camp and a number, like that of a convict'. 'Henceforth by this number only were you known, your name having been relegated to the past and limbo of all things.' Despite the search of the prisoners and their clothes, and the excavations in the *Spielplatz*, large amounts of contraband somehow did get through. A Canadian prisoner, Major John Thorn, had a map confiscated, though it was not a particularly significant loss since it did not cover the area where he now found himself, but a civilian cap, tacked to his undershirt, a black rubber coat carried in a strap over his shoulder and several hundred marks sewn into the lining of his clothes all escaped the searchers' notice. Had the German guard 'removed the heel of one of my boots,' Captain Jack Shaw observed, 'he would have found a compass protected by cotton wool.'

Shaw, a 'neat sailer' and a 'prominent oarsman who won many cups' before the war, had served with the 2nd King Edward's Horse, the Oxfordshire and Buckinghamshire Light Infantry and the Royal Flying Corps before being taken prisoner at Messines in 1917. He was also a gifted amateur musician, and at Freiburg prison camp, he became conductor of the camp orchestra, though his motive might have been less to share his love of music than to use it as cover for an escape attempt. While giving a concert in the

German guards' dining room, he pretended to have injured his foot during a comedy sketch, and when left alone in the dressing room while the concert continued, he climbed out of a window and escaped. He was soon recaptured and, after serving two weeks' solitary confinement for the attempt, was transferred to Holzminden in November 1917.

His younger brother, Lieutenant Wilfred Shaw, was also captured by the Germans, at St Quentin on 23 March 1918, and was briefly reunited with his brother at Holzminden. Their parents suffered the agony of being informed by the War Office that Wilfred, initially listed as missing in action, had been killed. More than a month later, on 12 May 1918, they got another letter from the War Office, telling them that a postcard had been received that 'contains the names of various British officers who are now Prisoners of War. Amongst those appears the name of 2nd Lieutenant W. R. Shaw, the Bedfordshire Regiment.'

Soon after being taken prisoner, Wilfred had had the unwanted distinction of being interviewed by the Kaiser and the chief of the German General Staff, Paul von Hindenburg, who were close to the front lines, following the progress of the great spring offensive, which, they hoped, would decide the war. Wilfred had been knocked out with a blow from the butt of a rifle when he was captured and when he came round was briefly interrogated by a German officer in a dugout. Then he was 'dragged out to a couple of blokes sitting in a sort of Victoria [carriage] with a white horse'. The Kaiser looked at Shaw, then turned to Hindenburg and said,

'The English are sending babies.' Shaw was only nineteen and looked even younger, but he 'didn't like being called a baby'. Asked what he knew about British plans and troop movements, Shaw replied that he knew nothing – as a nineteen-year-old junior officer that was hardly surprising. The Kaiser then told him, 'We'll be in Paris in seven days.'

'Best of luck,' Shaw said. 'Take me with you.' But he was told that 'a nice prisoner-of-war camp' was waiting for him in Germany. The Kaiser might have been speaking sarcastically, but the first camp Wilfred Shaw was sent to was, indeed, 'a damned nice camp'. One day he was summoned to see the commandant, who told him that his brother had applied for him to be transferred to his camp in Holzminden. Wilfred insisted, 'I'm quite happy here,' but he was duly transferred. 'So I went . . . to a bloody reprisal camp.' When his brother greeted him there, Wilfred 'wasn't very pleased to see him. I damned near knocked his ruddy head off . . . because it was a damned nasty little camp.'

Although all prisoners were searched on arrival, twenty-two men transferred to Holzminden from Clausthal after a failed escape from there had brought their escape equipment with them and successfully evaded detection. Lieutenant Cecil Blain 'palmed' his compass and some German marks and passed through the strip-search without them being found. Another man hid his equipment in a battered trunk. The German guards were so busy probing and measuring it to ensure it didn't have a false bottom that they neglected to check whether it had a false side.

Another group of twenty-five new arrivals did not reach Holzminden until midnight, after a day-long journey from Heidelberg. Despite the lateness of the hour, they were met at the gate by the commandant, and at first sight, Karl Niemeyer appeared to be an almost avuncular figure, 'a friendly, if over-familiar old bounder', as one of the new inmates described him. He told the prisoners that he was always glad to see any Englishman, had been a great friend to the English in the past and would be again when the war was over. Solicitously, he urged them to write to their friends and relatives, asking for warm clothes to be sent – the winters in Holzminden were very cold. He then concluded, 'So now, yentlemen, I expect you will be glad to go to your bedrooms. I will wish you goodnight. You will be searched in the morning.'

They had eaten nothing since leaving their previous prison camp early that morning and went to bed hungry. The next morning, when they paraded before him after the search, he was at first still apparently solicitous, asking if they had eaten and then dispatching a cook to procure breakfast for them at once. When it arrived, breakfast turned out to be a cup of watery lukewarm *ersatz* coffee, made from dried, roasted and ground acorns, 'neither pleasant nor nourishing', or burned barley – 'The burnt malt coffee gave us heartburn and the burnt acorn coffee upset our bowels.' The 'genial Karl' kept a close watch on their expressions as they struggled to drink their 'coffee' and greatly enjoyed their discomfiture, while pretending 'not to understand our disgust'.

At that morning's *Appel* Niemeyer paraded his entire complement of staff, who were drawn up facing the prisoners. 'These are not officers and gentlemen,' Niemeyer said to them, as he gestured towards the prisoners. 'They are criminals and I hope you will treat them accordingly . . . If I see any German speaking to them, he will immediately be sent to the Front.'

It rapidly became clear to the prisoners that the *Appels* were to be used not merely to check the tally of prisoners but as a form of collective punishment, especially in winter, when they were often forced to stand for 'from half to three-quarters of an hour in bitterly cold weather with snow and slush underfoot'. After an escape attempt, the *Appel* could last for hours. On one occasion when the roll-call revealed that five British officers were missing, Niemeyer kept the rest standing on the *Spielplatz* for more than two hours while a thorough search of the camp was made. He himself

sat comfortably in a chair, smoking the inevitable cheroot. The *feldwebels* also started smoking in order to tempt us to follow suit and become candidates for solitary confinement in the 'jug'. Several fell. A certain British officer of the right type fell foul of Niemeyer on this occasion and one of the sentries, under pressure from Karl, banged his toes time after time with the butt of his rifle. Our comrade must have suffered considerable pain, but he took no notice whatever of his assailant and, taking out his case, he carefully selected a cigarette and smoked it to the end.

The *Appel* was only brought to an end when the five missing officers were discovered hiding under the floor of the bath house, in preparation for an escape attempt that night.

Other collective punishments imposed by Niemeyer included additional roll-calls, the withholding of parcels and letters, confining prisoners to barracks and closing the exercise yard and tin room, where the officers' tinned food was stored. A senior British officer who had the temerity to complain to Niemeyer about the immorality of such collective punishments was penalized for his effrontery by being sentenced to eight days' solitary confinement.

In acting as he did, Niemeyer was merely enforcing the policy of his superior, General von Hanisch, 'an unreasonable and cruel man, endowed with a violent temper'. Known as 'The Pig of Hannover' by German soldiers, von Hanisch had been stripped of his active command following a battle against British troops and was believed, as a result, to be 'specially bitter against British prisoners. He also appears to be mad.' Another prisoner recorded his impressions of an inspection that von Hanisch had made at Schwarmstedt, observing that the general's 'reputation as a strafer preceded him and he certainly acted up to it . . . About the third room he looked into had several of the Allies' flags on the walls at which he went mad. Shouting that there was only one flag in Germany, he ordered them to be taken down. Shortly afterwards he nearly had a fit on finding some unopened tins in a locker and later distinguished himself by ripping a map of France off the wall.' When he toured Holzminden, 'there were no Allied flags for him to tear down, but he did not fall short of expectation'.

At best, the prisoners in the camps under von Hanisch's command were subject to numerous petty restrictions, and at worst to systematic intimidation and brutality. According to one escaped prisoner who made it across the border to neutral Switzerland, all the camps under General von Hanisch's control maintained order by

> a reign of terror. The German sentries and guards are instructed to use their rifles freely, not only to prevent escapes but also to maintain discipline. Very few officers and, of course, still fewer NCOs and men have more than a nodding acquaintance with the German language, yet it is no unusual occurrence in this Army Corps for a German sentry to shout an order in uneducated and unintelligible German at the top of his voice, then use his bayonet indiscriminately because he was not immediately obeyed. That there have not been more cases of bayoneting is due more to the agility of the British than to the forbearance of the Germans.

Yet whenever a guard used his bayonet on a prisoner, 'after all such cases, the Germans attempt to make out a case of mutiny against the prisoners'.

An 'organized system of coercion' was carried out in the four camps, which was sometimes imposed by the general himself and sometimes by his subordinates, including the Niemeyer twins, Karl and Heinrich, the commandants respectively of Holzminden and Clausthal, a former hotel in the Harz Mountains converted to a prison camp. Heinrich was almost as notorious as his brother at Holzminden, earning them the nickname 'The Terrible Twins'. As a British officer noted, it was difficult to believe that a system designed and carried out by 'three such cruel men' as General von Hanisch and the two Niemeyers was not 'deliberately devised to condemn the prisoners of war under them to a life of humiliation and outrage'.

> Whether from accident or design, the men selected as General von Hanisch's lieutenants were of a character admirably fitted to carry through efficiently his system of treatment . . . It can hardly be doubted that their character was throughout well known to him. It is certain that he was in close touch with all that occurred in both camps, not only by his own visits, but through those of his assistants, Generals von Brausing and Pavlowski, as well as through the reports of the Commandants; and he seems personally to have conceived many of the repressive measures employed against our officers.

Although some German commandants operated their PoW camps under a more enlightened regime and maintained a strict adherence to the agreed rules of war, at other camps the treatment of British prisoners could be brutal and even barbaric, and that was true of Holzminden above all others. Von Hanisch was said to 'shriek, quivering with rage', at the British officers there, calling them 'dogs and pig-dogs', telling them they were all 'barbarians and did not deserve to be allowed to live'. He also declared in the hearing of the prisoners at Holzminden, 'I am hoping every day to receive the order to send some of these people to be put up behind our lines to be shot by British shells.'

The general's threats were treated as mere bluster by most of the British prisoners, but the Germans under his command, including Karl Niemeyer, were plainly terrified of him. One Holzminden inmate observed that when von Hanisch was inspecting the camp, the German soldiers 'were at a perpetual salute, with eyes right or left, and constantly tripping up on the uneven parade-ground. We were convulsed. The Herr General gave us an address. No one listened, so it was announced that the Herr General had stopped our sports which were to have taken place the following day – loud, derisive cheers from the PoWs.'

The senior British officer at Holzminden, Major Wyndham, had the difficult task of raising the defects in the accommodation for his men with von Hanisch, who listened to the litany of complaints in the *Spielplatz* in front of the barracks. He was flanked by his junior officers, all in their dress uniforms and standing ramrod stiff. Whenever he addressed a remark to any of them, they raised their gloved hands to their peaked caps, as if shielding their eyes from the rays of the sun, and maintained that pose until the general turned away.

Von Hanisch treated Wyndham's complaints with

ill-disguised impatience and contempt before finally exploding: 'You dare to come before me with such trivial complaints when, if you British officers had your deserts, you should be shot?' He told Wyndham that the bath house and the second cookhouse would be completed as soon as possible, but requests for additional facilities, such as the public room and library that all German prisoners in Britain enjoyed, were dismissed out of hand. 'England is not Germany,' von Hanisch said. 'It is wartime and the English officers must learn to do without luxuries.' When asked if Holzminden was to be regarded as a *Strafe* – punishment – camp, the general replied, 'It may please the English officers to understand that.'

Most of those incarcerated at Holzminden would heartily have concurred with the view expressed by one prisoner that 'The worst feature of the camp was the Commandant.' When the camp first opened, Hauptmann Karl Niemeyer had been only the camp officer – the second-in-command – although the commandant, Colonel Habrecht, who was 'a kindly old dodderer of about seventy', had delegated everything to him. The 'old hands' told one new arrival that the commandant was 'all right, but the whole place was run by the Captain, Niemeyer by name, who was most antagonistic and did everything to make it as uncomfortable as possible'. Niemeyer made clear his displeasure at what he perceived to be Habrecht's laxity towards the British prisoners and said that he, Niemeyer, would 'put things right' at the camp if he was given control of it for only twenty-four hours.

When Flight Lieutenant Frank M. Olst arrived at Holzminden, the first two people he met were Lieutenant G. W. Armstrong and Hauptmann Niemeyer, 'two good pals', he said, with heavy irony, for 'the redoubtable, blustering and lying blackguard' Niemeyer was no British officer's pal. Almost a caricature 'Hun' with close-cropped grey hair, a florid complexion and 'fierce moustaches modelled on the Kaiser's', Niemeyer was described by one jaundiced British observer as 'the greatest exponent of the Prussian "blood and iron" policy that ever came into contact with British prisoners. His name is a household word among them.'

One of five brothers, Niemeyer had lived in Milwaukee for seventeen years before the war, leading the inmates to call him 'Milwaukee Bill'. So many of Milwaukee's inhabitants were of German origin or descent that there were said to be more German speakers than English speakers in the city, but while living there or elsewhere in the US – some people said he had been a barman in Milwaukee, others that he had been a billiard marker in New York when the war broke out – Niemeyer had picked up some English along with 'a good deal of American bar-room slang', and spoke 'bartender Yank', English with a strong American accent. His catchphrases – 'I give you three days [imprisonment] right away' and 'I guess you know I am the commandant' – soon became wearisomely familiar to his victims. 'Cost price' was another favourite phrase, often used in the somewhat baffling 'I tell you something straight, yes, cost price, I guess', and his misuse of the language and frequent malapropisms were a constant source of amusement to the prisoners.

With his twin, Karl Niemeyer was said to have left America with German embassy staff immediately after the US declaration of war and crossed the Atlantic to seek a commission in the German Army. Along the way, the pair reportedly evaded a search by British seamen, who boarded the ship on which they were travelling. Karl Niemeyer gave one Canadian prisoner a graphic description of his heroic escape from America, for which he said he had been awarded the Iron Cross by the Kaiser, but 'he had told this story in twenty different ways' and it was later suggested that he had actually made his way back to Germany, via Italy, before America had even entered the war and begun interning German citizens. As he also never tired of telling his captives, Niemeyer had seen action on the Somme, but allegedly 'one week of the Somme had been enough for him', and soon afterwards, whether as a result of wounds, an intervention by an influential friend or because of his relative fluency in the English language, he had secured a much safer post as camp officer, first at Ströhen, then at Holzminden, where he arrived as the camp opened in early September 1917.

Niemeyer invariably wore an ankle-length military greatcoat and cavalry spurs – though he was never seen on a horse – and carried a walking-stick. He had the paunch of a heavy beer drinker, was rarely without a black cigar in the corner of his mouth and wore his cap at a jaunty angle on the back of his head. Any impression of jocularity was soon dispelled, for Niemeyer could swear like a trooper and was 'noted for his ferocity'.

One Holzminden inmate called him 'the famous Niemeyer, about the biggest cad I've ever met in any walk of life'. Another described him as 'that notorious Hun bully. His vanity was colossal, and was only equalled by his uncouth manners, crass stupidity and ignorance in dealing with men and officers.' Yet another prisoner said that Niemeyer 'was clever, he was tricky and he had an ungovernable temper'. At roll-call he would 'stalk around shouting at everybody, trying to look as important as possible, with two revolvers stuck in each side of his belt, his sword dangling at his side'. 'The personification of hate, his manners and tongue were foul.' He would spit on the floor of an officer's room and he 'rejoiced in flourishing his revolver on all occasions', threatening officers with it. At times he was a constant presence and would 'swagger up and down the camp and demand to be saluted on every passage'; at others he would not be seen for days on end.

A bachelor, Niemeyer was said to 'loathe the sight of women', though there were also rumours of 'wild orgies' in his apartment and of regular drinking bouts – given some credence by a sighting of Niemeyer, supported by two of his *Feldwebel*s (sergeant), vomiting into the yard from an upstairs window. Others claimed that 'He used to take drugs and get very het up.' He played no sports, neither walked nor rode for exercise, nor had any hobbies or pastimes. His only real companion was his retriever puppy, but even that was 'the source of considerable annoyance to its owner', since it seemed to prefer the company of the prisoners to that of its master and had to be coaxed or cowed into following him as he went on his rounds.

Major Wyndham made strenuous representations to von Hanisch about Niemeyer, who had already been reported to and sternly condemned by the *Kreigsministerium* (Ministry of War) for his conduct when serving at Ströhen, a dismal PoW camp that was 'a morass' when wet and 'a place of dust-storms and stench' when dry. Niemeyer had arrived there on 4 August 1917 'in time to order the bayonet outrage of that evening'. When contingents of new prisoners arrived, 'most of the British officers would move to that part of the camp, opposite the Commandant's office where newcomers were received, searched and generally "messed about". Light-hearted badinage between old friends, previous escape-mates and long-lost relatives then floated gently to and fro through the fence. In short, new arrivals were given a suitable welcome.'

On that day 'a particularly popular batch' of prisoners had arrived, who had many friends in the camp, and a group of about forty inmates gathered near the camp gates to greet them.

Naturally enough there was a good deal of shouting between the parties on either side of the wire. Equally naturally, the Commandant, who was at that moment engaged on an addition sum, or something quite as absorbing, objected, as it transpired later, to the noise just outside his window. Tact, however, had never been his strong suit and he resorted to his old game of shouting . . . What he said was, no doubt, quite clear and well expressed, but ninety-nine per cent of his audience, not knowing his language, could only hazard a guess as to his meaning. Germans – the military at any rate – often shout. It is impossible, therefore, for the uninitiated to tell whether the shouter is really annoyed or is merely the victim of an untimely spasm of indigestion. On this occasion, however, most of us decided to be on the safe side and we sauntered back towards our huts.

Niemeyer, 'summoning a patrol by waving his cap, gave the men the order to charge the officers', and 'to use their arms if the prisoners did not move away quickly enough'. 'Evidently we did not move fast enough to please our over-lord, for the next thing we knew was that armed soldiers were in our midst.' As a prisoner was moving away, a sentry shouted at him in German to move faster. The prisoner did not understand and continued walking at the same pace, whereupon 'the sentry charged at him with his bayonet and stabbed him in the back below the shoulder blade, penetrat-ing the lung'. The same sentry, a young soldier 'just back from the front', also bayoneted another prisoner in the back and 'seemed as if he did this from the pure enjoyment of it'.

It was not an isolated incident: 'bayoneting was a common occurrence' at the camp, with at least 'eight well-attested cases of deliberate murderous attempts on British officers'. One of them, Captain Knight, was walking across the yard when Feldwebel Pohlmann shouted at him in German. Once more, Knight did not understand the command, but without any further warning or explanation, Pohlmann brought the butt of his rifle down on Knight's foot, then bayoneted him in the thigh. Severely wounded, Knight had to be carried into the camp hospital. In vain did the prisoners look to the commandant 'for protection, justice, fair play or redress. Niemeyer, indeed, is said to have congratulated the guard.' When Niemeyer passed through the camp hospital during his routine tour of inspection, Knight asked him for some brandy because 'he had lost so much blood'. Niemeyer refused, saying that 'if water was good enough for German privates, it was good enough for British officers'.

The prisoners at Ströhen, furious with the conditions in the camp, were determined to bring them to the notice of the authorities at home. Previous complaints expressed in letters to neutral ambassadors and the *Kreigsministerium* had 'got no further than the Commandant's office, so we decided to take the law into our own hands and go on strike'. They refused to write the two letters and four postcards a month that they were allowed to send home, and abstained from drawing any cheques on their banks in England, as many of them would normally have done to pay for items bought in the camp canteen. In addition to this, believing that Niemeyer was running the canteen for his own profit, they spent every penny we could spare for seven days, then, immediately he received a large fresh stock from Berlin, rubbing his hands the while, we refused to buy a single article of any description. The strike had the desired effect and it was not long before the Commandant implored us to buy his goods. Our people and the banks became agitated at the sudden cessation of correspondence from Ströhen and brought the matter to the notice of the authorities at home. Diplomatic negotiations then followed which resulted in a neutral ambassador being asked to report upon the conditions in which we lived.

Within a month of his arrival at Ströhen, Niemeyer was transferred to the new prison camp at Holzminden. That the transfer was not a punishment for his misdeeds at Ströhen but, rather, a reward for them became apparent when he was made commandant of Holzminden soon afterwards. The facilities and conditions at Ströhen, particularly in the bitter winter, were significantly worse than at almost any other officer PoW camp in Germany, yet the views of the inmates, as expressed by two escapees from Ströhen to the Government Committee on the Treatment by the Enemy of British Prisoners of War, was that 'From what we hear of Holzminden, we would rather remain at Ströhen all the winter . . . The reason British officers are reluctant to go to Holzminden is that the man who used to be second in command at Ströhen . . . is now commandant at Holzminden. The officers fear that any camp which is under him will be an uncomfortable place.'

A vindictive, splenetic 'holy terror', Niemeyer's mood was always particularly black early in the morning, when he would make unannounced random inspections of the camp and the prisoners' quarters, 'storming up and down in a black gust of bilious passion'. Such visits 'usually resulted in the Commandant bagging a brace or so more for "jug"', but his own men were almost as likely as the British prisoners to be the targets of his rage. 'He tried to intimidate everybody, but finding he was not successful with us, he would commence bullying the poor sentries until they did not know what they were doing.' He 'thundered and damned and cursed' so much that the prisoners could see German soldiers on parade 'literally trembling as he flayed them with his tongue'. As a result, 'The Germans all hated him too; all his underlings loathed him.'

A representative of the Dutch king visited Holzminden soon after it opened and described the behaviour of Hauptmann Niemeyer as 'disgraceful'. However, Niemeyer had a loyal and powerful supporter, being 'protected throughout by General von Hanisch; in return he lives in servile dread of his chief'. Von Hanisch's rejection of all complaints and representations about Niemeyer might have been – as was widely believed by the British prisoners – because a proportion of the exorbitant profits from the camp canteen and of the value of goods pilfered from parcels sent to the prisoners by their relatives, and by the Red Cross, was finding its way via Niemeyer to the general's pockets.

The first commandant at Holzminden, Colonel Habrecht,

had complained to von Hanisch of Niemeyer's 'insolence and discourtesy', and would have echoed the view of one senior British officer that Niemeyer was 'by temperament, totally unsuitable to command a unit of any kind ... in addition it is no exaggeration to say that "the truth is not in him"'. On the night of his first inspection of the camp, 1 October 1917, General von Hanisch brusquely rejected the complaints of Habrecht and the British officers, then announced that the 'dodderer', Habrecht, would be retiring with immediate effect, and that, as of 3 October, Niemeyer would replace him as commandant. 'He had been unpleasant as a camp officer; as commandant he was insupportable.' The first of many cases of Niemeyer ordering guards to fire into prisoners' rooms occurred just three days later, on 6 October, when a guard fired through a third-floor window in *Kaserne* A. The bullet 'crashed through the window, narrowly missed the officer aimed at, and passed between the legs of another officer in the room above.' 'Luckily he missed ... but the bullet went up into the corner and proved useful evidence later on.'

Another early cause of friction was the insistence of Niemeyer and his subordinates on reading out their orders in German:

Very few of us understood the language, yet those who failed to comply with them were punished. Those who did understand did not approve of acting as unpaid interpreters of unwelcome 'red tape'. We therefore insisted on an official interpreter being appointed and pressed the camp staff to accept the onus of ensuring that the orders were understood. We won our first point and several German aspirants for the post were tried out on parade. Their efforts, for the most part, were lamentable and their strange distortion of our language received such overwhelming applause that Hauptmann Niemeyer, in charge of the parade, determined one day to undertake the task himself. Accordingly, he carefully read out the orders in German and then attempted a translation at sight – a most unwise venture. He soon learned better . . .

He started off fairly well, although he amused us by introducing the phrase 'I guess you know' at the end of each sentence – he had, strangely enough, spent some time in the United States. Just when he appeared to be going to get through the ordeal with comparative credit, he made some incredible error, which drew forth much laughter and applause. Had he been a wise man he would himself have passed it off with a laugh, but instead of doing so, he made the fatal mistake of losing his temper and, in his rage, he gave birth to a winner – 'You tink I know notinks,' he yelled, 'but I know damn all!' He left the parade-ground hurriedly with hoots of derision ringing in his ears. An efficient interpreter was produced within twenty-four hours.

CHAPTER 4

SOLITARY CONFINEMENT

The Punitive Regime at Holzminden

Prisoners were often sent to the basement punishment cells on the most trivial pretexts.

ALTHOUGH THE PRINCIPLE that 'it is the duty of a prisoner of war to escape if he can' had been approved by the British and German governments, it was still a 'cardinal offence' in the prison camps under von Hanisch's control to attempt to do so. Before August 1917, the penalties inflicted on those caught in the attempt were 'most severe'. Prisoners were subjected first of all to a reprisal sentence of five months' imprisonment in retaliation for the supposed ill-treatment being endured by German prisoners in England. They then had to serve an additional personal sentence. However, on 1 August 1917, new regulations came into force, amendments to the Hague Rules agreed in July of that year. All previous sentences for attempted escapes were now to be annulled, although that provision was 'not readily accepted in the 10th Army Corps, at least by the Niemeyers'.

Paragraph 16 (a) of the new agreement, signed by the Allied and German governments, also declared that in future the maximum term of imprisonment for 'a simple attempt to escape on the part of a combatant prisoner of war, even if repeated, shall not exceed military confinement for a period of 14 days'. There were longer terms for burglary or criminal damage while attempting to escape than for the act of escaping itself and, as a result, there was virtually no disincentive to make an attempt to do so. In addition, whether ultimately successful or not, the mere act of trying to escape was damaging to the captor nation. As one First World War escaper noted, 'Those who break out of camp render the greatest service, for while they are at large, thousands of Germans are searching for them and every escape causes an increase in the number of guards', drawing off men who, of course, could otherwise have been drafted into the fighting units in the front lines.

Although the provisions of the new Hague agreement were 'loyally observed in some of the camps in Germany, no less than in England', those relating to the maximum sentence to be imposed for an attempted escape were routinely evaded at Holzminden and the other camps under General von Hanisch's control. It was done in two ways. First, the time before being charged and sentenced that escapees spent in cells on *Untersungschaft* (detention pending enquiry) or *Schutzhaft* (detention on remand), in conditions identical to those they faced under *Stubenarrest* (detention after sentence) was considerably prolonged, so that recaptured prisoners actually served a month or even more in solitary confinement for the escape attempt. Second, 'cumulative sentences' were imposed, so that, as well as fourteen days' imprisonment for the actual escape attempt, prisoners would receive additional sentences for being in possession of escape equipment or German marks, or for causing damage to Imperial Government property while making their escape. By also lengthening the periods spent on remand while these 'crimes' were being investigated, escapees could find themselves in solitary confinement for periods of up to six months.

Such punishments were not imposed 'only to maintain discipline or enforce regulations. It was a weapon with which to subdue the spirit of the British officer.' Prisoners were placed on a punitive dietary regime that alternated three days on black bread and water with one day on camp rations that were little more nutritious, which continued for as long as they remained in solitary confinement. They also served their time 'under the worst conditions of restriction and hardship'. They were incarcerated in long, narrow cells, eight feet high and six feet wide by fifteen feet long, with one small barred window high in the outer wall, at ground level. The only furniture was a small table, a stool, a tin basin, a jug for water, and a bare-boarded bed – although some prisoners were allowed to take their mattresses to the cells with them. The cells were dark, poorly ventilated, freezing cold in winter and suffocating in summer, and there the captives remained, 'sometimes without exercise, without light ... often deprived of the opportunity of washing, reading, writing or smoking, and condemned to exist on camp food'.

In theory, when not serving spells of solitary confinement, all British officers at Holzminden were allowed to leave the camp for walks on parole, but before doing so they were required to sign a parole card, printed in German and English, imposing other conditions in addition to those required by the Hague Rules. The Holzminden parole card stated:

> I herewith give my word of honour that I shall not, in case of my taking part in a walk, make an attempt to escape during such walk, i.e. from the time of leaving the camp until having returned to it, at the same time, strictly obeying any orders given to me by the accompanying officer, and not to commit any acts that are directed against the safety of the German Empire. I know that ... a prisoner of war who escapes in spite of the word of honour given is liable to death. I give also my word of honour to use this card only myself and not to give it to any other prisoner of war.

To modern eyes, the additions to the standard German parole card seem trivial and complaints about them petty, but the British officers took a different view: they believed that 'any attempt to interfere with our parole was in honour bound to be furiously contested'. In their eyes, a British gentleman's honour depended on him being regarded as a man of his word. Doubting his word by trying to impose additional parole conditions was effectively impugning his honour and was bound to be resisted. There was also a widespread feeling among the prisoners that if they conceded even an inch to Hauptmann Karl Niemeyer, 'he was pretty certain shortly to make overtures for an ell'. Major Wyndham had raised the issue with General von Hanisch during his tour of inspection of the camp and received a brusque reply. When neither side would give ground, Wyndham gave orders for the parole cards to be torn up. Unless and until a formal apology was received, no British prisoner would avail himself of the privilege of leaving the camp under parole. Attempts to leave it by other, less formal, means would continue.

The atmosphere in the camp was one of 'continual war between the Germans and ourselves,' said one prisoner. 'The camp staff were over-anxious to enforce petty and unnecessary orders, while we were, perhaps, too ready to fight for real or supposed rights. Our only weapon was that adopted by trade unions in civil life, namely, concerted action . . . some of our actions may appear childish, but most of them achieved their objects; at the least they kept us amused.'

One of Niemeyer's first acts as commandant had been to arrange the transfer of the troublesome Major Wyndham to another camp, Freiburg, sending him away on the morning of 7 November 1917. By no coincidence that was the very day when the Dutch ambassador, Dr R. Romery, was scheduled to make an inspection of the camp, so Wyndham was now no longer present to register his complaints. The lengths to which Niemeyer was willing to go to allay the suspicions of visiting neutral inspectors had been shown by the precautions he had taken before an earlier visit by a Dutch ambassador to Ströhen.

British regiments have sometimes been accused of employing 'eye-wash' on the eve of an inspection but, compared with that to which the Germans resorted, our efforts are infantile. The Ambassador was to be accompanied by the local General [von Hanisch] and, presumably, it was for the benefit of both that the programme was carried out . . . Not only was the whole camp thoroughly cleaned, for the first and last time during my occupation, but every stone in the place was whitewashed and a special paling was put up round the 'jug' only to be demolished and carted away the day after the inspection . . . In due course, the Ambassador, General and Staff arrived. The activity in the precincts of the camp increased till it resembled a London terminus during the rush hour. The Ambassador inspected the camp but, as all its deficiencies had been temporarily rectified in the days preceding his visit, he found little evidence to support our allegations of foulness.

In addition to his general inspection, the British War Office had also asked the Dutch ambassador to conduct an investigation into the excessive prices and profiteering in the Holzminden canteen, but to the disgust of the PoWs, Dr Romery was so won over by a charm offensive from Niemeyer – who, said Romery, 'most courteously received me and conducted me over the camp' – that he dismissed most of the thirteen specific complaints raised against the commandant as unfounded. The ambassador also made approving comments about the accommodation and the kitchens, and 'tested the bread which was of good quality'.

In response to the specific complaints about the 'exorbitant rates' charged for goods in the canteen – one senior officer imprisoned at Holzminden estimated Niemeyer's profit from the canteen between September 1917 and January 1918 to be 'certainly not less than 150,000 marks [and] possibly 250,000' – the ambassador accepted Niemeyer's assurances that the prices were a fair reflection of the quality of goods on sale. He had been 'informed by the camp authorities that, as special stress is laid upon selling goods of the very best quality only, the prices had had to be fixed at the rate noted' and went on to make the surprising assertion that 'the Canteen made no profit out of trading'. As a report prepared for Lloyd George's government in the closing stages of the war pointed out, with classic British understatement, 'In the light of the evidence, this statement must be received with great caution'.

Dr Romery did concede that the camp was run 'in a strict military manner', but insisted that 'there had never been any question of ill-treatment' and, in his conclusion, felt able to state that his general impression of Holzminden was 'of a favourable nature. All the officers looked well and appeared to be in good spirits. The majority of the complaints brought forward seemed to me to be of minor importance and the cause could be obviated with a little mutual goodwill. The Commandant, although maintaining strict discipline, appeared desirous of doing everything possible to render the life of the prisoners as bearable as circumstances would permit.' Had the prisoners been privileged to be party to the ambassador's thoughts, it is doubtful that they would have known whether to laugh or cry.

Major Sorrell-Cameron had become Wyndham's temporary replacement as senior British officer, although his reign lasted little longer than the Dutch ambassador's visit. He was replaced by Commander B. Bingham VC, RN, who became senior officer on 9 November 1917. He, too, earned Niemeyer's displeasure by accusing him of profiteering from the canteen, citing prices that were 'immense compared to other camps'. At Holzminden each prisoner was issued with a *Kontobuch* – a small account book – in which his credit and purchases were recorded. There was a daily charge of one mark ninety pfennigs for 'messing' (food), which was levied whether or not the prisoners actually ate anything, and there were monthly charges for hot water – whether or not there was any – the use of the kitchens to cook their own food and so on. Prisoners were also compelled to keep a monthly balance of at least eighty-five marks in their accounts; since there were normally as many as seven hundred prisoners and the numbers approached a thousand in the latter part of 1918, this added up in all

to a very large amount, permanently lent to the camp authorities without interest.' The prisoners were even charged one mark for the account books and since the guards had neglected to rub out the shop price paid for them, the prisoners were able to see that even the books in which they were compelled to record their purchases – bought for a few pfennigs each – were being sold to them at a substantial profit.

Niemeyer threatened Bingham with a court martial unless he produced concrete evidence of profiteering, but when Bingham returned on 10 December 1917, armed with sworn statements and 'damning price lists from other camps', Niemeyer refused to see him and had him transferred, at two hours' notice, to a camp in Silesia, hundreds of miles away. Major A. E. Haig replaced Bingham as senior British officer, but was perhaps even more trenchant in his criticism of Niemeyer's 'robbery and extortion'.

A written report by a Captain Christie-Miller about Niemeyer's profiteering prompted a War Office official in London to suggest that 'this might offer an opportunity of getting rid of the Niemeyers by an official complaint. The *Kriegswucherant* (War Usury or Extortion Office) might be glad to get its fingers on this gang. It would be worth trying to ungum Niemeyer.' That view was over-optimistic, even naïve: protected as he was by General von Hanisch, it would take more than a few complaints about canteen prices to 'ungum' Karl Niemeyer. Another senior British officer imprisoned at Holzminden, Colonel Charles Rathborne, made a more realistic assessment when he remarked that 'I do not consider it will ever be possible to get any real improvement at Holzminden so long as Niemeyer is there and . . . I saw no sign whatever that his position was any less secure, or that there was any intention of improving things generally in the 10th Army Corps.'

Freed of even the modest restraints imposed on him by his predecessor, Niemeyer had become a complete tyrant. He routinely ignored the Anglo-German accords on the treatment of PoWs and meted out draconian punishments to the prisoners for the most trivial offences: 'The ordinary three days' jugging for small offences is always being inflicted right and left; there are almost daily rows of one sort or another.' One prisoner recalled that he was cooking when the commandant approached him. 'I was more interested in cooking than the Commandant and didn't stand to attention and I was put into solitary confinement for seven days.' The punishment cells in the basement corridors were soon full of officers whom Niemeyer had incarcerated for 'an innocuous stare, a failure to salute at thirty paces' distance or more than likely for no reason at all'. One man received three days' cells 'for looking out of a window', another for having 'a bottle for hot water' in his room, and a third served five days for having a piece of cord that had been tied round a box of his possessions during his transfer from another camp. Another prisoner recorded 'the latest dodge for getting us up at 8 o'clock. Various fierce Huns rush in and tear the clothes off anyone who is in bed, take his name and he gets three days' cells, so all that one has to do if wanting three days' rest in bed is to stop there in the morning. Truly the working of the German mind is wonderful.' Yet another prisoner was in solitary confinement for twenty-seven days without being charged or even told why he was being punished.

The penalty for not saluting a German officer was three days' solitary confinement. The prisoners 'did not feel inclined to admit inferiority to our jailers, especially as some of them were younger and of inferior rank. We invariably waited, therefore, for some form of salute from them which we acknowledged at leisure, but many had to serve a term in "jug" as a result.'

As a consequence of the wholesale imprisonment of men for trivial offences, the cells were soon so overcrowded that the names of fresh offenders had to be placed on an ever-lengthening waiting list, greatly reducing the deterrent value of a spell in the cells. 'No prisoner objected to being awarded a term of solitary confinement to be carried out in, say, three months' time – the war might be over by then – so the camp staff had to find other ways of punishing us.' Nor were Niemeyer's attempts to send men to the cells always crowned with success. On occasions he would deliver some miscreant to his guards and stalk off while his victim was led away, but on one occasion, the officer condemned to the cells ducked away from the guards, ran into the *Kaserne* and rushed up the stairs to the top floor. He was able to transform himself from a flying officer to

an old sea skipper in about two minutes, and walk down coolly past the poor bewildered guards, who were puffing and blowing about in their podgy way on the first and second floor, looking for a young '*flieger*'. On such occasions the Commandant would come in, suffering from liver and hate, and look around for another victim. Wherever he rushed, however, the crowd would disperse and he would be reduced to making funny little dives among us to try and find out who was laughing so loudly and shouting one of his numerous nicknames. Some poor devil would at length be marched off in triumph by Niemeyer himself amid much cheering from the spectators.

Such 'public-school pranks' were one of the few weapons available to the prisoners and they used them to taunt Niemeyer unmercifully. Indeed, while trench warfare was a brutal demolition of the 'play up and play the game' idea that war was only an extension of the conflict on school playing fields, the atmosphere at some officer prisoner-of-war camps bore at least a passing resemblance to public-school life: an 'us and them' mentality, impotent youthful rebellion against an all-powerful authority, elaborate escapades involving great ingenuity and improvisational skill, furtive expeditions outside the 'dorm' and, of course, abysmal food. One British officer even described his first prison camp as 'very like being at school again'.

However, although taunting Niemeyer might have amused the British officers at Holzminden, they were also storing up trouble for themselves. The commandant was undoubtedly short-fused, irascible, arrogant and spiteful, but plaguing him with a continual series of schoolboy and even infantile pranks was no way to improve that. There was

Prisoners line the windows and the yard outside *Kaserne* A, one of the two accommodation blocks at Holzminden PoW camp. The foliage on the trees and the relative health and good humour of the inmates suggests that the photograph was taken soon after the camp opened in early September 1917.

Below: *Kaserne* A during the bitter winter of 1917-18, one of the coldest of the century. Prisoners were charged an exorbitant sum for firewood and were often left to shiver in unheated rooms.

Right: The wooden cookhouse in the *Spielplatz* (exercise yard), winter of 1917-18. There were only two small stoves for the 700 to 1,000 men housed in the camp.

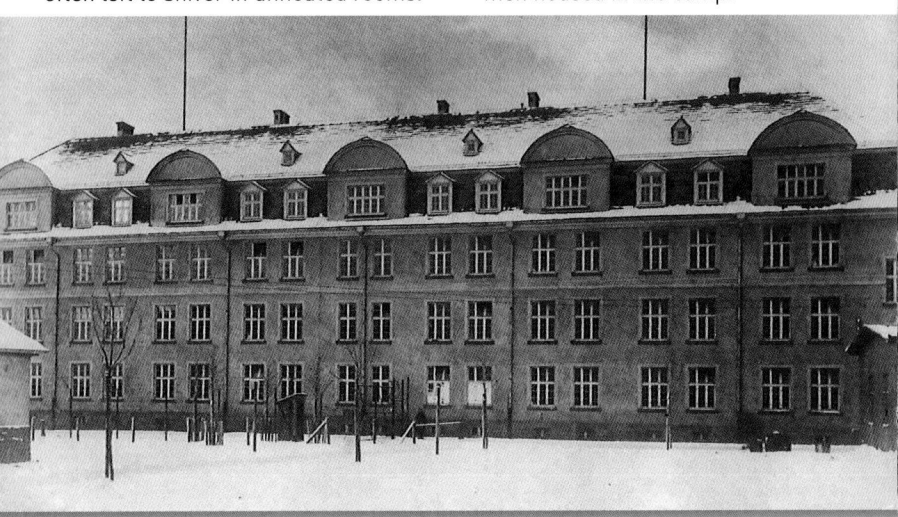

Below: *Kaserne* B seen from outside the perimeter wire. The escape tunnel began beneath the entrance doorway at the far end of the building and was driven sixty yards under the perimeter wall and fence, into the crop field beyond. The building on the right was the gymnasium for German troops. The low wooden shed was the cookhouse.

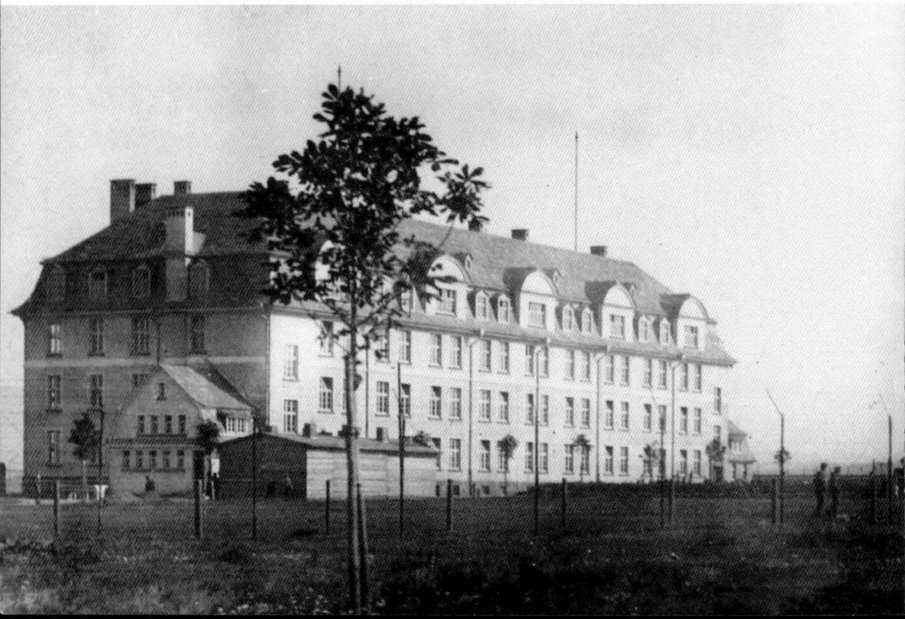

The infamous commandant of Holzminden, Hauptmann Karl 'Milwaukee Bill' Niemeyer – 'the personification of hate'.

Above: Prisoners making the icy trek to the bathhouse. Niemeyer initially forced the prisoners to wash in the horse trough in the yard. Even when they were finally allowed to use the bathhouse, they were only permitted to shower twice a week, in cold water and with only two working showers for the 700-plus prisoners. The cartoon was drawn by James Whale, a Holzminden inmate who went on to become one of the leading directors of Hollywood's Golden Age.

Left: Prisoners were issued with 'camp money', valueless outside the confines of the PoW camp. The aim was to make it impossible for them to bribe their guards or the civilian workers, but it also allowed Niemeyer to extort a penal rate of exchange when converting the inmates' 'real money' sent from Britain.

Above and left (centre and bottom): Interior views of the cramped barrack rooms, shared by up to fourteen men. There were no curtains and the prisoners in ground-floor rooms were not permitted to open their windows, even in the most torrid summer heat. The food tins on the table (**centre left**) were from Red Cross parcels, a vital supplement to the dire camp rations. The wind-up gramophone was a rare luxury and must have cost the officer a fortune in camp money or bribes.

Right: Wilfred Shaw, one of two brothers involved in the Holzminden tunnel. Wilfred played no part in the digging, but he acted as go-between with a guard who pocketed huge sums in bribes, in return for supplying maps and German currency to the prisoners.

Any sport or pastime was seized upon as a respite from the boredom and monotony of camp life, though for many prisoners, the favourite recreation of all was planning and making escapes.

Above: The Holzminden Camp Orchestra. Vernon Coombs is at the front left, holding the double-bass. The conductor, the Italian Count di Balme, is in the centre of the front row, with the drums.

Below: The cast of one of the fortnightly plays staged at the 'Gaiety Theatre' at Holzminden – one of the larger barrack rooms. The chance to forget the misery of their surroundings for a few hours made the plays hugely popular with the prisoners: 'There was nothing that we would less willingly have foregone than our "shows".'

Above: During the icy winter of 1917-18 the frozen *Spielplatz* at Holzminden became an impromptu ice-skating rink, though the cold was so severe that few prisoners availed themselves of it.

Below: Games of hockey, football and tennis were staged on the *Spielplatz*. Attempts to play cricket were less successful: so rough was the surface that 'the game is more dangerous than amusing'. As lack of food and poor conditions took effect, prisoners had less energy to spare for such pursuits.

Left: Jack Shaw's leather football, used in games on the *Spielplatz* and signed by all the Holzminden escapees, was one of his most treasured souvenirs.

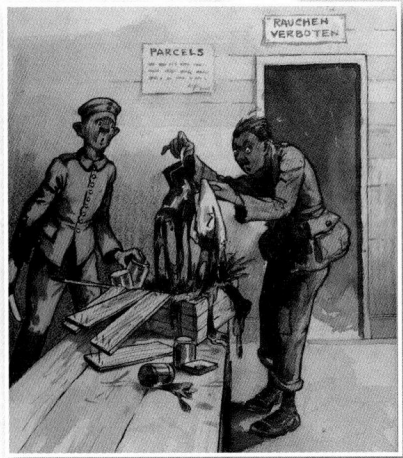

Below: 'You have der tins? – Yes? No?' Prisoners showed great ingenuity in hiding contraband food, money and escape equipment. Most of it remained undiscovered despite frequent searches by camp guards and even civilian detectives.

Prisoners at Holzminden displayed boundless humour in the face of their hardships. (**Above**): 'Prisoners' Parcels: Aunty's home-made jam runs amok.' Food parcels sent by families and the Red Cross kept prisoners from malnutrition and even starvation.

Right: While most of their peers struggled to find enough to eat, a few officers who had private funds accumulated enough gourmet food and wine to lay on special dinners for their friends. Other less wealthy inmates performed miracles of improvisation, such as 'Doubtful Soup' and 'Kish Fakes'.

Whether or not they had any food to cook, in bitter weather prisoners congregated around the stoves in the cookhouse – 'the only warmth obtainable'.

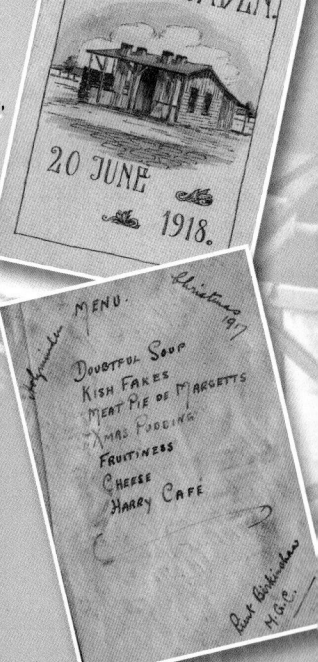

HOLZMINDEN.

20 JUNE 1918.

MENU.
Christmas 1917
DOUBTFUL SOUP
KISH FAKES
MEAT PIE OF MARGETTS
XMAS PUDDING
FRUITINESS
CHEESE
HARRY CAFÉ

also an undoubted whiff of British arrogance and con-
descension in many of the comments that the British PoWs
recorded about him: Niemeyer's crime was not only to be an
arrogant Prussian, it seems, it was also to be a lower-class one.

William Leefe Robinson, the young pilot who became a
British hero and won the Victoria Cross for being the first
man to shoot down a German Zeppelin, would have
struggled to empathize with those who saw the camp as
merely a harsher version of public school. Leefe Robinson
was brought into Holzminden on 13 May 1918 and, because
of his fame, was subjected to a more than usually brutal
regime. Before he had even arrived, Niemeyer was gloating
to the other prisoners that the 'English Richthofen was
coming'. Leefe Robinson did not help his cause by escaping
almost immediately with Captain W. S. Stephenson. They
were quickly recaptured, and Niemeyer raged at Leefe
Robinson, swearing 'to avenge the death of [the Zeppelin
commander] Wilhelm Schramm, whom he falsely claimed
to have known well'. From then on, 'the Boche harried and
badgered and bullied him in every way possible'. Among
others of Niemeyer's 'pet escapees', Leefe Robinson was
continually given 'small sentences of cells for absolutely no
reason' and was kept 'so restricted that few prisoners ever
saw him'. One Holzminden inmate 'didn't know he was
there. I never saw him.' He was generally in solitary confinement, and even a prisoner who lived in the same barrack
block never saw him: 'He was very much confined.'

The camp adjutant, Second Lieutenant Hugh Durnford,

saw Leefe Robinson dragged out of his bed at seven thirty a.m. on the excuse that as 'an Inspector General was coming, officers should be out of bed particularly early. His clothes were pulled off him, and he was forced on to the floor, and a table nearly overturned. Captain Robinson was subsequently punished with three days' arrest for absolutely nothing. Niemeyer absolutely persecuted him. He said he should answer five *Appels* a day and he was not allowed to go from one barrack to another.' Accused of disobeying an order, he was 'whipped to the point of collapse'.

When challenged about Leefe Robinson's treatment, the *Kriegsministerium* claimed that 'Captain Robinson was more closely watched than other officers because he was strongly suspected of making preparations for escape and had already been punished for such attempts as well as for bribery and unseemly behaviour. The non-commissioned officers and men at the camp have been repeatedly instructed by the commandant to deal with imprisoned officers in a correct but firm manner and up to the present no similar complaint has been made by the officers.'

Like Leefe Robinson, Algernon Bird, another airman imprisoned at Holzminden, was singled out for particularly harsh treatment. Bird had been Baron Manfred von Richthofen's sixty-first victim; after being shot down and captured, he was introduced to the 'Red Baron' – an encounter filmed by the aircraft designer Anthony Fokker. Bird strongly resented this; he disliked von Richthofen treating him as if he were a trophy of battle. For the rest of his life, he 'never, ever, talked' about his time at Holzminden, and his son believed that his father had had 'a very bad experience' there.

Although Leefe Robinson and Bird were particular targets, Niemeyer's hostility to the prisoners in his charge was so widespread and his rages so notorious that most prisoners avoided encounters with him if at all possible. One orderly, Private George Dellar, opened his door at six thirty one evening, saw the commandant approaching along the corridor and promptly closed it again. A moment later it was reopened and a guard pulled him out into the corridor, where Niemeyer asked Dellar what he wanted. 'I told him I wanted to go to the latrine,' Dellar later said, to which the commandant replied, 'You can shit where you like. You can shit yourself. You can shit the bloody bed but you will not go to the latrine tonight.'

Taking their cue from their commandant, many of the camp guards also behaved in what one patrician British officer described as 'a most unbecoming, familiar and offensive manner'. There were frequent incidents and regular claims of violence and brutality. When a German NCO and four guards were sent to evict three British officers from a room to make way for some fresh arrivals, 'the first officer was seized by the throat and shaken, the second was struck with a rifle and the third one chased down the passage, his pursuer jabbing at him with his bayonet'. Others 'were kicked downstairs, repeatedly hit with the butt end of the sentries' rifles for the least offence'.

Some prisoners responded to rough treatment by barracking Niemeyer or turning their backs on him and one, E. L. Edwards, even emptied a bucket of potatoes over him – which earned him 108 days on bread and water in solitary confinement. At the end of that term, he was sentenced to a further eighteen months' imprisonment for disobeying an order and insulting the commandant.

The prisoners, incensed at the attitude of the commandant but impotent to act without risking draconian punishments, could only register their anger by going on *Appel* in 'a very disrespectful manner. We wore no head-dress; we wore very casual clothes; we had our hands in our trouser pockets.' Niemeyer promptly ordered the prisoners back to their barracks and called out the guard. 'They were pointing their guns at us and he threatened to shoot us, but people didn't seem to take any notice. They either didn't believe him or else they were going to show him that they didn't care, and we all sort of very casually sauntered over to Barracks, taking as long as possible,' even though 'there was some firing going on'. 'Milwaukee Bill retaliated by lining up his men and ordering them to loose a volley' at the building.

On that, as on several other occasions, Niemeyer had responded by ordering his guards to open fire. 'There were people at the upper windows of the building, looking over the parade-ground, and I don't know whether they were laughing, or what it was, but he suddenly told the soldiers to fire at these people up there . . . without any warning at all. He thought they were mocking him, I suppose.' There was 'some slight improvement' in his conduct in the spring of 1918, 'simply due, I think, to Niemeyer happening to be in a better temper; but that has quite worn off'.

Next to Niemeyer in the chain of command were the officers in charge of the two cell blocks. There was a *Feldwebel-offizier* and four *Feldwebels* who all 'take their tone from Niemeyer' and were 'all harsh', though Oberleutnant Lincke was said to be the worst of the four, 'an absolute worm'. Feldwebel Groner, who had charge of *Kaserne* A, was a paunchy, sallow-skinned man with a heavy moustache and a permanent scowl. Feldwebel Ulrich, in charge of *Kaserne* B, was a more jovial figure. A married man with several children, he had been wounded at Passchendaele, but was widely believed to be 'swinging the lead' – avoiding further active service at all costs. Whenever a senior officer came into view, Ulrich's normally brisk and upright gait would become slow and halting, his back stooped and his expression doleful. As soon as the officer had departed, Ulrich would experience a miraculous cure and resume his normal gait and demeanour.

Feldwebel Leutnant Welman – 'most offensive' – was in charge of the quartermaster's store and the canteen, where prisoners could exchange their camp money for additional food, if there was any, fuel for heating, tobacco, writing paper or other 'luxuries' at suitably inflated prices. Camp money (notes of various values printed with the name of the prison camp) was issued instead of German marks because, being valueless outside the camp perimeter, it couldn't be used by the prisoners to bribe guards or civilian workers; it also provided a further opportunity for defrauding the prisoners when swapping 'real money' for the camp substitute at a penal rate of exchange.

'Clouded' wine was sold in the canteen, for eleven or twelve marks a bottle, when the normal price for a decent bottle was only three or four. That aroused the fury of Captain Douglas Lyall Grant, a substantial consumer of the product, who denounced it in his diary as 'nothing less than a SCANDAL. The wine is sold unnamed and the quality is abominable . . . No good (or even bad or indifferent) wine merchant would dare to see wine thus "clouded". It would be poured down the sink.' A document pinned to the camp notice-board cited the 1915 Army & Navy Stores Wine List as proof that prisoners were being grossly overcharged and claimed that over a three-month period, on the sale of 100 bottles of wine a day, 'someone – one knows not whom – has pocketed Mks 36,000 on 9,200 bottles'.

At least one senior British officer made no objection to that – just one of many 'flagrant and shameful instances of exploitation' – because he thought that 'the higher the price of wine and the worse its quality, the better it was for the officers as they would buy less', while Niemeyer 'undoubtedly encouraged heavy drinking for the purpose of making money'.

Feldwebel Leutnant Welman was said to pocket 50 per cent of the profits from the canteen, though it seems unlikely that Niemeyer would have allowed his subordinate such a large percentage. The remainder was passed up the line to Niemeyer and part of it probably found its way to von Hanisch. Feldwebel Schneider, 'one of the greatest nuisances in the place, who ... takes his tone from Niemeyer and is most offensive', ran the parcel room and took his commission in kind: parcels either failed to arrive at all or, if they did so, were lacking some of their contents. 'It was fairly common for two or three parcels every day to have something taken out of them and bricks or straw put in their place.' Boots or shoes and tobacco were routinely removed but canvas shoes with rope soles were 'most useful and do not get stolen'. 'It was never possible to get a pair of boots sent to you in the same parcel' because they would invariably be stolen. 'You had to have the left and right boots sent in separate parcels . . . and I had to have 16lbs. of tobacco sent out per month in order to have two ounces.'

One of the previous camp *Feldwebels*, an old farmer who wore horn-rimmed glasses and was known affectionately as 'Square Eyes', had been a kindly soul, but unfortunately for the prisoners, he did not last long: it was suspected that he had been transferred for being too friendly with his charges. Others who failed to show the necessary rigour in their dealings with the prisoners also departed. Most of the camp officers who remained were unbending disciplinarians or worse.

Like the rest of the rooms, those allocated for dining on the second floor of the barrack blocks had bare, roughly whitewashed walls and square pillars supporting the central roof beam. They were not large enough for all the officers to use, so some ate in their rooms, even though it was against the camp regulations. The food supplied to the prisoners was 'worse than you would feed to pigs', 'prepared in such a way as to be almost inedible'. Breakfast was at eight o'clock and consisted of 'a hunk of the sourest black bread' and a bowl of acorn or burned barley *ersatz* coffee, without sugar or milk. For lunch at twelve thirty, 'they called it soup – water with a few vegetables thrown in and on Sunday a bit of horseflesh'. The soup 'changed in colour, but not in taste', and was variously described as 'a very nauseous paste', made of barley, stewed mangels, or 'any kind of vegetable they could lay their hands on – mostly turnips', or 'different varieties of greasy water, christened with the names of certain standard dishes'. Occasionally there was sauerkraut, and sometimes a potato. Dinner at six thirty was more 'soup of a different colour from the morning, but still tasteless; a small dish of sour red cabbage, and more stewed mangels'.

At Holzminden, three British orderlies were on permanent fatigue duty in the potato cellar in the basement of *Kaserne* B, peeling the daily ration. The potatoes were then tipped into one of the two large coppers in the cook-house and boiled to extinction along with turnips or whatever other ingredients were available that day, then ladled into pails for distribution to the dining rooms. When one group of new arrivals at the camp lined up to collect their lunch, they were astonished to see a five-course menu:

Soup was there in a large pot and we went to help ourselves. Then we found we had to buy our crockery and cutlery from the canteen at fairly fancy prices. When we came back, the soup was still there, but decidedly cooler. We managed to get some of it down, though it was not too tasty, and waited for the next course. The older prisoners, expecting this, had come in to lunch for a change, but merely sat and talked at their tables. Then one asked why we were waiting and of course we said for the next ration to come along. Then it was explained to us in a very nice way that the menu card ran something like this: soup, meat, potatoes, butter (I query this last commodity) and prunes. AND THE WHOLE LOT HAD BEEN IN THE SOUP.

Having provided their campmates with their entertainment for the day, the new prisoners abandoned thoughts of five-course dinners and returned, hungry, to their quarters.

In the early days of the Holzminden camp there was an occasional piece of fish or meat, or sometimes 'a little of the celebrated German sausage' in their soup. One prisoner recalled, 'One German would fling a few potatoes into the dish, while another thrust his dirty hand into a great cauldron to deposit a piece of fish upon the plate. Niemeyer, thoroughly pleased, stood by to taunt his victims, saying, "Ach, it is not so goot as Piccadilly, zo?"' On some days there was nothing but plain sauerkraut or sometimes barley, which many prisoners saved and made into porridge for breakfast the next day. Sometimes the only protein was 'horse's lights' or 'meat which one of our guards told me was seal', and on a couple of memorable occasions a cow's head, complete except for its skin and ears, and 'half a horse's head, complete with eye', were seen floating in the cooking pot. By mid-1918, even such dubious sources of protein were unavailable and the prisoners' soup was almost exclusively 'turnip skins, dried almost to resemble chips of wood, chopped up like sawdust and mixed with boiling water'.

The prisoners were charged sixty marks a month for this foul fare. It was probably no coincidence that this was the exact amount fixed by arrangement between the German and British governments as the maximum amount that a subaltern might receive as his pay while in captivity. The Germans converted it 'very unfavourably' into camp money before passing it on. If an officer needed more money, he had to draw a cheque on his own bank in England, which was then discounted by the Germans with a neutral agent, once more 'at a ruinous rate of exchange' that left a substantial profit for everybody involved in the transaction, apart from the hapless prisoner. Inmates were charged for the camp food whether they took it or not. Since at least four hundred prisoners never did but were charged almost two marks a day – in fact it was not even provided for them – the commandant could make a profit of at least eight hundred marks a day.

Complaints about the quality and quantity of the food supplied were met by Niemeyer's standard response to criticism: 'All officers who complain about food in their letters are given several days' solitary confinement in cells.' The inadequacy of the camp food was not always, as prisoners believed, a product of German indifference or malevolence. The Allied blockade of the North Sea ports had placed an even greater stranglehold on the German economy than the U-boat campaign had done on the British food supply. German imports of food, fertilizer and agricultural equipment had been stifled and a scarcity of fuel and transport, coupled with a lack of manpower to work the land as more and more men were sucked into the armed forces, led to food shortages so severe that the winter of 1916–17 was known as the 'turnip winter' by German civilians, since there was virtually nothing else to eat. By late 1917 and early 1918 the shortages had reached crisis point. Although there were almost a million prisoners of war and foreign internees working as forced labour on German farms, trying to improve the harvest yield, the low productivity of such a reluctant workforce, the lack of competent managers to direct their efforts and the chronic shortages of fertilizers, fuel and transport, led to little improvement in the food supply. With German troops existing on barely adequate rations and civilians close to starvation, it was beyond reason to imagine that the country's rulers would divert food resources to improve the diet of prisoners of war. Had they done so, there would undoubtedly have been riots. The food served to the German guards at Holzminden was only marginally better than that fed to the prisoners. Pilfering of the food parcels sent to inmates was widespread, and once more Niemeyer was indifferent to prisoners' protests. 'A complaint was made that the German cook had been seen eating our rations. Niemeyer said he would see to it. Result: the cook remained and the kitchen windows were painted white to obscure our view.'

Most other-ranks prisoners had to subsist on the near-starvation rations in their camps. Some officer prisoners – at least, those at the camps where their parcels from home were not intercepted and pilfered in huge quantities – lived in a style that made a mockery of any idea of hardship and also infuriated the guards and the local populace, who were forced to exist on a far more restricted diet. One inmate at Gütersloh camp, Captain Douglas Lyall Grant, described a breakfast of 'Fruit and Cream, Porridge, Fish, Sausages, Bacon, Tomatoes, Various Potted Meats and Game, Toast, Butter, Jam and Marmalade – all from parcels of course'. On another occasion he gave a dinner for which the menu was 'Asparagus Soup; Sole; Duck or Goose with potatoes and greens; Plum Pudding; Sardines on Toast; Coffee'.

Officer prisoners at Gütersloh were also able to indulge themselves in games of hockey, tennis, fives, football, cricket and rugby, and there were country walks on parole, theatricals, art exhibitions, entertainments, a daily camp newspaper and a monthly magazine with short stories and illustrations. In the early stages of the war prisoners with money could buy food and a range of other items from itinerant salesmen who were permitted to visit the camps with their wares. 'One such vendor did a brisk trade in copies of the *Baedeker Guide to North Germany* – a volume that, since it contained maps, was eagerly snapped up by prospective escapers.' Although the maps it contained did not cover the entire route of those making for the Netherlands, 'it seemed that the road was not too difficult [and] there appeared to be plenty of woods and forests' in which they could hide by day.

In the face of similar self-indulgence by some inmates at Krefeld prisoner-of-war camp, the guard at the camp had to be doubled in the summer of 1917, not to prevent the inmates from getting out but to prevent the local inhabitants, who had been staging a protest demonstration in the town, from storming the camp and liberating the prisoners' stores of food. Two days later, the threat of riots had become so serious that, in addition to the doubled guard, there were also 'two machine guns in the fields outside and two on the roof of the buildings'.

Even after he was transferred to the far harsher regime at Holzminden, Lyall Grant was still able on occasion to indulge his appetite for the finer things in life. There was a camp doctor on site at Holzminden and a dentist visited at intervals, but those with very serious medical conditions or with more specialized requirements were sometimes sent off-camp for examination or treatment. When Lyall Grant and two other prisoners were allowed out of Holzminden on parole in order to visit an 'oculist' in the nearby town of Brakel, they made a day out of it with the co-operation of their easily bribable guard. As Lyall Grant recorded:

It was just over an hour by train and made a pleasant outing, particularly as after the interview we lunched at the village pub and it was a treat to get something that didn't come out of a tin. Menu as follows: vegetable soup, hare with potatoes and vegetables, gooseberries and milk, cheese and bread (no butter available), all washed down by Château Laon ... The guard who went with us had rather a heavy day. Going there, our train had to wait half an hour at a junction and we insisted on getting out and visiting the refreshment rooms, with the result that when the other train came in, we were missing and they had to keep our train waiting until they found us. At lunch, when we wished to order more wine the guard refused on the ground that the money given to him to pay expenses was finished and, as we only had camp money (issued for us in camp and no good outside), nothing could be done. We rather surprised him by producing 180 marks of *real* money and so were able to get on with the good work.

While other prisoners at Holzminden complained about Niemeyer's brutality, the complaints of the blimpish Captain Douglas Lyall Grant, as noted in his diary, centred chiefly on the petty rules, regulations and restrictions enforced by the commandant, the lack of the sort of recreational facilities he had enjoyed at Gütersloh and Krefeld – the latter possessing no less than fifteen tennis courts – the pilfering of parcels that made his lavish breakfasts and dinner parties harder to arrange, the poor quality of the wine in the canteen and the excessive prices he had to pay for it.

Lyall Grant was not the only one to indulge himself now and then. Joseph Allen, who was imprisoned at Holzminden after being shot down during a bombing raid on 26 February 1918, produced a menu for a dinner on 20 June 1918 'to celebrate the birthdays of D. C. Doyle and A. Clouston', that read:

Soup
Tomato

Fish
Herrings

Poultry
Roast Duck

Game
Jugged Hare

Vegetables
Roast Potatoes
Boiled Potatoes
Peas
Onions

Sweets
Marmalade Pudding
Stewed Peaches

<u>Cheese</u>

<u>Coffee</u>
Holzminden Wine
Cigarettes by Abdullah

Although Lyall Grant and Allen were able to indulge themselves from time to time, most prisoners were far less fortunate and many were severely malnourished. Even making allowances for Germany's food-supply problems, the diet at Holzminden was so inadequate that most prisoners lost stones in weight and were suffering from malnutrition to varying degrees; the faces of all newly captured prisoners 'assumed a pale-green hue, due to the initial stages of starvation'. Only when food parcels began to arrive for them from England did a little colour return. 'Our [Red Cross] parcels kept us going,' one prisoner said. 'People formed Messes of about six people and we shared all our parcels.' Without those supplies, it is probable that many prisoners would have starved or died of illnesses exacerbated by malnutrition, and that was indeed the fate of many enlisted men held as prisoners of war by the Germans. Taken as a whole, though, the sufferings of British prisoners paled into insignificance beside those of the hundreds of thousands of Russian captives. As their country dissolved into revolution and civil war, they had no access to the sort of food parcels that British officers enjoyed and were treated with a barbarity that their German captors would rarely have displayed towards British prisoners.

As the deputy commissioner of the American Red Cross in Switzerland lamented,

It is a fact beyond dispute that the ravages of disease due to malnutrition, even starvation, have killed tens of thousands of prisoners in the hands of the German forces. Other thousands have been interned in Switzerland or repatriated to their homes, human wrecks as a result of the failure of the German Government to properly feed and clothe them. Neither treaty nor humanitarian consideration induced the German Government to treat its prisoners of war as human beings, or make much effort to preserve their lives.

The International Red Cross and Red Crescent was founded in 1863, its prime mover a charismatic Swiss businessman, Jean-Henri Dunant. In 1858, aged thirty, he had moved to the French colonial territory of Algeria and set up a flour-milling company. When his attempts to purchase land on which to grow wheat were frustrated by colonial officials, Dunant's response was to travel to Paris to petition Napoleon III. When he discovered that the emperor was in Lombardy, leading his armies into battle against the Austro-Hungarian forces of Emperor Franz Joseph, Dunant travelled there himself. What he saw changed his life. He arrived in June 1859, in the immediate aftermath of the battle of Solferino. The Austro-Hungarians had been routed, but even the victorious French soldiers were paying a terrible price. Many of their wounded were simply left on the battlefield to die, but even the nine thousand who had been brought or had made their own way to the town of Castiglione discovered that there were just six army surgeons to deal with them.

Appalled, Dunant sat down to write the polemic, *Un Souvenir de Solferino*. He described the horrors he had witnessed and the indifference of army commanders to the sufferings of their men, and proposed establishing, 'in time of peace and quiet', relief societies composed of 'zealous, devoted and thoroughly qualified volunteers' to provide neutral and impartial care for the wounded of all sides in time of war. Published in 1862, his book was an immediate sensation, and in February 1863 Dunant, with a distinguished Swiss jurist, Gustave Moynier, and three other men, founded just such a relief society in Geneva, choosing as its emblem a red cross on a white ground. The following year, 1864, he and his associates organized the first Geneva Convention, at which delegates of the leading powers agreed to recognize the status of medical services and of the wounded on the battlefield, and accepted the Red Cross emblem as a universal symbol of neutrality.

Although the principal focus of the Red Cross was always on providing medical care, the organization also established centres to record the names of the wounded and missing and, by extension, prisoners of war. In the Franco-Prussian War, a centre set up in Berlin and staffed by eleven volunteers dealt with sixty thousand enquiries about missing French military personnel and processed 186,000 letters to and from prisoners of war. A Tokyo office during the

Russo-Japanese War of 1902 handled information on seventy thousand prisoners of war and also supervised, with scrupulous honesty, the return of personal effects found on dead soldiers, including more than a million yen and two million roubles.

A British version of the Red Cross had been set up in July 1870, following the outbreak of the Franco-Prussian War with all its attendant horrors. Concerned British citizens formed the British National Society for Aid to the Sick and Wounded in War and, operating under the rules laid down by the Geneva Convention, they helped to give aid and relief to both sides in that war and in a number of other conflicts over the remainder of the century.

The Society was formally reconstituted as the British Red Cross in 1905 and granted its first Royal Charter in 1908 by King Edward VII and Queen Alexandra, who became its president. A system of local branches was set up covering the whole country, and in 1909, as war clouds began to gather, Voluntary Aid Detachments were formed in every county in England to provide aid to the army medical forces in times of war. All were trained in first aid, and some individuals were also trained in nursing care, hygiene and sanitation, and cookery.

When war broke out in August 1914, the British Red Cross and the Order of St John pooled their financial and human resources to form the Joint War Committee, working under the emblem of the Red Cross. The committee formed Voluntary Aid Detachments in hospitals, convalescent homes, rest stations, packing centres and medical-supply depots. Children and other volunteers were encouraged to gather sphagnum moss from the moors, which was used to make wound dressings – two million dressings were supplied by the British Red Cross in 1918 alone. The Joint War Committee was also the first organization to provide motorized ambulances for the battlefields, in place of horse-drawn vehicles. The greater speed of transferring the injured to casualty-clearing stations and field hospitals led to much improved survival rates.

The Red Cross was also heavily involved in providing aid and comfort to prisoners of war and their families. The British Section of the Red Cross in Geneva had a staff of eighty-three people, working in shifts twenty-four hours a day. There were four sections: the first dealt with amassing information about PoWs and passing it on to the men's families; the second handled the forwarding of parcels, letters and money; the third inspected conditions in PoW camps; and the last arranged repatriation and supervised the welfare of internees held in neutral countries, like Switzerland and the Netherlands. A standard card was issued to all combatants on which PoWs entered their name, rank, home address and the details of the prison camp where they were held. By the end of the war, the British Section alone had processed half a million of these cards.

The efforts of the Red Cross were supported and supplemented by those of regimental associations, 'Care Committees' and other community organizations and individuals in Britain. Helped by fund-raising events and public meetings, with escaped PoWs as guest speakers talking about their experiences, they raised large sums of money and helped to collect and dispatch gifts of food and clothing. Many people also 'adopted' individual PoWs, sent them gifts and corresponded with them, boosting their morale. One indomitable Englishwoman, Lady Evelyn Grant Duff, the wife of a government minister, took on the task of supplying bread to British PoWs in Germany. She imported flour from Marseille to Geneva, where it was baked into bread, then sent by rail to a depot in Frankfurt for distribution to the various camps. More bakeries in Denmark and the Netherlands supplemented the effort. Despite their best endeavours, the bread took up to a week to reach the camps, and though it was still palatable in winter, in summer it often arrived covered with mould. As a result, rusk-like biscuits were substituted for bread during the hotter part of the year.

The German government had undertaken to deliver parcels from individuals and voluntary organizations to prisoners of war but 'very many things are difficult to get through, printed matters, woollens and various other things being forbidden, except necessary clothing'. Germany's rulers also took cynical advantage of the system, both as a channel for communication between German agents in Britain and Berlin, and as a means of evading the blockade of Germany's ports. Some parcels sent from Britain addressed to fictitious prisoners of war in Germany were intercepted by the British government and found to contain messages for German military intelligence or contraband strategic materials, including rubber, which was in such short supply in Germany that the High Command was even reduced to requisitioning the cushions from billiard tables.

The activities of the various volunteer organizations in Britain had been co-ordinated to some extent by the Prisoners of War Help Committee, formed in early 1915, which had submitted a proposal to the War Office to concentrate the packing and dispatch of all PoW parcels in one place to eliminate the waste and duplication inevitable when so many different bodies were otherwise involved. The War Office, in its wisdom, promptly rejected the idea. However, partly as a result of the German abuses of the system, the Army Council later decided to adopt the plan. The voluntary groups were placed under the direction of a single unit, based at a central depot in Thurloe Place, South Kensington. Eventually, dubious that the Help Committee had the necessary expertise and manpower to take on such a responsibility, the Army Council put it in the hands of the Red Cross.

It employed 750 people, with the stated aim of ensuring that every British prisoner of war in Germany received a fortnightly ten-pound parcel of food and thirteen pounds of bread. During the course of the war, they packed and dispatched millions of parcels. The scale of shipments was astonishing: a Swiss haulage firm in Berne alone carried two million parcels between 1914 and 1918. The food included porridge oats, tea, milk, cocoa, 'bully' (corned beef), processed cheese, jam, marmalade, margarine, potted meat, bacon, sugar and rice pudding. Although 'all of it tasted of tins', it was far more palatable and nutritious than the normal prison-camp rations. Expert advice was given on what the food parcels should contain:

> The British Science Guild has appointed a committee to make suggestions relating to food ... A prisoner of war doing moderate work requires a daily ration which has an energy value of 2500 calories, and may be made up of proteins, 100 grams; carbohydrates, 400 grams; and fats, 50 grams. It is possible to combine all these constituents in a single foodstuff, or to see that the ratios are roughly supplied by the combination of several things in a parcel.

The Red Cross also distributed emergency parcels of iron rations and biscuits, like the old naval 'hard tack', which were kept as a reserve in case ordinary parcels went astray or the German frontiers were closed, which happened once or twice a year for a period of up to a month.

In addition to providing, packing and distributing food parcels for PoWs, approving shops – such as Harrods, Selfridges and the Army & Navy Stores – where parcels could also be packed and dispatched, and arranging transport of goods that could not be trusted to the normal postal service, the Red Cross had responsibility for co-ordinating and controlling the work of the various volunteer organizations concerned with the welfare of PoWs, gave financial and other assistance, where necessary, to local groups and regimental care associations, and formed a Care Committee to look after the interests of men from regiments that had not formed such associations. They also dealt with all enquiries from the public on any matter relating to PoWs in enemy hands and also, at the direction of the Military Intelligence branch of the War Office, carried out the examination and censorship of letters and parcels being sent to PoWs. Their dedication was exemplary. When the workforce at the firm of box-makers that supplied the cartons for the prisoners' parcels went on strike, twenty Red Cross workers at once occupied the factory and carried on manufacturing the cartons themselves.

The parcels sent by their families and the Red Cross were the only things that kept the prisoners from malnutrition, and so grateful were the officers and orderlies at Holzminden for the parcels sent to them that during Christmas 1917 they took up a collection for the Red Cross. The imprisoned men contacted their banks or relatives in Britain and arranged donations that raised the then considerable sum of £2,289.

Despite the best efforts of the Red Cross, not all parcels reached their intended recipients. There were constant complaints from prisoners that parcels had been stolen by German guards, with tins of biscuits, coffee and tobacco particularly vulnerable. Red Cross estimates suggested that on average four out of five parcels reached their intended target, but that was an average across all the PoW camps in

Germany and in some, including Holzminden, the proportion was much lower. While many prisoners were not receiving sufficient food, others had a considerable surplus: one estimate suggested that a German division of troops could have been fed comfortably on the spare and waste food sent to British prisoners of war.

Prisoners at Holzminden who complained of thefts from their parcels might find themselves in the cells. Lieutenant Burrows remonstrated with the parcel-room attendant when he discovered that the butter from his Red Cross parcel had been stolen and replaced with wood shavings. His reward was three days in solitary confinement. Prisoners also claimed that not only was much of their food pilfered, but that guards took a malevolent pleasure in spoiling what was passed on. Parcels had to be collected from the parcel room and every item was subject to scrutiny by the guards, reducing the flow of parcels from the room to a trickle and causing endless frustration and irritation to the prisoners.

Even worse, all tins of food had to be opened in the presence of the guards and examined by them, so any tinned food from a parcel that was not immediately required – and almost every edible item in a parcel was tinned – had to be stored in the tin room in the cellars of *Kaserne* B. A visit to the parcel room showed a prisoner what he should eventually be getting from the tin room, but there was 'considerable leakage' on the journey from parcel room to tin room and much of the food disappeared. When a prisoner wanted one of his tins, he joined an endless queue of his peers that stretched from the tin room along the cellar corridor, up the stairs and often out of the door of the block into the yard. It took an average of five to ten minutes to 'serve' each man in the queue and the last ones to join it in the morning were lucky to be given anything before the evening roll-call.

Every tin was opened, its contents tipped into a bowl and probed for contraband until the food was barely edible. All packets of tea and sugar were 'stabbed several times with a long skewer' or were emptied out. The guards would take food parcels and 'slash them to pieces to see if there was anything hidden', which must have been almost as painful for them to witness as the prisoners, with Germany so desperately short of food. The guards hated this wanton destruction – 'They were very badly fed and we could get practically anything out of them in exchange for food' – but Niemeyer was a frequent sudden visitor to the tin room, and any guard who had failed to show the necessary rigour when examining the contents of tins got at best a savage tongue-lashing and at worst a few days on fatigues.

On several occasions Niemeyer took out his own penknife and the prisoners had to watch him 'hack to mincemeat' a ham or tongue that had been left too whole for his liking, 'threatening dire things to his staff, if ever such an object was let off so lightly again'. In this he was merely aping his superior: General von Hanisch had enlivened one of his inspections by telling the tin-room attendants to see that 'not a tin, not a bit of paper or string or anything but the bare contents fall into the hands of the prisoners'. Then, picking up a knife that had been 'used promiscuously', he hacked a steak and kidney pudding to bits, saying, 'That is the way to treat all their food before you deliver it.' Following the lead of von Hanisch and Niemeyer, 'privates who were none too clean in their methods' cut up 'meat, butter and every other article of food with the same knife without wiping it', and 'sugar, jam, sardines, rice, oatmeal, cigarettes, tobacco, etc.' were tipped out of their containers in 'a dirty and useless manner', often mixing them and leaving them barely fit for consumption. 'Cigarettes were frequently broken, and puddings and cakes cut till they were crumbs.'

The finding of contraband items served only to heighten Niemeyer's vigilance. One prisoner, A. J. Evans, found 'watching a German open a parcel in which you know there is a concealed compass one of the most exciting things I've ever done'. Evans managed to smuggle his compass out of the room, but another prisoner, Jack Shaw, had to stand and watch as

one of my tins, opened in my presence, was found to contain my Mark IV Prismatic compass, value £4 10s., on which my name was engraved ... I endeavoured to persuade 'Milwaukee Bill' that I must have been the victim of a cruel hoax on the part of someone who did not like me in England, but he was not having any. At the same time, the German who was opening my packages mixed tea, coffee, pepper, sugar, salt and ground rice all together in one heap on a piece of paper, which he pushed to me with a grin. I threw the whole lot into his face, to his discomfiture, and was immediately placed under arrest and, for the day's work, the commandant awarded me three weeks in solitary confinement.

In the early days of the camp, the prisoners were largely preoccupied with finding something to eat. There was no 'common box' – a store of tins of food on which newly captured prisoners or those transferred from other camps could draw while waiting for Red Cross parcels to reach them. The German canteen 'had nothing edible for sale', the commissary was empty, the catering facilities for each block were wholly inadequate for the numbers they had to serve and the cookhouses were closed at nightfall – four p.m. in winter – putting the prisoners under even greater strain. At nine o'clock every night the lights had to be extinguished, and if this was not done at once, the sentry outside would immediately report it to the *Unteroffizier* of the guard, which usually resulted in yet more restrictions being imposed on the prisoners.

Fuel for the stoves, the only form of heating in the barrack blocks, was also in very short supply, provided, 'if at all, in wholly insufficient quantities'. The only time it was freely issued was when the Dutch ambassador was inspecting the camp. On that day Niemeyer announced that a mistake had been made over the issue of fuel, which was now freely available. A few days later the fuel was again withdrawn, and Niemeyer denied ever making the statement.

The weather was severe enough in the winter of 1917–18 for the parade-ground to be turned into an impromptu ice rink from the beginning of January onwards. 'There has been a certain amount of skating on a flooded part of the square and one or two people are to be seen with bandaged heads.' 'Great care was taken of the rink, and it was religiously brushed and reflooded at the end of each day of the seven weeks that the frost held.' However, most of the men shivering in their virtually unheated prison blocks had little appetite for skating or even for venturing outside. There had been heavy, driving snow, sleet and savage frosts since the start of December, and by the turn of the year firewood was very scarce. What little the prisoners received they had to 'pay through the nose for, with the result that one is very cold in this bitter weather'. Desperate for warmth, prisoners burned the stools from the dining rooms and even some of their own bed boards, while those with sufficient money paid the extortionate rate of from forty to as much as 250 marks for a cubic metre of firewood. One prisoner complained that Niemeyer 'reckoned to charge 10,000 marks for 39 cubic metres of wood, all loosely piled'. The German guards gathered the wood from the forests around the camp, and Niemeyer took the lion's share of the profits, which were very substantial; it was estimated that, by the end of March 1918 alone, 55,000 marks in fuel charges had been extorted from the British officers at Holzminden.

Occasionally a wagon-load of coal briquettes – fuel for the *Kommandantur* and guardroom – would arrive and be discharged into the coal cellars under *Kaserne* B. It was the cue for every British officer to help with the unloading. Clad in their 'British warms' and trenchcoats with capacious pockets, they ensured that not all the coal found its way to the cellar, and for a night or so the stoves in the prisoners' rooms gave off a little heat. When a load of wood underwent the same treatment, each of the prisoners was charged the equivalent of six shillings for the extra wood ration they had appropriated. As one remarked, 'That must have been a valuable wagon load.'

Although often the difference between life and death for other-ranks prisoners who had no food parcels on which to draw, the black bread supplied to the officer prisoners as part of their rations was 'fourth-class bread, composed of sawdust and potato' and so unpalatable that, rather than eat it, many officers kept it to supplement their wood for the stoves: 'When hard it made excellent fuel.' On one occasion the guards raided all the prisoners' rooms and took all the spare bread they had stored as fuel. They carried it to the cookhouse and began to burn it in the cooking stoves. The man who had the job of stoking was shovelling a loaf at a time into the stove, without realizing that a prisoner behind his back was just as quickly taking them out again and throwing them to his comrades, who took them away to hide them more securely. 'It was only when he began to wonder how many more loaves the stove was going to take that he jumped to the ruse. Then he lost a few more out of the sack while he recovered from the shock.'

Other deliveries were also vulnerable to the depredations of the prisoners. On one occasion a four-wheeled wagon full of potatoes was backed up to the cellar of *Kaserne* B and guarded by a sentry on each side:

> Poor chaps. They wanted six on each side. A growing crowd of prisoners watched the orderlies unloading the potatoes for a few moments and then one prisoner 'made a rush at one end of the wagon. The sentry darted after him, only to find fellows all along the unprotected side. They lost a lot of those potatoes. To crown it all, some fellow took a few with him upstairs and managed to drop one plumb on the spike of the sentry's helmet. The weight forced his helmet over his eyes and even his own pals were almost in tears at the comical sight he presented.'

The bath house at the far side of the *Spielplatz* was eventually completed, but instead of allowing the prisoners to use it, Niemeyer promptly turned it into a kennel for the prison guard-dogs, claiming there was no room for them to be housed elsewhere. He then put up a sign reading, 'When a more suitable place in the camp can be found for the dogs, officers may have baths on Tuesdays and Fridays.' While the dogs had the run of the bath house, the prisoners either went unwashed or used the icy water from two pumps intended for filling the horse-troughs on the *Spielplatz*. Even then, they were forbidden to strip completely: 'Officers washing naked were imprisoned.' When the bath house was eventually turned over to the prisoners, 'the loathsome state of the floor when we went for a hot shower inclined most of us to bathe in the open'. Even when the stinking traces of its previous occupants had been removed, the men discovered that 'the so-called hot showers are ... usually cold and always only a dribble', and there were never more than two showers working at any one time. Including the orderlies, that left one shower for every 350 men, who competed for 'the few drops of lukewarm water which trickled feebly from whichever of the six shower-baths happened to be in working order'.

CHAPTER 5

BARBED-WIRE FEVER

The Monotony of Prison Life

Prisoners often had to queue for hours for everything, including cooking and washing – 'Hot water being at a premium, it was annoying, to say the least, when the next man in the line poured the fiery liquid over your slippered foot.'

POOR FOOD AND miserable living conditions were a fact of life for prisoners at Holzminden, but boredom could also be a debilitating factor, often leading to what the prisoners termed 'barbed-wire fever', which 'replaced energy and hope with lethargy and cynicism'. Although bulletins were sometimes passed around, building a vague picture of what was happening in the outside world from a combination of hints and rumours, the gossip of German camp guards and civilian workers, and the knowledge and experiences of recently captured soldiers, prisoners had few sources of information. Just like the letters they wrote, the ones they received were subject to censorship and, with the exception of the *Lager Poldhu* – the inter-camp rumour mill – they were utterly dependent on their captors for news of the progress of the war and the success or failure of offensives and counter-offensives. Information about the British attacks on the Somme and at Passchendaele, or the German *Kaiserschlacht* offensive (also known as 'Operation Michael') in the spring of 1918 came to the prisoners via the commandant and the guards. As the German attacks launched by the *Kaiserschlacht* swept through the British lines, 'our hosts are distinctly "uppish"', one prisoner wrote. 'There has also been much shouting in the approved style and the usual display of tact – flags have been hoisted on our building. On evening *Appel* an officer waved a special evening edition [of the newspaper] to us and then pinned it on the notice-board – never before have we seen an evening paper in the camp and needless to say it told of the taking of Bapaume and another 15,000 prisoners.'

Although this news came 'through German spectacles, so to speak,' one prisoner said, 'and this depresses some people, personally, it cheers me because I can't help dividing all their successes and multiplying all their defeats.' In the same way, although news of the peace treaty between Germany and Russia was circulated in the same month, March 1918, not all the prisoners were downcast by it. 'Russian peace news has depressed a lot of people and of course the flags are all out, but I don't see what there is to be depressed about. It is a pity, of course, because it will no doubt prolong the war by fifteen or twenty years, but the delightful German terms will show the few remaining neutrals that all their talk about "no annexation" is up to their usual standard and will cause them to cease to be believed anywhere.' But few others felt able to adopt such a consistently optimistic view. News of reverses or even pyrrhic victories, such as that in November 1917, when the blood-soaked third battle of Ypres had finally ground to a halt in the mud around the village of Passchendaele – a name that ever afterwards was to evoke shudders of horror in veterans – increased the prisoners' feelings of isolation and depression.

During his incarceration at Holzminden, the poet F. W. Harvey observed that it was not the physical hardship but 'the purposelessness of it, and the awful monotony, that sickens the heart'. Prisoners also often felt a sense of shame that they had surrendered and been captured, rather than fighting to the death, and this contributed to the depression and lassitude that many exhibited. 'The silent battles being waged in these drab backwaters of war' were not so much against the German guards as against 'degradation and despair, physical collapse and mental stagnation'.

Some men were further isolated by their characters, or lack of social graces, increasing the risk of depression and even suicide. 'Little cliques developed,' one prisoner said. 'There were so many people, you couldn't get on with everyone'. 'Certainly there were very morbid people there,' another prisoner recalled. 'It depends entirely on your personality how you take these things. To some people, it was the worst thing in the world. To others, if it was bad, you tried to make the best of it'. 'One quite often gets down in the dumps through sheer monotony,' another inmate noted. 'But it is useless to allow oneself to get like this or else one generally ends up in an asylum, like one or two from this and other camps have done.'

The monotony of prison life only made those feelings worse. As one prisoner noted, with resignation, 'In future letters are to be given out for an hour daily. This means another queue – life is principally composed of queues at the moment.' Standing in lines was 'always a prominent feature of prison life, and always a nuisance; but at Holzminden it was not merely a prominent feature and a nuisance, it was the whole ugly face and a damned nuisance'. One prisoner who had been waiting for two hours in the queue for the parcel room was unwise enough to mention the fact to the commandant as he passed. Niemeyer turned a baleful eye on him and declared that 'he didn't care a damn if he waited ten hours'.

> You stood in queues for parcels, you stood in queues to draw out what had come in the parcels, and again to cook it at one of the open-air stoves. You stood in queues for letters. You stood in queues for cells, and to take food to those who were in the cells. You stood in queues for baths. You stood in queues to be robbed at the canteen. You stood in queues for firewood, which they sold at an exorbitant price when you were unable to steal it from them, as you had a perfect right to do, since they should have provided reasonable warmth free. You stood in queues for your bread-card and for your wine-card, and again when you bought either of these most detestable mixtures, and again to be inoculated with whatever they decided to pump into your system, and again when you wanted to report sick and be excused from attending *Appel* as a result of standing in any of these other queues, but especially the bread and wine ones. If a man had had to stand in them all, his whole day would have been taken up

with waiting about in the cold; but by sharing the work, and getting, e.g., your friend's letters when you got your own, it was possible to escape with about four hours each *per diem*.

When not queuing, one well-read captain recited Molière to relieve the boredom and, when not required for roll-calls or in solitary confinement, other prisoners played football and hockey or exercised on a set of parallel bars. A group of them also dug, cleared and levelled an area of the *Spielplatz* for use as tennis courts, and in spring they put up a cricket net, 'but there is no matting and it is quite impossible to make anything like a true pitch so the game is more dangerous than amusing'. Teams from the two *Kasernen*, which included a number of Canadian prisoners, also played an occasional game of baseball, though for the most part 'the teams consisted of people who had either very little or no notion of the game'. On a couple of other occasions they even staged a race meeting on the *Spielplatz*, with the more athletic prisoners acting as horses while the inveterate gamblers placed or accepted bets.

Football games were the most popular recreation, though the cramped space only left room for nine-a-side matches, held under FA Rules 'so far as they applied'. Captain Jack Shaw was honorary secretary of the camp football competitions, which included teams drawn from the officers and the orderlies. The games helped the prisoners to keep fit and were good for their morale, but were banned by Commandant Niemeyer after an arc light was accidentally broken, even though the prisoners paid for the damage out of their own funds. Less energetic prisoners played bridge or other card games, and chess also 'proved a good way of passing away a few hours'. Others merely 'walked round and round the prison yard', whiling away a little time; anything was better than 'to allow oneself to become like some people who spend most of their days in bed and are quite beyond doing anything'.

A library of five thousand books had been accumulated in the camp from the parcels sent by families and the Red Cross, and some prisoners claimed to have read every one of them in their attempts to stave off the boredom. There was also a camp orchestra, conducted by the Italian Count di Balme, with Vernon Coombs on double bass, and the Reverend Bernard Luscombe – though 'he wasn't a reverend at the time' – on cello and several other instruments. The orchestra members bought their own instruments, using some of their prison pay. Coombs was a professional musician and orchestrated the music for their concerts and shows, as well as learning a few new instruments himself. 'There was one man there who seemed to be able to play anything,' he later said. 'He taught me the double-bass and the trombone. The orchestra kept me going . . . It kept our spirits up; it would have been terrible if we'd just had to mooch about all day long.'

The second-floor dining room in *Kaserne* B doubled as a concert venue, lecture hall, church or theatre, as required. Theatrical productions and revues were regularly staged there, and though the patrician Captain Douglas Lyall Grant rather sniffily declared of one poorly received production that 'to put it bluntly, it was rather above the average *Kriegsgefangener* [prisoner of war] brain, which prefers to cope with light comedy or lighter music', as a whole the shows were a hugely popular diversion, allowing the prisoners to forget the misery of their situation for an hour or two. As one said, 'There was nothing that we would less willingly have forgone than our "shows".' Whenever a performance was to be staged, the dining tables were pushed together to form a platform at one end of the room and the wings and drop-scene were hastily erected. The productions staged at the 'Gaiety Theatre, Holzminden', included *Home John*, *The Crimson Streak*, *The Just Impediment*, *An Irish Sketch* and the Galsworthy play *The Pigeon*, and the prisoners even staged a Christmas pantomime, *Sleeping Beauty*, though 'unlike other pantomimes, there was no comic element to it and it chiefly consisted of ragtimes'. The Germans didn't often come to the concerts but they came to see the shows – the commandant at Trier prison camp even took his daughter with him. 'They used to laugh at the jokes but they didn't see the underlying smut in them.'

Elaborate costumes were made – there was a gentleman's agreement that items from such costumes were never to be used as part of a disguise for an escape kit – with men playing the female roles. One prisoner, dressed as the 'Artist's Model', fancied that he 'must have looked rather sweet as the "Model", in a small ballet frock and tights, with a wreath on

One of the many shows put on by prisoners in the Holzminden Gaiety Theatre – one of the barrack rooms.

my head', and another prisoner described the female impersonators as 'most voluptuous', before hastily adding that there was no homosexuality in the camp – 'never heard of such a thing'. Nonetheless, as another cross-dressing female lead, F. W. Harvey, noted,

> The attitude of officers towards other officers dressed as women in plays, etc., was very peculiar. [When in costume, I] noticed with surprise how attentive officers were in keeping me supplied with refreshments and also that (quite unconsciously) their manners completely changed when speaking to me. They were most careful in avoiding the usual camp language and most fastidious in their choice of adjectives. They insisted on giving up their seats to me, and it was quite pathetic to see the efforts made to engage my female interest in subjects no sane prisoner of war (if any of us are sane) would consider. How pretty the room looked! And the costumes, so picturesque, weren't they? Perhaps a glass of lemonade . . . I had to pull them back into reality by swearing vigorously, and so far had they fallen under the illusion of my femininity that I fear I shocked them by doing so.

Among the amateur thespians was James Whale, a lieutenant with an infantry regiment and a prisoner at Holzminden for fifteen months. He devoted his time there to producing plays, 'for which he could design and paint scenery, act, and participate in the writing of original material. He later said that this had been his introduction to stagecraft, and it was at Holzminden, in the heart of enemy territory, that 'drama began to gain its hold on him'. The plays were very popular, and Whale found the enthusiastic response of his captive audience 'intoxicating'. He also drew charcoal portrait sketches of his fellow inmates and played bridge so successfully in high-stakes games that he cashed in about four thousand pounds' worth of IOUs when he got back to England after the war. He went on to direct *Journey's End* for the London stage; a play about the First World War, initially starring the twenty-one-year-old Laurence Olivier, it was a global success. Whale also directed the play on Broadway and the movie that followed, launching a Hollywood career that made him one of the most celebrated directors of Hollywood's 'golden age'.

There was also a debating society at Holzminden, The Wrangler's Club, for 'the free discussion of subjects of vital interest and of problems likely to confront us after the war'. There were lectures on tea-planting in India, Japan, the evolution of man, and the formation and government of the German Empire, and a wealth of vocational courses, including book-keeping, building construction, horse management, town planning and elementary and conversational French, Spanish, Italian and German; for obvious reasons, the latter was the most heavily subscribed. Some of the feats of learning by prisoners during their time at the 'Escapers' University' were astonishing. Harold 'Homer' White was a true polymath. An Oxford classics scholar before the war, he was 'a pioneer in aerial cartography', and while incarcerated in Holzminden, he 'acquired a reading mastery of French, German, Italian, Spanish, Portuguese and Russian'. He was also a member of the camp orchestra, 'a good flute player and a high tenor well practised in *lieder*, part-singing and folk song'. After the war, he became a school teacher and also found time to be a 'knowledgeable astronomer and meteorologist, a fine photographer and enthusiastic motorist and mountaineer'. He took up the piano in his forties, 'with remarkable success', and in his retirement 'read the Old Testament in Hebrew' and made 'skilful watercolour sketches'.

Holzminden inmates would do almost anything to alleviate the boredom – 'prisoners do quaint things e.g. take up fancy needlework and knitting' – but the most popular recreation of all was 'making illicit escaping gear' and planning and preparing for escapes, with schemes of varying inventiveness and credibility continually being mooted. Yet the idea that prison camps were hotbeds of enthusiastic escapers is false. As one inveterate escaper, Captain J. L. Hardy, complained, 'I used to talk sometimes about escape to the others, but one mostly got laughed at for one's pains . . . One was made to feel oneself not quite a gentleman! It simply was not *done* to be breaking out of camps and travelling about Germany dressed as a tramp.' Not all men were the stuff of heroes and some, frankly admitting to relief at being out of the killing zone of the trenches, had no desire to do anything that would hasten their return there. Captain J. R. Ackerley, taken prisoner in mid-1917, later recalled that

'Not only did I not try to escape myself, but I do not remember that anyone else tried to escape from any of the three camps in which I found myself.'

The majority of PoWs seem only to have wanted a quiet life and many were perfectly content to sit out their captivity until the war's end, or until they had been incarcerated long enough to qualify for a prisoner exchange that would see them interned in neutral Holland. The least speculation or rumour about a fresh exchange of prisoners to Holland created a fever of excitement among the prisoners. 'The much vaunted British phlegm is conspicuous by its absence when moves to neutral countries are concerned, and a child going to its first party is a rational being compared with a p. of W. preparing to leave for Holland; so infectious is "Hollanditis" that not only all those who think they may get there succumb to it.' One party of forty men who left on an exchange to Holland in the greatest of high spirits had the mortifying experience of being sent back to Holzminden from the Dutch border because 'our government has not sent enough German officers to cover the British officers already across the border. Needless to say we all sympathize with them, but it certainly has its comic side – seeing people roll up again to whom we had recently waved adieu.'

Captain Douglas Lyall Grant was one who settled into PoW camp routine as if he had been born to it. A Scot who had won the Military Cross at Messines, Lyall Grant had then been rewarded with the sinecure of embarkation officer at Boulogne, but was captured after being shot down when the pilot flying him back from leave in England lost his way in poor weather and strayed over the German lines. The diary Lyall Grant kept while incarcerated in four prison camps, including Holzminden, is a near-endless recitation of luncheons, dinners, drinks parties, sporting contests, theatrical performances and celebrations of Hogmanay, Burns Night and the feast days of St Andrew, St George, St David and St Patrick.

Although he described one escape attempt from Holzminden as 'an extraordinarily stout show', he showed little inclination to try it himself. In the main, he was content to wait out the time until he qualified for a prisoner exchange, then spend the rest of the war interned in Holland, though he complained, 'All agree that Holland is most expensive. The fashionable thing seems to be to spend all your money in about three days and then retire to a sanatorium.' To such men, escapes were often an unwelcome disruption to the normal routine of the camp, leading to reprisals and loss of privileges. The senior British officer at Clausthal, Major General Ravenshaw, had even tried to prevent his men from making any escape attempts. Lieutenant Tom Mapplebeck, who ran the Escape Committee, was summoned by Ravenshaw, with two other officers, and given 'the order that all attempts to escape were to stop' since they always led to severe retaliation by Heinrich Niemeyer against all of the inmates. It was even alleged that Ravenshaw had threatened those planning to escape with reprisals of his own – court martial – when they returned to Britain after the war.

* * *

Whatever the threats from the Germans or their own senior officers, some prisoners, albeit a minority, were inveterate and indefatigable planners and attempters of escapes. Almost all were officers since, unlike the enlisted men working as orderlies, they had less fear of reprisals: unlike officers, orderlies could be sent back to camps for enlisted men and compelled to do forced labour. Officers also had sufficient time, leisure and means to devote to planning escapes and assembling the necessary equipment, and it is arguable that, for many, the chance to relieve the monotony of camp life, boost their morale and also 'outwit the Hun' was almost as much of an attraction as the prospect of eventual freedom.

Every time new British prisoners arrived at Holzminden, they were paraded in the *Spielplatz* where the commandant addressed them. 'Shaking his fist under our noses he bawled: "You are very clever? Yes? Well, I make a special study of this escaping."'

'I am Niemeyer. I have constructed the camp so that you cannot escape. It is a waste of time trying.'

'You damn well do as I tell you. If you think you can get out – try.'

A score of prisoners promptly took him at his word. It was 'generally recognized that those who are first to attempt to get away from a *Lager* [prison camp] have the best chance of escaping, as every succeeding effort becomes more difficult owing to the increased vigilance, and there also being one less place to get away from . . . providing the exit is always discovered.' Those prisoners eager to escape therefore lost no time in making a minute examination of the buildings, the perimeter fence, the gates and the security procedures, looking for any signs of fallibility, however slight.

To improve their chances of escape, they also set about generating a series of false alarms. The electric wires powering the arc lights around the camp were not insulated and, even 'at risk of getting shot', the prisoners would open a window at night and throw a length of wire or a piece of some other metal over these electric wires, creating a short-circuit that blew the fuses and extinguished the lights. 'Then the fun began. Whistles blew, guards dashed out, rooms were entered to see that they contained the right number of inmates and, as often as not, the three-shot signal was fired [alerting the guards on the bridge over the River Weser in the town of Holzminden to the possibility that an escape had been made from the camp]. Then it would be realized that no one had gone.' After a string of false alarms, the lights were often left undisturbed when a genuine escape attempt was being made – almost always at night – in the hope that, as a result, the guards would be less alert.

The would-be escapees soon detected an initial weakness in the Holzminden camp's security. Although officers on inspections, intelligence agents seeking information from prisoners and civilian tradesmen carrying out repairs made regular visits to the camp, and all contractors and workmen were issued with a camp permit – a small printed ticket that was supposed to be given up when leaving the camp – no log appeared to be kept of their comings and goings. Furthermore, although passes should have been shown by everyone using the gates, the sentries had an understandable reluctance to challenge officers and NCOs. When turned up, the underside of the collar of a German officer's uniform jacket revealed a scarlet lining. 'This splash of red marks out the officer very clearly at any distance . . . and the German soldier who sees it coming either bolts for cover or, if too late, shakes himself together for a terrific salute.' Having observed all this over the course of a few days, a group of British prisoners in *Kaserne* A formed their plans.

The *Kommandantur* was separated from the prisoners' quarters on each floor of the building by barricades of two-inch planks, 'solidly nailed together and fastened with wire'. On the top attic floor, the corridor ran the whole length of the building, and the double doors at the head of the staircase were sealed off by planks nailed across them. However, one of the lower panels of the door had been left exposed, and on their first night at Holzminden, as soon as the guards had made their final inspection of the night, Major John Thorn and another Canadian prisoner, Lieutenant Wilkin, set to work on the panel with a penknife. In less than two hours they had removed it. More stout planks had been fixed on to the other side of the door, held by six-inch nails driven right through them, then bent and flattened on the reverse side. However, Thorn saw at once that by straightening the nails and severing them with wire-cutters, they would be able to push off the lower boards, and squeeze through the gap. Since they had no wire-cutters, they carefully replaced the panel on their side and concealed the marks they had made when removing it, trusting to luck that no one would notice anything before they could make their escape.

The next morning they spread the word among their friends that they needed something to cut the nails, and one prisoner pointed out a soldier working in the courtyard, who had a pair of wire-cutters in his pocket. 'It took exactly two hours to steal the cutters from the unsuspecting soldier.' That night, they again removed the panel, straightened the nails, cut them off, and at length prised off the two lower boards, opening the way into the German quarters. They tip-toed far enough along the corridor to make sure that it would be possible to get out of the building down the stairs, then retraced their steps and replaced the boards and panel.

The next step was to make fake German uniforms. The following day, by cutting up a pair of his old grey trousers and 'using red quilting for the piping and for the band, we made a fairly decent Boche cap'. More red quilting made the requisite stripe down each side of their trouser legs, and with two coats owned by the orderlies who had been working in the kitchen, they had outfits that would pass for German in the half-light of dusk. They then collected enough dried food – hard biscuits, beef cubes and chocolate – to last the twelve days they estimated it would take to walk to the Dutch border. One of the British officers gave them a 'Tommy's cooker' – a spirit stove, with some blocks of solidified methylated spirit for fuel – and they had empty cigarette tins to use as pans for boiling water. They also took cigarettes with them: 'It is remarkable that no matter how hungry or thirsty a man is, he will always be comforted by a cigarette or a pipe of tobacco.'

The escape attempt was set for the following evening. When Thorn's original companion, Lieutenant Wilkin, fell ill and became too weak to go, a 'Major Gaskell of the Indian Army' was recruited in his place. At the evening roll-call on the day of the escape, Thorn had an unpleasant shock when he was summoned to the *Kommandantur*. On the day he had arrived at the camp, the guards had taken some French and Belgian francs from him; when he had asked for a receipt for the money, Niemeyer told him that the money was '*verboten*' and had been confiscated. When Thorn argued, Niemeyer sentenced him to three days in the cells as soon as one became vacant; they were already filled to capacity with men who had previously earned the commandant's wrath. When Niemeyer sent for Thorn, the Canadian assumed that he would have to go straight into solitary confinement, frustrating his plan to escape, but after calling him 'a *Canadischer Schweinhund* and a few other pet names', Niemeyer instead ordered him to report for his three days' imprisonment at ten o'clock the next morning.

One hour after the order was issued, Thorn and Gaskell, clad in their fake German uniforms, 'passed the commandant at the foot of the stairs, and all his guards who were in the small courtyard, carrying in our right hands two water jugs, stuffed with civilian clothes, and in our left hands packets containing our food'. Niemeyer and his guards did not even glance at them and the sentries on the gates let them pass without challenge. Scarcely believing their luck, Thorn and Gaskell walked up the road, then cut across the fields, circling round behind the camp before striking west. When they reached the River Weser they spent some time looking for a boat they could steal but then made their way into town. As soon as an escape from Holzminden was detected, camp guards would fire the signal of three shots, warning the guards on the bridge over the river to be on the alert, but the alarm had not yet been raised and, finding the bridge unguarded, Thorn and Gaskell simply strolled across. Using the North Star as a guide, they walked for ten or fifteen miles through hilly, wooded country, but then got completely lost in a forest. After wandering around for two or three hours, they eventually found themselves back at where they had first entered the forest. They set off again in a new direction and by daybreak, although they felt they must already have walked at least forty miles, they were still no more than twenty miles from Holzminden. Even by the most direct route, the Dutch frontier lay 150 miles to the west. When they reached a stretch of forest fenced off by signs warning '*Verboten Ingang*', they decided it would be a good place to hide until dark. They found a stream of clean water, where they filled their bottles and cigarette tins, then washed themselves before finding a safe hiding place deep in the forest. They boiled some water in the cigarette tins on the Tommy's cooker, made beef tea using an Oxo cube, ate some biscuits and a piece of chocolate, then settled down to wait out the daylight hours.

Back at Holzminden, one of Thorn's Canadian comrades, Captain Bellew, had won a little more time for the escapers by answering for Thorn when the morning roll-call was taken. Although the prisoners were lined up in fours and sentries were posted to prevent them moving from one group to another during the head-count, when the tally of prisoners was made, Bellew managed to move around so that he was counted twice and Thorn was not missed. Major Gaskell's absence was even easier to conceal: the German guards 'did not take much trouble in counting the senior officers'. Had Thorn not been due to report to the cells for his three-day punishment, the escape might easily have passed unnoticed for another twelve or twenty-four hours, but just after *Appel*, Niemeyer appeared and, when the under-officer had reported everybody present and correct, Niemeyer called Thorn's name to remind him to be in his office at ten o'clock ready for his 'strafing'. After Thorn's name had been repeated three times, to be greeted only with silence, Captain Bellew stepped forward and politely informed the commandant that Thorn had left the previous evening on a journey to Holland. As a result of this *lèse-majesté*, Bellew found himself marched off to take Thorn's place in the cells.

The roll was called again, and Major Gaskell was also found to be missing, at which point an incandescent

Niemeyer ordered all the officers back to the barracks, where they were locked in for the rest of the day. Knowing that Niemeyer was certain to use bloodhounds to track down the escapees, several of Thorn's other Canadian comrades then decided to make the hounds' task a little more difficult. Major Colquhoun, of the 'Princess Pat's' (Princess Patricia's Canadian Light Infantry), who had himself escaped several times, carefully emptied some cayenne pepper into a pair of Thorn's old shoes, swapped his socks for some belonging to another officer, and hid the rest of his clothes. When Niemeyer and his staff searched Thorn's room and took the socks into the courtyard for the hounds to get the scent, they began to chase around without discovering a trail to anywhere except to various parts of the camp. Then they were brought back and given Thorn's shoes. After a noseful of cayenne pepper, they tore around the yard with a hapless German soldier trying to hang on to their leashes, eliciting roars of laughter from the windows of the blocks, which were lined with prisoners. Niemeyer drew his revolver and threatened to shoot, and those officers he recognized were immediately given three days in the punishment cells.

Niemeyer then turned his attention to discovering how the two men had managed to escape and 'called in the local police and police dog to smell out the mystery. After a lengthy search they pushed the wretched animal down a drain; the animal, seeing light at the other end and being pushed from behind, walked through the drain. This satisfied them: they had discovered the method of escape!

They actually announced to us that they now knew how it was done and spent the day busily filling up the drain. As a matter of fact, I doubt if it was big enough for a man to get down at all.'

Twenty miles away, Thorn and Gaskell had spent the day taking it in turns to sleep for a couple of hours while the other kept watch, and just before sunset, having dined on more beef tea and a biscuit, they moved on. They avoided roads and travelled cross-country, wading through streams, splashing through marshes, climbing steep hills and forcing or cutting their way through dense underbrush. Every time they crossed a road, they paused, listening hard and straining their eyes into the darkness to detect any sound or movement, before slipping across and disappearing back into the fields and woods. 'We wondered if the bloodhounds had yet been put on our tracks. These did not worry us very much, however, as we had waded through too many streams for the dogs to be able to follow our scent.' From time to time, they found themselves facing the perimeter wall surrounding some extensive country estate, and as they were determined to keep walking due west for at least three days, rather than detour and risk losing their direction, they climbed the walls. As a result, they often found themselves 'in a private garden with a watch-dog barking at our heels ... While we carried heavy sticks for protection against these animals, at the same time the barking used to get on our nerves, and many a time we ran for miles to get away from them.'

In the early hours of one morning, they lost track of each other while crossing a large field. It was a moonless, cloudy night, so dark that they could not see more than two or three feet ahead and, unable to call out for fear of discovery, had they not been wearing wrist watches with luminous dials, they might not have found each other again. When Thorn caught sight of a flicker of light in the distance, he thought at first that it was a firefly, but then realized it was his companion, who had been searching desperately for him.

On most nights they found a good source of water but on a few occasions they had to be content with a stagnant pool and were thankful for the spirit stove to boil its water and the Oxo cubes to disguise the foul taste. Often their daytime hiding place was deep in a forest or dense undergrowth, but there were times when, as dawn approached, they found themselves in open country or close to buildings and had to make do with whatever shelter they could find. On one occasion they had to lie up on the outskirts of a village and had children playing close to them throughout the day.

Navigating without a compass and travelling across country on moonless or overcast nights caused them numerous problems. On one occasion, without seeing it in the darkness, Thorn stepped over the edge of a cutting and tumbled right down the steep slope to the bottom some fifteen or twenty feet below. He was badly winded but, luckily, had not broken any bones. Looking up he could see the dark shape of Gaskell outlined against the night sky as he searched for his comrade, and scrambled back up the slope just in time to stop him suffering the same fate. Later the same night, they were following a railway track running in a north-westerly direction when they found themselves on the outskirts of a large town. They left the railway at once and tried to circle around the town, but lost their bearings. Instead of reaching open country, they found themselves closer to the centre. 'Every turn we took seemed to bring us into more populated streets, and when at last we came across a street-car line, we began to think we were going to get caught.' Fortunately, after wandering around for almost two hours, they found their way back to the fields and moved on, vowing not to go within a mile of another town.

They had no idea where they were, and when they came across a signpost, Thorn climbed the iron pole, and risked using the small electric torch he carried to read the inscription. Even so, it took him some time to make out 'Horn – 5 Km'. As soon as it was light, they scoured their map until they found the place. Horn lay forty-five kilometres from Holzminden, and as they were a further five beyond it, they felt that they had travelled far enough to be outside the search zone. They decided to risk travelling along the roads, enabling them to make much faster progress. By now they had thrown away their fake German soldiers' caps and coats, and torn the red stripes off their trousers. Wearing civilian coats and with a few days' growth of beard, they looked more like tramps than escaped prisoners. The few people they encountered hurried by – 'No doubt our appearance frightened them, as in the moonlight we looked two veritable scarecrows. Having to sleep on the damp ground, our clothes were covered with mud, and not having shaved for four or five days, it was no wonder they passed quickly by, especially as we carried in our hands thick sticks which we had cut from the forest.'

Using the roads, they estimated that they would now be able to cover between twenty and twenty-five miles a night, but they were still about a hundred miles from the Dutch frontier. A range of hills lay ahead, and beyond them they would be entering a much more densely populated region where evading detection would prove doubly difficult. Around midnight that night, they heard firing. They were at once afraid that they had been spotted and that a local garrison had turned out to find them, but they eventually realized that they were passing through a district where large numbers of troops were being trained, and the shooting they had heard had come from soldiers on the firing ranges. They decided their best course was to leave the roads and take to the hills. Eventually they found themselves in empty moorland, but they could find no water and by daybreak were so thirsty that they were reduced to licking the dew that had settled on the leaves of the bushes during the night. The next night they came down from the hills and found a stream of fresh water, and fertile land, including a large orchard, where they gorged themselves on apples and plums, and carried away more with them in their packs when they moved on. Each time they passed a signpost, they drew heart from the fact that the distance to the frontier was steadily diminishing.

They had now been on the run for six days. At four the following morning, while detouring around a village, they strayed into a garden in the pitch darkness, and disturbed a dog that rose from the ground almost under their feet and began barking furiously. Frightened that the noise would rouse the occupants of the house, they took to their heels. As they ran, they saw lights moving along the road towards them. They sprinted on, towards the safety of a nearby forest, but again lost each other in the darkness. Thorn hid among some bushes, and when things had quietened down, he retraced his steps to where he had last seen Gaskell and was spotted by his comrade, who was hiding nearby.

As they moved on, they again saw lights but realized they were on the bicycles of workers coming to and from a nearby factory – the road surface was so bad that they could travel at no more than walking pace, which had led the two escapees to imagine that the lights were the lanterns of a search party.

On this and subsequent nights it was harder to find safe refuges to wait out the daylight hours. Now they found a small, sparse wood, and cut down enough bushes and saplings to make a natural-looking thicket in which they hid. It was as well they did for, it being a Sunday, the inhabitants of all the surrounding villages were out for a stroll. All day they heard 'the continual sound of voices and we had to hug the ground very close to keep from being seen'.

They moved on again that night, resolving to leave the road and take to the fields at the first sight of anyone ahead or behind them, in case the alarm was raised about 'two dirty-looking strangers on the road, who might be escaped prisoners of war'. Even so, they were taken by surprise when a cyclist approached from behind them but 'had to laugh when the man passed us pedalling for dear life, dropping things as he went in his hurry to get by us. He was evidently far more afraid of us than we were of him, no doubt from our appearance thinking we were out robbing the neighbourhood.'

To avoid getting lost once more, they resolved to go straight through the big industrial town of Bielefeld, which, as the crow flew, was still only forty-five miles north-west of Holzminden, though they had walked many more miles than that. They reached the town at two the next morning. They could scarcely have been more furtive, for every time they passed a large building they crept into the road, or crossed to the other side of the street, or stood motionless before continuing. Had anyone been watching they could hardly have failed to take them for escaped prisoners or criminals, but Thorn and Gaskell were pleasantly surprised to find that, at such an early hour, there were no police or soldiers on the streets and they did not meet a single person on their entire journey through the town.

Beyond Bielefeld they made fast progress through gentle, well-cultivated country. Towards morning, they again picked fruit from an orchard, and saw a signpost revealing that during the sixth and seventh nights they had walked fifty-five miles and, if all went well, were now just three days from the Dutch frontier. Over the next two nights they moved on rapidly, and estimated that they had walked more than a hundred and ninety miles in total, but even now with the border so close, a combination of tiredness, hunger and a strange over-confidence was threatening their success. Such an impression was heightened by their decision, when they found a stream of good water just after midnight, to take a bath. 'It would have shocked the natives to have seen us at this hour of the night, stripped and enjoying ourselves like two porpoises in the water.' Still over-confident as they walked on later that night, they were whispering to each other about what they would do when they reached Holland. Thorn had just said that the first thing he intended to do was to order a thick steak, underdone, with French-fried potatoes, and a whisky and soda, when both men were startled by a shout of '*Halte! Hände hoch!*' and found themselves 'looking down the barrels of two rifles held by two rather ferocious-looking soldiers'. As they looked around, they realized they had just crossed the railway using a level crossing, something they would not have dreamed of doing had they thought about it for even a moment. 'Imagine our feelings,' Thorn later said. 'After having walked over two hundred miles, and having passed through all of the most dangerous districts, only to be caught within twenty-five miles of the frontier, which we had hoped to pass the next night. Our dreams of beefsteak, underdone, and whisky and soda faded away, and in their place came visions of German bread and water.'

They were taken to the jail in a nearby town. After being searched and stripped of their remaining food and their maps, they were locked up for the night in separate cells, where they took what rest they could, lying on bare wooden benches. The next morning they were given a breakfast of *ersatz* coffee, 'made as usual from burned acorns, a piece of war-bread, which I must say was better than that supplied to us in the camps, being composed, no doubt, of only two-thirds potato peelings instead of the usual nine-tenths, and it was not held together by sawdust, as was the bread supplied to us before'. The guard also brought them a bowl of bean soup, and Thorn was 'quite astonished to find therein a piece of potato'.

The next day, Thorn and Gaskell were transferred first to a military prison at Osnabrück, and four days later they were returned to Holzminden. 'I could picture in my mind,' Thorn said, 'what kind of reception we should get on our arrival there.'

It was pouring with rain when they arrived at Holzminden station, and they were soaked to the skin by the time they reached the camp under heavy guard. They soon discovered that, in the interval since their own escape, several other prisoners had got out by the same means: the guards had still not worked out how the escape had been made. Niemeyer had had the entire camp thoroughly searched, but the removable panel in the attic door had eluded the soldiers' notice and Niemeyer 'had no idea at all how we were getting out. He went nearly mad. The sentries were doubled, then trebled. They were ordered to shoot at sight. But still every morning there were two or three officers missing at roll-call. Poor Niemeyer must have had visions of being sent to the Front himself; yet it was perfectly simple. We just walked out of the main gate at dusk when the guard was being changed.'

Most of the escapees carried sacks on their shoulders, to make them look like Germans who had been on some working party, 'the sentry taking them for Huns carrying sacks of rubbish, whereas the sacks really contained civilian clothing and food'. Among the steady stream of prisoners making use of Thorn and Gaskell's escape route had been Thorn's original escaping partner, Lieutenant Wilkin, who had recovered from his sickness by the third day after they had departed, and wasted little time in following them. He first picked the padlock of a room where an old sewing machine was stored, and during the night, when no Germans were around, he took it down to his room. Although very few of the prisoners would have handled a needle and thread before, let alone used a sewing machine, he and several other officers made convincing fake German soft caps and, like Thorn and Gaskell, fixed red quilting to their trousers. With the addition of 'a pyjama jacket dyed in coffee . . . it was good enough to pass muster in the dusk'.

On the sixth day, having 'taken the elementary precaution of placing the most realistic dummies in our beds', to delay discovery of their absence until roll-call the following morning and, 'choosing the time when all eyes were on the guard-mounting ceremony', four of them, including Lieutenant Wilkin, went through the panel. Carrying their food and clothing in sacks slung over their shoulders, they walked along the corridor, down the stairs of the *Kommandantur,* crossed the yard and strolled past the sentry on the gate. 'No one paid any attention to us. I can still remember the thrill of it,' Sir Brian Horrocks later recalled, 'that wonderful moment when, from outside the wire, we could look back at the camp with its sentries, its arc lamps, its barbed wire. We were free.' More men escaped on several subsequent nights. Some did not even trouble to make their own replica German uniforms, but simply stole genuine officers' coats hanging in the hall of the *Kommandantur* and then strolled out of the main gates of the camp as the sentries snapped to attention and saluted them.

By the time Thorn and Gaskell were brought back to the camp, a total of sixteen officers had followed their example, making their way through the panel, down the stairs and out of the gates, and still Niemeyer did not know how any of them had escaped. When Thorn was brought into the guard-room, he greeted Niemeyer with '*Guten Tag, Herr Kommandant. Schlechter Wetter, nicht wahr?*' (Good day, Commandant, bad weather, is it not?). 'At this the storm burst, and after calling me a few pet names, such as *Englander Schweinhund,* etc., he roared at us that our punishment would be so severe that no other officer would dare to attempt to escape from his camp.' After being thoroughly searched, they were taken to the punishment cells. They were already so filled with other officers – more than thirty were now in solitary confinement, sent there as Niemeyer vented his spleen over the escapes – that extra space had been created for them by partitioning off parts of the coal cellars.

On their second day in the cells Thorn and Gaskell were summoned to Niemeyer's office for a court of inquiry into the escape. Despite a fierce cross-examination and threats of a longer term of imprisonment, both men remained tight-lipped, leaving Niemeyer still no hint wiser about the means of their departure.

On Thorn and Gaskell's fourth or fifth day of solitary confinement, Captain Bellew managed to bribe one of the guards and smuggled some food in to them. Cigarettes arrived by a more direct route. After lights out that night, they were sitting in their cell talking about 'what we would give if we could only get a cigarette or a pipe of tobacco, when I noticed through the bars of the window an object swing to and fro, and putting my hands through the bars I was delighted to find a packet of Players' cigarettes swinging on the end of a piece of string which had been let down by one of the officers from the top floor of the building'.

More of the officers who had escaped through the panel were gradually being recaptured and brought into the cells. If they had sufficient warning of being apprehended, escapees tried to destroy or conceal their maps and the smaller items of their kit, and many gave away what was left of their concentrated rations to the police or soldiers who recaptured them. By so doing, they avoided drawing the attention of Niemeyer and his guards to the uses to which certain foods in Red Cross parcels were being put. Had Niemeyer realized, the items would at once have been added to the banned list.

Among the recaptured escapees was Lieutenant Riley, who was brought back on 13 October 1917. His attempt had come heartbreakingly close to success – he'd thought he had already crossed the Dutch frontier when he was apprehended by sentries patrolling a level crossing, still three miles inside German territory. A week after Riley's recapture, five more officers attempted to escape by the same route. The first two – Lieutenants Ure and Tasker – managed to get away, but a guard became suspicious and apprehended the next three, Lieutenants Hope, Bevan and Garland, before they could follow their comrades out of the gates. Three others tried a different route in early November, hiding under the floor of the parcel room, but the sentry beyond the barbed wire heard them as they tried to break out that night and fired at them, forcing them to surrender.

After a month in solitary confinement, without a bath, a change of clothes, or any exercise, Thorn wrote a letter 'in my best German' to Niemeyer asking to be allowed to have a bath,

> otherwise we should soon be visited by those little friends who would not be welcome at that time. The next day the commandant put his head in the door and I asked him for two or three small things, such as a little coal to heat up the

cell, and another blanket, as it had begun to get extremely cold. He looked at the bed and the surroundings and said, '*Das ist schön für einen Englander,*' [That's good enough for an Englishman] and, with these words, walked away. However, a few days later we were conducted from our cell into the courtyard, and allowed to have a shower bath, which had been fixed up for the officers of the camp.

After seven weeks in the cells, Gaskell and Thorn were told that they were to be transferred to another prison camp. When they were marched into their former quarters to collect their belongings, Thorn discovered that almost everything he possessed had already disappeared. 'Before escaping I had told several officers that if they did not hear that I was recaptured in ten days they could take it for granted that I had succeeded, and could distribute the various parts of my uniform, my underclothes and socks among the newly captured officers, and the day before I was returned to camp most of these officers had been sent away to other camps, and with them went my belongings.' All that he was left with after his remaining clothes were returned was 'a tunic, an old pair of riding-breeches and puttees, no socks, and no underclothes, so that it did not take me very long to pack'. At six o'clock the next morning they left Holzminden, under strong guard. A few months later they accepted the chance of a PoW exchange and were interned in the Netherlands until the last days of the war.

CHAPTER 6

INVETERATE ESCAPEES

Impossible to Confine

'Three More Out' – Prisoners showed astonishing ingenuity and daring in their attempts to escape; some attempts were even made through the main gate under the noses of the guards.

ALTHOUGH ALL THE men who had made their escape by way of Thorn and Gaskell's removable panel in the attic doors of *Kaserne* A were eventually recaptured, Niemeyer 'nearly went crazy with rage' that the escape attempts had been made at all. He was now 'beginning to appreciate that his charges were, of their own necessity and inclination, becoming "gaol-breakers" whose spirit it was hard to subdue'. As a result, security was made even more draconian. Within three weeks the former *Landsturm* guards – the militia of former reservists and men who, because of age or infirmity, had not been called up for regular military service – had been replaced by younger and fitter *Soldaten*. The perimeter wire was heightened, the no man's land free-fire zone created inside it and conditions for the occupants were made even more intolerable. The ground-floor windows nearest to the prison gates were whitewashed to stop prisoners seeing the passes and permits used by visitors to the camp and the camp personnel as they came and went past the guards on the inner gate: if the prisoners had been able to see or, even better, steal a pass, they could then have forged copies. A further restriction was also imposed: Niemeyer required the ground-floor windows to be closed at all times, another source of grievance for the prisoners, especially in hot summer weather. With all these new measures in place, Niemeyer felt confident enough to tell his charges, as they assembled for an *Appel*, 'You see, yentlemen, you cannot get out now. I should not try it; it will be bad for your health.'

The system of permits and passes had also been tightened in the wake of the original escape and every individual from the highest to the lowest of the camp personnel was supposed to show a pass when entering or leaving the camp. When a sentry let Niemeyer through without asking for his pass, the commandant gave him a savage dressing-down, to the vocal pleasure of the British prisoners within earshot. The next time Niemeyer – in a hurry – attempted to go through the gate, the same sentry demanded to see his pass. The result was a fresh tirade, more raucous laughter from the prisoners and a seven-day spell in the punishment block for the hapless guard. By such means did Niemeyer alienate not only the PoWs but his own men as well. So unpopular was Niemeyer with his own men, and so desperate were they for the once-commonplace goods like soap, beef dripping and chocolate that the British blockade of Germany had made almost unobtainable, that the prisoners found a number of allies within the German ranks. In return for a share of the delicacies that British officers received in their parcels, some of the disaffected guards and camp employees were willing to pass on information and all manner of contraband goods.

Their most useful ally was a young German soldier universally known as 'The Letter Boy', since one of his main tasks was sorting and distributing the mail. He also acted as Niemeyer's confidential clerk, the bearer of his messages and relayer of his orders. He spoke some English and rather more French and, despite his nationality, had a fervent hatred for his country that was only exceeded by his detestation of his commanding officer. As a result, in return for a regular supply of foodstuffs from Red Cross parcels, he was willing to commit almost any treason that did not involve excessive risk to himself, and even took to giving five 'hardened and inveterate escapers' a daily briefing, filling them in on all the camp news and gossip over a cup of coffee and some biscuits in Room 83, in the attic of *Kaserne* A. He was also willing to procure anything that would fit in the pockets of his great-coat and, though he must have known to what ends the requested items would be put, he only ever betrayed the confidences of his colleagues, never those of the prisoners. Though less trustworthy than his counterpart, 'The Electric Light Boy' proved a useful source of pocket torches and an occasional bottle of 'Kriegs Cognac'. The camp sanitary man – the only civilian allowed access to the camp without a military escort to watch his movements – was another fruit-ful source of contraband until a raid on his house uncovered a larder full of English tinned food, after which he was not seen in the camp again.

A woman typist in the *Kommandantur*, who was conduct-ing a passionate but completely unrequited love affair with an Australian flying officer by means of letters dropped from the window and delivered to the prisoner by a bribable guard, proved another fruitful source of intelligence. An 'obliging canteen attendant' and a member of the parcel-room staff, who was a patriotic native of Alsace-Lorraine, the territory seized from France at the end of the Franco-Prussian War, were also willing to bend the camp rules in the prisoners' favour on occasion. One of the three camp interpreters, Kurt Grau, who had lived on a hill station at Nilgiris, in India, before the war, would do almost anything for anyone who might be able to help him return there when the war was over. Surprisingly, even a professional man like the camp dentist, Rudolf Hoffman – 'quite good but not too gentle' and given to wearing his ceremonial sword at all times, even while examining and treating his patients – was also open to bribery, though he had the misfortune to be apprehended as he was smuggling in contraband, and was charged with associating with the prisoners 'for the purpose of treason'. Fourteen prisoners were summoned to give evidence against him at his trial, but all refused to testify and as a result were each fined 300 marks.

Even with the intermittent help of these unofficial allies, the task of escaping from Holzminden remained formidable, but despite the heightened security measures imposed by Niemeyer, British prisoners continued to make brazen attempts to flee. Captain Harold W. Medlicott, of the South African Infantry, was 'an almost legendary figure among the prisoners of war, known as the man who had escaped more often than any other and whom it appeared impossible to confine. He was equally well known to the Germans – it was quite usual to find that his name was familiar even to the junior other ranks of the German camp staffs in camps to which he had never been sent.' About half past three one soporific Sunday afternoon, Medlicott and a Captain Walters, having closely observed and timed the sentries' routine patrols, chose the handful of seconds when a section of the perimeter fence was out of sight of all the guards to emerge from the shadows by the cookhouse and run across no man's land between the two barrack blocks. Two sentries patrolled the area between the rear walls of the blocks and the main fence. Their beats met at the midway point between the two buildings, in the centre of no man's land, but after turning about, both had their backs to Medlicott and Walters and would not reach the end of their beat for another fifteen seconds. The average man would not even have been aware that the possibility of escape existed, but Medlicott 'not only saw the possibility but put it into practice with a coolness which was staggering . . . He was continually in a position in which at any moment he was liable to be shot at the shortest range without any line of retreat or any sign of cover, and in spite of this, his movements and bearing showed no indication of haste or even that he appreciated the enormous risk he was taking.'

While the guards continued on their way, pacing towards the end walls of the two *Kasernen*, Medlicott and Walters, 'dressed in old Burberries', climbed one of the brick pillars that stood at intervals along the wall, cut the barbed wire between the steel palings, and threw the wire-cutters back to waiting accomplices in the yard, who promptly hid them ready for a future escape attempt. Fearing that the guard might have heard the twang of the cut wires, the two men froze for a moment, but first Medlicott and then Walters clambered over the palings through the gap in the barbed wire and dropped silently to the ground outside the fence. They stood close to the pillar while they put on their rucksacks and pulled Homburg hats from their pockets. Medlicott, having 'dented the crown to his satisfaction' and put his hat on, even took out a cigarette case and 'lighted a cigarette with a perfectly steady hand' before they moved off.

As the guards turned to resume their inward beats, all they saw through the fence was two men wearing civilian clothes and hats, with rucksacks on their backs, strolling along the road to Holzminden that ran past the camp. Only sheer bad luck prevented the two men getting clean away. It happened that the German attendant in the punishment cells was looking out of one of the rear windows at that moment and immediately recognized Walters and Medlicott, since both had just completed under his supervision the sentence of imprisonment imposed after a previous escape attempt. The attendant ran upstairs, raised the alarm and then 'assisted in hoisting a sentry over the fence after them. He fired one shot and started in pursuit, followed by most of the rest of the garrison and numerous dogs and small boys.' Realizing that they had been spotted, Walters and Medlicott made a run for it. They 'displayed great staying powers and outdistanced their pursuers, watched by an interested mob from all the windows', and sprinted towards the level crossing, making for the shelter of the forest on the far side of the railway. However, the duty officer in the *Kommandantur* had already phoned the crossing guard and he emerged from his hut holding a rifle and blocked their way. With the camp guards also close on their heels, the two escapees had no option but to give themselves up. They returned to sympathetic cheers from their comrades and a further spell of imprisonment in the punishment cells, while Niemeyer gave the attendant three months' leave as a reward for his alertness.

As was his regular custom, Niemeyer vented his fury at the attempted escape by ordering his guards to fire at any windows in which prisoners showed themselves. Although 'not a single officer' went near them, 'many bullets were fired through the windows'. Several prisoners witnessed Niemeyer order the guards to fire: 'they saw him and heard him give the word of command'. Luckily 'no one was hit and broken glass and ceilings were the only damage done.'

The Walters-Medlicott attempt had a tragic footnote. Transferred to another camp at Bad Kolberg, they once more escaped but this time both were shot dead after being recaptured. Their captors claimed that once the two Britons had been handed over to their prison escort, they made a run for it, despite stringent warnings, and were mortally wounded. There was no independent confirmation of that and many of their contemporaries suspected that the inveterate escapees had simply been executed after recapture.

After minutely studying the disposition of the various sentries around the camp and their habits and beats when on duty, another group of escapers also succeeded in cutting the Holzminden perimeter wire. Captain Strover, Lieutenant Bousfield and Lieutenant Nichol identified another weak spot in the defences: a section of fence immediately behind the parcel room, which was very close to the wire. Helped by a milling crowd of fellow prisoners, who distracted the attendant, the three men managed to hide in the parcel room and remained there, undetected, when the attendant locked the door and went for his lunch.

As soon as he was out of the way, the three men emerged, cut through the back wall and made a hole in the fence. Having wriggled through it while the sentry was patrolling away from them, they closed the gap so skilfully that it was almost invisible. They then strolled nonchalantly past the German married quarters, out of the gate and away down the road towards Holzminden, intending to cross the River Weser by the town bridge and then make their way to the Netherlands. However, by sheer bad luck, as they rounded a corner in Holzminden, they came face to face with the tin-room attendant at the camp, who was returning from an errand in the town. He recognized them at once but, out-numbered three to one, allowed them to pass unchallenged, then tracked them, recruiting more and more people to join the pursuit until the escapees, realizing the game was up, surrendered. On returning to camp they refused to reveal how they had made their escape, and, despite a minute search, the hole in the perimeter fence was not found until several hours later.

An Australian who also attempted to cut the wire persuaded Jack Shaw and another prisoner to stage a fight at the opposite end of the *Spielplatz* to distract the guards' attention. The two men 'set to in real earnest and had been doing our best to punish each other,' Shaw later said, 'when Feldwebel Caston, who I think was a good fellow at heart, strolled up and patted me on the shoulder. "*Das ist sehr gut, mein Herr*, but 'e is caught."' When he turned around, Shaw saw the Australian being marched off to the cells. Since the laundry house lay outside the perimeter wire, another escaper arranged to be carried out of the camp in the laundry basket. He avoided detection by the guards at the gates, but as he tried to emerge after dark that night, he was spotted by a sentry who fired at him and hit him in the jaw, forcing him to surrender.

Second Lieutenant A. T. Shipwright made a similar attempt, persuading an orderly, Arthur Coleman, to roll him up inside an old carpet and then trundle him out of the camp gates in a wheelbarrow. The ruse worked, but Shipwright was recaptured soon afterwards. The same fate befell two officers who tried to escape by hiding in the 'muck cart' that cleared the refuse of the camp once a week. It had been the idea of one officer, who recruited the help of the orderlies on 'that unpleasant fatigue'. They played their part by dumping rubbish on top of him and, 'buried under all this filth', he would probably have got away with it, but having observed this, another 'inconsiderate chap' made a last-minute attempt to escape in the same way, using the other cart. 'Things were so rushed that he was not covered properly' and was spotted by the guard as he checked the cart. Further none too gentle prodding and probing with bayonets of the refuse in the first cart persuaded the original officer to reveal himself and, after a brief halt for a shower that was as much in the interest of their captors as the would-be escapees, the pair were marched off to the cells.

In January 1918, 'a most bitter night with frost and snow on the ground', three Australian officers cut the wire and got away while the freezing sentries huddled in their shelters for warmth. One escapee sprained his ankle and was caught when trying to board a train. The other two gave themselves up almost three weeks later 'owing to lack of food and the severity of the weather'. Norman Barlow escaped by jumping from a moving train while being transferred to another camp but was also recaptured and sent back to Holzminden. 'I was given fourteen days' solitary confinement and an extra eight days for having a map in my possession.' He was then brought before Niemeyer who greeted him by slapping his hand on his chest and saying, 'All my boys come back to me.'

The most daring and celebrated escape attempt of all was that made by an officer with a gift for impersonation, who disguised himself as the fearsome commandant while Niemeyer was 'attending some function in the town':

'Imitating his appearance and manner, as well as his voice, and wearing a German uniform, [he] walked straight out of the camp, pausing only to curse the sentry who had opened the gate for being slack. Then he waved his stick, Niemeyer-wise, in the direction of the friends who were watching him, spat on the ground and disappeared. It was several days before they recaptured him.'

Other escape attempts ranged from the daring to the eccentric and the downright farcical. 'There was always some plot being hatched. The climax would be a bold dash, scaling the wall, shrieking whistles, barking dogs and an escaper brought ignominiously back . . . It was a silly thing to do; obviously a sudden dash from a place like Holzminden couldn't succeed.' Nonetheless, there were continual attempts and 'People used to think of wild ideas.' One man proposed to leap from a top-floor window on a windy night holding an improvised umbrella, which he hoped would act as a parachute, carrying him over the wire. Had he done so, he would probably have broken his neck but, fortunately, saner counsels eventually prevailed and the idea was abandoned. A nineteen-year-old pilot then announced his intention of pole-vaulting to freedom from the upper windows, with the aid of a pole made from 'the spars of deck chairs tied together with string . . . They had hopes that the pole would be long enough to carry the jumper over the outer railings. The weak spot in the plan was that the pole was to be steered by guys [i.e. guy ropes] from a lower window . . . Apart from the very fragile condition of the pole, windows had to be opened after dark on two landings and that was a proceeding for which one might get a bullet if the sentry was on the alert.' Although the windows were opened without provoking gunfire, the pole snapped as soon as the young pilot launched himself from the upper window. He plummeted twenty feet to the ground and was fortunate not to impale himself on the steel railings of the palisade. The commandant and three or four of his men were on the spot moments later, and the speed with which they had appeared convinced the prisoners that Niemeyer had had prior knowledge of the attempt.

Another almost equally eccentric attempt was made after carpenters left a length of timber, intended for the manufacture of some cupboards, in the dining room of *Kaserne* B overnight. The enterprising Captain Jack Shaw and two fellow prisoners, Lieutenants Capon and Clouston, at once calculated that, reinforced with a wooden bench, this 'slippery board' was just long enough to bridge the gap between the sill of the first-floor window and the top of the palisade, which was twenty feet lower than the sill and only six feet from the wall of the building. They reasoned that 'if properly supported by six people from the inside', they could slide down it and jump to the ground on the far side of the palisade, in the road outside the camp. 'There would, of course, have been immediate discovery and considerable danger from the sentries' fire, but life was becoming so unbearable as to merit the risk.'

It was a dark and foggy night for the attempt but,

unfortunately, they had either underestimated the manpower required to hold the chute steady or, when burdened with the weight of an escaping prisoner, how quickly the end of the timber would drop below the level of the palisade. In either event, the result was the same. The first would-be escapee, Lieutenant Capon, slid down the improvised chute, with his kit strapped to his front to save his face in the event of a fall, but the chute began to buckle when he was halfway down and he fell straight into the yard on the wrong side of the fence, almost at the feet of the startled sentry a few yards away. Jack Shaw was already out of the window and sliding down the board after him and could not go back. The sentry saw him, levelled his rifle and fired. The shot missed Shaw but hit the chute, which broke under the additional strain, sending him tumbling into the yard alongside his fellow escaper. They were marched off for 'three weeks below' in the punishment cells. The third escaper, Lieutenant Andrew Clouston, had not been spotted by the guard and escaped punishment. As they began their solitary confinement, the would-be escapees could reflect that they had been lucky not to be shot dead by the furious guard. A Canadian airman who was trying to escape through the wire was less fortunate. The sergeant major on duty spotted him, 'called to the sentry to fire and the officer was shot through the arm. He immediately put up his hands and advanced towards the sentry, but the sergeant major ordered the sentry to continue firing and four more shots were lodged in him.'

Niemeyer retaliated to the latest escape attempt by locking the men out of the dining room all day as a collective punishment, but 'he had reckoned without the morning liver of "Broncho" who had spent long years in tropical climates'. Broncho's plates were shut inside the dining room and it was only when he wanted them for breakfast that he discovered the door was locked. 'Growing a trifle more livid, he seized a stool and battered down the door. He would have battered down Niemeyer himself in such a mood, or the Kaiser himself for that matter, any morning before 10 a.m.' As punishment for the carnage wreaked upon the door, the prisoners were locked inside their barrack block. After twenty-four hours, perhaps hastened by a boycott of the canteen by the men in the other *Kaserne*, which was adversely affecting his profits, Niemeyer relented and normal service was resumed.

For all the would-be escapees, getting out of the camp was only the first, and in some ways the least, hurdle they had to overcome. They then had to try to pass undetected through a vast swathe of hostile territory, living rough for two or more weeks, usually with inadequate food, footwear, clothing and maps, and in complete ignorance of the lie of the land and the customs and language of the inhabitants. Vernon Coombs, who had been badly wounded in the leg and was too lame to make any attempt to escape, was 'quite certain that if I had escaped, I would have been caught. If you escape, you go into a part of the country you know nothing about and you meet Germans. Some people can get out of situations like that but I don't think the majority can.'

Every new escape attempt led to fresh tirades from Niemeyer and a further tightening of camp security until every potential avenue through or over the wire had apparently been blocked. Lieutenant A. V. Burberry was the last to try to escape by cutting the wire and almost paid for it with his life. Niemeyer 'had wind of' the attempt, and as Burberry began cutting the wire, a sentry sneaked up on him. Burberry lay still, 'supporting himself on his hands with his body just off the ground', as the sentry walked to within five yards of him, 'aimed at his heart and fired', but he was 'evidently aiming at the groundline, with the result that, the fellow's body being just off the ground, the bullet touched his wrist and passed through the front of his coat, without further damage'. Burberry had only just begun cutting the twelve strands of wire so 'there was no need whatever to fire'. The conclusion most prisoners drew was that Niemeyer was seeking to deter further bids for freedom by making would-be escapees pay with their lives.

Escape by way of the gate or the fence now seemed all but impossible, but 'the efforts crystallized at last with twenty of the most daring spirits getting together to make a really scientific, fool-proof planned escape'. This group of officers formed the ambitious plan – 'the brainchild of a Canadian officer, Major Colquhoun', according to one, or 'Lieutenant Ellis, who started the work nine months before the escape', according to another – to drive a tunnel under the wire. As an Army Escape & Evasion instructor later said, 'The Poles, to escape, always storm the wire, the French disguise themselves, usually as nuns or whatever, but the British always dig.'

'After each tunnel I worked in before, I swore stolidly that I would never work in one again,' said one prisoner. 'But these vows were of no use – amusement had to come from somewhere, and I enjoyed this sort more than any other. It was a slow job, but in a cheery working party I found the work great fun!'

The place chosen for the start of the tunnel was at the foot of the staircase in the orderlies' quarters of *Kaserne* B, the closest point in either block to the perimeter fence. The officers first had to find some way of gaining access to the orderlies' quarters. There were heavy barricades on each of the floors, sealing off the orderlies' part of the building, and the only way for officers to reach it was to walk out of the door of their own quarters, pass along the outside of the building and go in through the orderlies' entrance. However, this was strictly forbidden: the orderlies' quarters were off-limits to all officers because of the proximity of that end of the building to the outer fence, and 'anyone trying it would come under the gaze of three armed sentries just twenty yards away'.

The would-be tunnellers somehow had to find a way to avoid detection by the guards in the prison yard, and the sentries stationed just outside the perimeter fence, who had a clear view of the officers' and orderlies' entrances, and who

– in theory at least – knew most of the orderlies by sight. In practice, the numbers incarcerated at Holzminden – more than seven hundred officers and orderlies – the turnover of personnel among guards and prisoners, and the regular rotation of 'beats' among the guards, all combined to diminish the risk of the tunnellers being detected. They therefore borrowed spare uniforms from the orderlies and waited inside their own quarters until one of their comrades signalled that the guards had either been distracted or were pacing their beats some distance away. Wearing their orderlies' uniforms, the tunnellers could then slip out of their own doorway and make their way along the building and in through the orderlies' entrance. While a couple of genuine orderlies kept watch for guards approaching from the yard, the officers began looking for a feasible site for a tunnel.

There was a small lobby inside the entrance to the orderlies' quarters from which a staircase on the left went up to the first floor and another, shorter, flight of steps to the right led down to the cellars. At the foot of the steps was a door, kept locked, that opened on to a passageway running the length of the building. The punishment cells were on the far side of the passage and the potato store, tin room, bread store, and the other cellar rooms on the near side. The initial plan had been to gain access to this passageway by picking the lock or making a skeleton key, and then to try to drive a tunnel out of one of the cellar rooms opening off it, even though there seemed little hope of avoiding detection by the jailer in charge of the punishment cells. However, just as a dummy key had been made to open the locked door at the bottom of the cellar steps, one of the prisoners had a brainwave. On the left of the steps down to the cellar, a partition of stout six-inch planks shaped like a 'V' on its side, 'which the Huns had put up to prevent a sentry being attacked by an escaper jumping out on him', completely blocked the space beneath the stairs leading to the upper floors. The small space it concealed was never used and was so heavily barricaded that it was never uncovered to be inspected. On its own, that space would not have been large enough to serve as the starting point for a tunnel. However, the prisoner reasoned that the space under the stairs to the first floor must also open on to a square cellar directly under the ground-floor lobby, bounded on the north by the wall of the cellar corridor, to the west by the wall of the adjoining potato cellar, and on the other two sides by the external walls of the building.

Before they could investigate the truth of that, they first had to make a concealed entrance in the barricade, but the planks were frequently inspected and any visible tampering with them was certain to be detected. The tools that they could improvise were also inadequate for the task. They therefore took steps to obtain proper carpenter's tools. A door was deliberately smashed in the officers' quarters in the knowledge that a civilian carpenter would be summoned to repair it. He worked under the supervision of an armed guard and his tools were checked and counted on arrival and departure, but as he worked, the prisoners staged a diversion by picking a quarrel with the guard. While shouting, jostling prisoners surrounded him, several of the carpenter's tools vanished. 'It was a real schamozzle and they just disappeared.' The theft was discovered almost at once, but there was no trace of the tools and the guard then faced a dilemma: if he told his sergeant or, even worse, the commandant about the theft, he would be punished with fatigues or worse for his dereliction of duty. Instead, 'to save his own skin', the guard kept his mouth shut and silenced the carpenter's grumbles, probably with a bribe paid by the prisoners, while they made off with their bounty.

The tunnellers' greatest asset was the slavish devotion of all the camp personnel, from the lowliest guard to the commandant, to the sanctity of the midday meal. With the exception of those compelled to remain on guard duty, all the German personnel disappeared from sight at noon for two to three hours. So sacrosanct was this luncheon interval that even Niemeyer rarely appeared during it, and the camp routine did not resume until about three o'clock. When breaching the barricade, the escapers therefore chose the time when the Germans working in the cellars and in the *Kommandantur* had disappeared for their lunch. While their comrades kept watch for guards, two officers disguised as orderlies used the stolen tools to remove the entire barricade. They succeeded in doing so, despite having to work in near-total silence to avoid alerting the attendant in the punishment cells and the guard standing just outside the orderlies' entrance.

As they peered into the void behind the partition, the prisoners saw that their supposition about the space had been correct. In addition to the cramped area under the stairs, there was a larger space under the ground-floor lobby. In total, it measured about four yards by five, with a ceiling height of less than six feet. The planks had fitted the aperture perfectly except for a narrow gap, no more than half an inch deep, at the top of the one next to the corner post, which had been cut slightly too short by the carpenter who had made the partition. The nails that held that board and the one next to it were carefully pulled out and cut off, leaving only the heads, which were then replaced, so that the barricade appeared untouched. Those planks were fixed together on the inside with battens and hinged to form a secret door, less than a foot wide. They then replaced the barricade, including the secret door, which was held shut by a bolt that slid into the corner post. The bolt was accessed from outside by the gap at the top of the plank. It was so small that only a couple of the men had fingers slim enough to operate it, and so well concealed that it survived the daily scrutiny of the guards undetected. Had the gap been even a fraction smaller, the tunnellers would have had to enlarge it and the newly cut timber would have increased the likelihood of discovery.

The tunnellers now had secure access to the cellar space and could work undisturbed, knowing it was never inspected. From then on, every day they went to Room 24, a little room near the door of the officers' quarters. There they changed into their orderlies' uniforms and dirtied their faces and hands – partly to look more like orderlies and partly to disguise their features. This was to the irritation of the orderlies, who resented the implication that they were dirty, since their personal hygiene was often much superior to that of the officers they served. A system of pickets was set up, one outside the 'Dressing Room' to give the alarm if a guard approached while the officers were changing into their orderlies' uniforms. Another waited in the yard, keeping the *Kommandantur* and guardroom under surveillance, another kept watch on the postern gate, while yet another, roving, picket was available to intercept any camp personnel emerging from unexpected directions. The tunnellers waited while a genuine orderly checked that the Germans working in the cellars were not on their way out. He then signalled the all-clear by stepping out of the doorway and scratching his head. A waiting officer relayed the message to the tunnellers and they slipped out of their own door, passed along the front of the building to the orderlies' door and, a few moments later, were through the secret entrance in the barricade, at which point the men on watch outside moved away.

At the end of the day's digging, they used the same subterfuge to slip out of the orderlies' quarters and back to their own. If necessary, the attention of the guards in the yard or outside the fence could be distracted by a staged diversion or by men talking to them, but often they were simply pacing around to ease the monotony of their turn on sentry duty and failed to notice anything untoward, even when the tunnellers were carrying concealed pieces of wood or other equipment under their clothes. If, as sometimes happened, a guard or one of the camp interpreters emerged from the *Kommandantur*, or the attendant for the punishment cells decided to take the air, as the tunnellers were about to enter or leave the chamber, officers in the yard or orderlies loitering in the lobby of the building would intercept them and, using any pretext, delay them with complaints, questions or conversation until the danger was past. The greatest danger to the tunnellers was that Karl Niemeyer might choose to make one of his sudden, un-announced appearances through the postern gate, to which he held a key. Since the postern was only ten yards from the orderlies' entrance, there would be no more than a few seconds' warning if he appeared. However, despite one or two close calls, the system of pickets and lookouts worked so well that the tunnellers were never caught in the act of enter-ing or leaving the chamber, and in all the long months of tunnelling, only once was an officer recognized while he was wearing an orderly's uniform.

The work of digging the tunnel was carried out in com-plete secrecy. The tunnellers cleaned themselves every day before leaving the orderlies' quarters and even those who shared rooms with them, though they must have suspected that 'something was up', remained unaware of exactly what their roommates were doing. 'No tunneller ever spoke of his work, not even to his brother officers, that was quite definite

– not a damn word. A man might be working on the tunnel for months and his roommates – the men he lived with – would not know.' One prisoner in *Kaserne* A 'really didn't know anything about what was going on in B House. I knew nothing about the tunnel – and it was being built for months. I didn't know anything about it until after the escape had taken place.' He was not unique, for almost no one knew about the tunnel other than the tunnellers themselves and the orderlies who had to be complicit in the escape plan, though they would take no part in it.

CHAPTER 7

THE RAT-HOLE

Tunnelling Under the Wire

'Double-Decked Beds' – So many bed-boards were removed by the tunnellers for use as roof-supports in the tunnel, that the unwitting occupants sometimes found their beds collapsing beneath them.

THE HOURS DURING which the officer PoWs at Holzminden would work on their new tunnel were restricted. All the buildings were locked at night and the tunnellers could dig only during the day between the nine a.m. and four p.m. roll-calls. Even then, the morning inspections and the issue of the daily potato ration from the adjoining cellar along the basement corridor meant that they could not get near the tunnel until around eleven thirty in the morning. They also had to allow plenty of time to clean themselves and hide all traces of their activities before finishing for the day, so work had to end well before the four o'clock *Appel*.

The only natural light in the chamber behind the partition came from chinks in the planking and was so feeble that it took several minutes before men coming into it from outside could see anything at all. The smell that greeted them was much more immediate, a fusty combination of bad air, damp earth, mildew and stale sweat. Their eyes slowly grew accustomed to the gloom, as they changed out of their orderlies' clothes and put on the filthy, permanently sodden and mud-stained rags that they kept in the chamber and wore when digging the tunnel.

The cellar floor was concrete and they decided that, rather than digging down through that, they would first drive the tunnel through the outer wall just below ground level, then tunnel down to a safer depth as soon as they were past it. The ceiling height in the chamber was level with the ground outside, and the roof of the tunnel was only three feet below it as they began to dig outwards directly under the orderlies' entrance door. However, even though they had avoided breaking through the concrete floor, they still faced a major obstacle: in order to drive the tunnel towards the fence, they had to break through the concrete foundations of the building, on which the outer wall was resting, and which in turn rested on solid rock.

Their only tools were 'whatever suitable appliances came to hand' – 'kitchen knives', 'penknives, spoons, a breadknife', sticks, pokers from the stoves in the barracks, pieces of sharpened tin or anything with a sharp edge, plus a cold chisel purloined from the carpenter, which was used to dig around stones and concrete. 'No patent gadgets were used at all. We dug with table knives where there was soil and progged [prodded] about with a cold chisel and bits of rake through the stone.' Progress was painfully slow. Although the concrete could be chipped away in tiny fragments, the steel reinforcing rods within it could not be bent or severed with the tools they had. However, as one prisoner patronizingly remarked, 'Ten months in the Fatherland had shown us that the conscience-price of the average working-class German was very dear at fifty marks,' and a large bribe was sufficient to persuade a civilian workman to bring some sulphuric acid into the camp among his other equipment. The tunnellers then used the acid, held against the steel in 'cups' moulded from clay, to burn through the reinforcing rods. Once through the foundations, they turned the tunnel to the north, the shortest distance to the perimeter fence.

The tunnel was 'merely a rat-hole', just sixteen inches wide by twelve inches high – 'about as wide as the average fire-place' – and so constricted that the tunnellers had to wriggle rather than crawl along it. It could not be made larger since the only place to store the extracted earth was the limited space in the cellar, and that was barely large enough for all the soil they would be digging out. The tunneller lit one candle – there were none to be had at any price in the camp canteen and all the hundreds of candles they eventually used came in Red Cross parcels from England – and left it at the entrance, where another man waited to remove the spoil. The digger then crawled along the tunnel in pitch darkness and lit another candle when he reached the face, placing it on a rock before setting to work. He lay prone, cutting at the clay and soil with a carving knife or one of their other crude tools and putting the excavated soil into an enamel bowl with holes drilled in opposite sides of the rim and a long rope tied to each.

When the bowl was full, the tunneller lifted himself on all fours – or, at least, as high as the twelve-inch ceiling would allow – and pushed the bowl back underneath his body. He then tugged on the rope to signal to the man at the other end of the tunnel, who hauled the bowl back, emptied the soil into mattress-cases stolen from their living quarters or 'bags made of old shirts', and these 'sacks' were stacked against the cellar walls and under the steps leading to the ground floor. Such was the volume of excavated material that, by the time the tunnel was complete, the cellar was filled, floor to ceiling, with sacks of spoil, leaving only the narrowest of passage-ways through to the mouth. When the cellar was beginning to fill with soil, the tunnellers also made endless journeys to the attic to dispose of some: 'We carried it upstairs in our pockets to shove under the roof tiles.' Having disposed of the spoil, the man in the chamber then tugged on the rope to signal to the tunneller to haul the bowl back again.

Roof falls were an added, potentially fatal, hazard. They were not only a risk to the life of a tunneller trapped under-ground, but in any major roof-fall, the subsidence caused in the ground above them would almost certainly have led to the detection of the tunnel. As a result the diggers also had to revet the tunnel at regular intervals using bed-boards stolen from their quarters and smuggled in under their clothes. All the beds had an iron frame across which wooden boards were laid, supporting the mattress, which was filled with paper or wood-shavings. Many of the bed-boards had already been used for firewood during the winter, and many more were now taken by the tunnellers, leaving not just their own beds but those of most of their often unwitting companions in a highly precarious state. The missing boards were the cause of much complaint, since very few knew of the tunnel, but the diggers joined in the chorus of disapproval, and neither their fellow prisoners nor the guards appear to have suspected the actual use to which the boards were being put.

Fitting the boards in place in the tunnel was an exhausting process. Having smuggled them into the tunnel chamber, they then had to cut them to exactly the right length for the space they were to fit – and all to different lengths because of the varying depth and width of the hand-dug tunnel. After dragging the boards along the tunnel with him to the point that needed support, the tunneller had to roll on to his back, hold the ceiling board in place with one hand and then, using his other hand, wedge an upright board under one end to brace it. Usually a prolonged period of trial and error ensued, cutting away a little more soil and stone at the foot of the tunnel wall, until the upright board could just be forced against the wall. The process was then repeated for the other end of the ceiling board. When complete, the bracing, in an inverted U-shape, was wedged so tightly that, even without nails or joints, it would hold up the tunnel roof and not be dislodged by the tunnellers brushing against it as they wriggled to and from the tunnel face. There were nowhere near enough bed-boards in the entire camp to revet the whole of the tunnel so, except in places where the roof was particularly unstable and it was revetted every foot, the wooden bracings were only used at intervals of two or three yards, leaving the possibility of roof-falls between them dangerously high.

The man working at the face was able to dig for a maximum of an hour before exhaustion and the foul air forced him to go back – there was no room to turn round so he had to wriggle backwards all the way – and make way for the next man. At the end of each shift they usually had pounding headaches as a result of the poor air they had been breathing. Their prodigious efforts were all the more remarkable, considering that they had been existing on a near-starvation diet for months.

No later than a quarter to four in the afternoon, all three men had to be clear of the tunnel and changed back into their orderlies' clothes. Just as when they entered the chamber in the morning, an orderly was stationed outside, with two or three of the other tunnellers keeping watch in the yard, while more officers and orderlies watched the door to the cellar corridor, the postern gate, the guardroom and the sentries outside the fence. Sometimes the signal to come out was given at once, but occasionally there were delays while German guards took prisoners to or from the punishment cells or ferried potatoes to the store in the cellar.

When the coast was clear, the orderly sang, 'Come out now', as if it was a line from a music-hall song. The three men at once emerged through the secret door and the orderly bolted it behind them as they made their way up the steps. They then waited just inside the entrance while another orderly made a last check of the yard outside, and exchanged glances with the men on picket. When the orderly said, 'Right', they slipped out of the entrance and made their way back to Room 24 inside the officers' quarters, where they changed back into their normal uniforms and joined the rest of the prisoners for the four o'clock *Appel*. If a guard or officer made an unexpected appearance from the guardroom or the cookhouse, or Niemeyer appeared through the postern gate, one of the loitering officers would intercept him and engage him in conversation or even argue with him, at the risk of three days' solitary confinement, until the tunnellers were safely back in their own quarters.

The escapers' original plan had been to dig a short tunnel, covering the ten yards from the outer wall of *Kaserne* B to the perimeter and emerging in the open ground a few yards beyond it. On a dark night, with the perimeter wall and palings partly blocking the view of the sentries within the compound, they would be almost invisible and there seemed every prospect of a successful escape within a very few weeks. As a result, Christmas was a cheerful occasion for those 'in the know' and the menu for their 1917 Holzminden Christmas dinner displayed to the full their ingenuity and mordant humour:

Doubtful Soup
Kish Fakes
Meat Pie de Margetts
Xmas Pudding
Fruitiness
Cheese
Harry Café

The prisoners also gave each other home-made Christmas cards produced from scraps of cardboard. One from Lieutenant T. R. Kirkpatrick to Norman Birks wished him 'Good cheer. And may ye wake up in a Homelier clime 'ere Yuletide come again.' Birks, who had been a prisoner of war since being posted as missing in action on 5 April 1917, had some hope of that, for he was on the list of escapers waiting to make use of the tunnel, once the working party who had actually dug it had made their own escape.

That Christmas, other Holzminden inmates were in far less cheerful mood. One described it as 'the worst I ever experienced. Parcels had not been coming very regularly about this time and I was down to a very low ebb; my Xmas dinner consisted of a tin of corned beef and some dried apricots, with not even a drink of [sic] consolation.' Others, including Captain Douglas Lyall Grant, fared better, even though Niemeyer had banned the sale of wine on Christmas Day; whether that was for disciplinary or religious reasons was not revealed. The prisoners 'showed our appreciation by making sufficient noise to be heard in the town' leading Niemeyer to ban the sale of wine for a further two days, but since 'most people had laid in a stock beforehand' they were not greatly inconvenienced by the prolongation of the ban. Inevitably the gregarious and affluent Lyall Grant and his roommates held a party, which was 'a great success', though he plaintively noted that 'a party here costs just about ten times as much as it would at the Carlton [Club in London]'. He and his comrades went on to celebrate Hogmanay in the traditional style, with 'the usual midnight procession with the [bag]pipes, and for once the Germans behaved sensibly – in other words, kept out of our way'.

There was no Christmas break for the tunnellers, but early in 1918 they suffered a bad blow. 'One of the originators of the tunnel', B. G. Austen, who had 'started to write home for pyjamas to be used as overalls so that mud would not show on our clothes', had begun to fear that Niemeyer was becoming suspicious. Austen had been taken prisoner after being shot down in flames and was so badly burned and wounded by shrapnel that he came close to losing his leg. However, while in the prison hospital at Cassel prisoner-of-war camp, a Russian doctor told him that 'It wouldn't be necessary to remove my leg; he would save it.' The doctor was as good as his word, and though Austen was on crutches for some time, he was sufficiently recovered by the time he reached Holzminden to be as active in digging as any of the other tunnellers. However, Niemeyer's suspicions had indeed been aroused and one day in February 1918, with no prior warning, Austen and six other tunnellers were abruptly removed from Holzminden and transferred to Schweidnitz at 'the other end of Germany'. Undeterred by this, 'more or less the same crowd' began work on a tunnel there and ultimately escaped through it, although Austen was eventually recaptured on the Austrian border. The Holzminden tunnel was in jeopardy for a little while, but Niemeyer's actions seemed to have allayed his suspicions, and work on the tunnel resumed without the need for fresh men to be drafted in to replace those who had gone.

As the harsh winter at last began to ease its grip and the fields beyond the wire started to green at the approach of spring, the escapers reached the target area, having driven the tunnel perhaps fifteen yards beyond the perimeter fence. They then cut a square chamber at the end, large enough to receive the earth excavated during the final drive to the surface. However, the chances of evading discovery as they emerged from the tunnel were then reduced almost to nil when Niemeyer, either prompted by his own fears or by rumours of another escape attempt, suddenly increased the number of guards outside the perimeter, including one stationed almost directly over the place where the tunnel was to emerge. As a result, the tunnellers were forced to abandon the furthest section of the tunnel, including the chamber to receive the excavated earth on the last push to the surface. The original route of the tunnel had curved to the west, but a new shaft would now be driven due north, covering a much greater distance towards a patch of cultivated ground outside the fence that, by high summer, would be covered with ripening crops.

Already beyond the camp perimeter, the rerouted tunnel would now have to be driven beneath the first forty or fifty yards of cultivated ground, which had been planted with vegetable crops that were already sprouting but were too low-growing to provide adequate cover. However, beyond them was a row of bean plants and then a field of rye that, when full-grown, would be dense and high enough to give good cover. That was now their objective, but so slow was their progress that they could make no more than an absolute maximum of two feet a day. Hindered by stubborn rocks, clearing roof-falls and having to revet the walls and roof with wooden boards, they often fell short of even that modest target. It was the best that could be achieved with their primitive tools in such appalling working conditions, but it led to a race against time to drive the tunnel all the way to the edge of the rye crop before it was harvested – in early August at the latest.

Morale at the camp was already plummeting as hordes of fresh prisoners began arriving and describing the rout of British forces during the great German offensive, 'Operation Michael', also known as the *Kaiserschlacht* (Battle for the Emperor), that had been launched on 21 March 1918. A hundred thousand Britons had been captured during that single offensive, considerably more than had been taken in the entire course of the war until then. The deluge of men, who 'arrived looking like scarecrows and were lucky if any of their own clothes arrived from home inside six weeks', led the existing prisoners to donate all their surplus clothes to help the newcomers, and the Red Cross also sent out large quantities of 'new and very good underclothes which, although not sufficient, went a long way towards fitting out the numerous prisoners taken during that time'.

Faced with the apparent possibility of more long years of war or even a British defeat, and with the prospect of months' more digging to push the tunnel as far as the shelter of the crops, most of the original tunnellers – many of them '1914 men' who had now been in prison for three years – were so disheartened that, 'rather than wait for an escape which might never succeed', they decided to abandon the attempt and instead take up the offer of an exchange of PoWs to neutral Holland, as agreed between the British and German governments.

When a Dutch representative chaired a conference between British and German delegates in 1917, he opened it by tabling an offer from his government to accept up to 16,000 British and German combatants or civilian internees on to Dutch soil, providing the costs were met by the belligerents. The Dutch government also proposed to supervise a more lenient system of repatriating those combatants who were too sick or wounded ever to be likely to take up arms again, allowing many more men to return to their homelands. It was further proposed that prisoners who had been at least eighteen months in captivity and were suffering from 'barbed-wire disease' – 'a form of neurasthenia that became so prevalent and well defined that men were . . . unfit for further military duty because of it' – should, after examination by a panel of three Swiss doctors and three doctors from the captor state, be declared suitable for internment in Switzerland or some other neutral country. If after three months their health had not considerably improved, their disease would be regarded as serious and they would be considered for repatriation. However, for the duration of hostilities, all those repatriated were not to be 'employed on any front of military operations, or on lines of communication, or in occupied territory'.

It was also proposed by the Dutch and agreed by the combatants that, irrespective of their medical condition, all officers and NCOs who had been in captivity for at least eighteen months were to be offered the opportunity to be interned in a neutral country, 'unless they desire to remain'. To maintain parity between the two sides, they were to be interned or repatriated 'head for head and rank for rank'. The belligerents also agreed to repatriate all captured medical personnel, to reduce the punishments for those prisoners who attempted to escape and immediately to release all prisoners serving long sentences for that offence. The combatants also confirmed that punishment for 'attempts to escape from arrest or prison or camps', even if repeated, was to be a maximum of 'fourteen days' military confinement' or, if combined with theft or damage to property or persons, a maximum of two months' imprisonment. If escapees were recaptured, they were not to be subjected to 'unnecessary harshness ... and they are to be protected from violence of every kind'. Collective punishments for the 'misconduct of individuals' were also forbidden. After an intervention by the International Red Cross, the combatants also agreed to abandon the practice of exacting reprisals on prisoners of war in retaliation for perceived offences committed by the other side. It was a policy that the British government conceded 'operates indiscriminately and unjustly', and after citing 'outrages committed or countenanced by the German government', they accepted the appeal by the Red Cross for 'neutral Powers to impress on the enemy considerations of humanity and justice'.

Those prisoners who accepted the offer of exchange would therefore be interned in the Netherlands or Switzerland until the end of the war. Many spurned the offer, for internment meant that they could play no further part in the fighting, and as part of the agreement, the respective governments undertook to return any men who escaped from internment and made their way back to Britain or Germany without permission. However, after all the privations they had endured, for many prisoners at Holzminden and elsewhere 'Holland looked too good a place to refuse to go to.' The first party of twenty officers had left Holzminden on Boxing Day 1917 and a further twenty-six, including many of the original tunnellers, departed on 24 March 1918. The senior British officer, Major Haig, went with them, and was replaced by Colonel Charles E. H. Rathborne, the latest in the lengthening line of senior British officers at Holzminden. Rathborne had previously been in Schweidnitz prison camp and, despite his portly figure, had escaped from there earlier that month, but was soon re-captured and sent to Holzminden, where he showed an immediate interest in a further escape attempt.

The prisoners being taken to the Netherlands were warned that if they made 'any demonstration which could be displeasing to the officer in charge of the escort, on crossing the frontier, we could be, and would be if necessary, sent back to Germany, as even while in Holland we remained German prisoners'. The British NCOs in the party defiantly gave a cheer as they crossed the Dutch frontier and Major Haig was subsequently informed that the *Hauptmann* in charge of the escort was so 'much annoyed with this anti-German demonstration' that he was going to report it to the *Kriegsministerium*. A month later, the bibulous gourmand Captain Douglas Lyall Grant was among another batch of prisoners exchanging captivity at Holzminden for the relative freedom of internment in Holland. He left 'after a final scowl at the Commandant, who was trying to be friendly, and no one shook hands with him'.

Those German and British PoWs who were interned in Holland took their animosities with them, and during the first few weeks of the exchange programme,

> many clashes took place between the Germans and ourselves, whenever we chanced to meet ... The sight of a German uniform to our men after the treatment they had received was like a red rag to a bull. Many an officer and non-commissioned officer returned to Rotterdam somewhat disfigured until at last no permission was given to wear a uniform outside the area, either for ourselves or the Germans. But even after that, if our men heard anyone speak in German, they were suspicious and waited around for hours to find out if he had been in the German Army; if he had been, the result was always disastrous for the German.

As a result of the exchange of prisoners, only three of the original tunnellers now remained at Holzminden and, having decided to carry on, they recruited a further ten officers to share the work and escape with them. The thirteen-man group now included Lieutenant Walter Butler, Lieutenants Frederick Mardock and Colin Lawrence of the Royal Naval Air Service, Captain William Langren, Lieutenant David Wainwright RN, Lieutenant Neil MacLeod, Captain Clifford Robertson, Lieutenant Andrew Clouston, Lieutenants Arthur Morris and Robert Paddison, and three pilots, Captain David Gray, Lieutenant Cecil Blain and Lieutenant Caspar Kennard, who collectively and individually had already made several previous escape attempts from Osnabrück, Clausthal, Ströhen, Neunkirchen and Krefeld before arriving at Holzminden. There was also an auxiliary list of another six men who were helping the escapers in one capacity or another. Among them was Lieutenant James Bennett, the son of a Somerset farmer, who had been invited to join the escapers in February 1918, 'presumably because I was tough and a bit of a daredevil'.

Cecil Blain had been taken prisoner on 7 August 1916 after his aircraft developed engine trouble well behind the German lines. Fair-haired and blue-eyed, with a round face and unremarkable features, he could have passed for German. He had spent time in South Africa before the war where he had learned Cape Dutch (Afrikaans), and although he was not a fluent German speaker, he understood the language perfectly.

Caspar Kennard, the son of a Kent landowner who had worked in Argentina before the war, 'learning the cattle business at the behest of a well-known meat-extract company', had been captured when his aircraft was forced down behind enemy lines in October 1916. Tall with a moustache and thick black hair pushed back from his forehead, he had a slightly distant and rather impatient manner and, though he spoke fluent Spanish, he was the only one of the pilots with no German whatsoever.

David Gray, who had been shot down and captured near Bapaume on the morning of 17 September 1916, had spent most of his pre-war life in India. Always immaculately turned out – even with only a prison-camp wardrobe – he was dark-haired with a neat moustache and a complexion dark enough for him to be mistaken in a poor light for a native Indian. He had a rare gift for languages, speaking impeccable French, German, Russian, Hindustani and several other Asian tongues. He had been known as Munshi – Hindustani for language teacher – in India, and it became his permanent nickname. His Indian roots made him a friend to the camp interpreter Kurt Grau. When identity cards and passes were needed for copying, Grau supplied his own and his name was even used on one of the fake identity cards that the three men made. Gray, Blain and Kennard had already garnered considerable experience during their previous escape attempts and Gray in particular had come heartbreakingly close to completing a 'home run' – a successful crossing of the border with Holland – after escaping from

Krefeld. His escape map showed a place called Brecklen Kamp just inside the Netherlands border, and when he reached a village bearing that name, he walked straight up to a guard post to announce himself to the soldiers there. Too late, he realized that they were wearing German uniform. He then discovered that there were two villages called Brecklen Kamp, one on either side of the frontier and, although no more than a hundred yards from the Dutch border, he had unwittingly delivered himself back into German hands.

The first few yards of the Holzminden tunnel that Gray, Blain and Kennard were now helping to dig sloped downwards, then levelled and rose again as it approached the point where the original exit was to have been made, just outside the perimeter wall. As the tunnellers crawled through this section, they often had the unnerving sensation of hearing the thud of a sentry's boots echoing through the earth as the guard paced his beat just three feet above their heads. Past that point, the tunnel again descended and, although running an average of eight or nine feet below ground level, it rose and fell by several feet in places as the tunnellers struggled to maintain a level while trying to avoid large rocks or difficult strata. It also wound from side to side like a snake since the diggers had no means of maintaining a dead-straight course with compasses that were 'not so finely accurate' as to allow precise bearings to be taken.

The tunnellers worked in three-man teams, and

rotated their jobs every hour with the third man acting as timekeeper. Their daily routine was unchanging:

1. Change from orderlies' clothes to working clothes.
2. No. 1 lights candle and puts in pump chamber just round bend.
3. Crawls to tunnel face with other candle which he lights and sticks on suitable stone. Takes rope with him. Very slow as tunnel only 18 inches wide.
4. No. 2 enters pump chamber and starts working home-made pump. Air forced along tube of biscuit tins.
5. No. 3 at tunnel mouth, hands basin attached to rope to No. 2 who puts it in front of him.
6. No. 1 loosens stones and earth, drags up basin, gets it in front of him, fills it and gets it back behind him. Gives signal on rope to No. 2.
7. No. 2 hauls back basin, passes to No. 3, who stacks away under stairs and returns it to No. 2.
8. By this time, No. 1 ready with fresh load and pulls up basin again.

To lie motionless in the stifling heat and foul air of the claustrophobic tunnel was gruelling enough; to dig away at the stubborn clay soil and prise free the rocks and stones that studded it, while lying in that cramped, prone position was absolutely exhausting – and conditions now became even worse. Until this point, the soil they had been excavating had been mainly a yellow clay, which was relatively easy to dig, but they now encountered a formidable obstacle: a dense, deep layer of large, flat, water-worn rocks, laid down in an ancient riverbed, bound together with sticky, unyielding clay and so compacted that they were very difficult to remove. So obstinate was the layer that the tunnellers tried to bypass it by digging deeper, but after descending a further four feet, they still faced the same apparently endless barrier of stones and reluctantly decided that their only course was to dig their way through it.

The stones they had to excavate were unpleasant enough, but the ones left in the floor, walls and roof made life even more uncomfortable for the tunnellers. They often caught their elbows, shoulders, knees and heads on projecting rocks, and all of them had almost permanent open sores on their knees and elbows, while the sharp-edged rocks also caused the rope used to haul the bowl containing the excavated soil to fray and break with monotonous regularity. Dragging the bowl round all the twists and turns in the tunnel's course and over the rough surface of its floor often caused it to jam or overturn and spill its contents. 'Towards the end, the tunnel was so winding and humpbacked that it was no longer possible to use our rope-and-basin method for disposing of the rubble, so we had to resort to filling the sacks where we were working and dragging them back through the tunnel.' It was a wearisome task in that confined space, for every time he filled a sack with spoil, the tunneller at the face now had to begin wriggling backwards a yard at a time, dragging the heavy sack – weighing around a hundredweight (about fifty kilos) – after him, all the way back to the chamber under the stairs. However, it gave them 'some good practice for the night of the break-out, for then each man had to crawl forward on his elbows, pushing his pack in front of him – which was even more difficult!' Inevitably the sacks wore through fast and had to be regularly replaced.

As the tunnel lengthened, it took longer and longer for the diggers to worm their way to and from the face, reducing the time in each 'shift' that they could actually spend extending the tunnel to not much more than an hour. 'The most agonizing time was when the tunnel had reached fifty yards or so. It would take half an hour to crawl there and an hour and a half to wriggle back.' In addition, the further the tunnel was driven, the worse the air became. When it grew so bad that a candle would not stay alight, work had to be suspended while a system to provide air was devised. Tins of biscuits were a regular component of parcels from home or forwarded by the Red Cross and one of the tunnellers went round the camp collecting every empty tin he could lay his hands on. He knocked the bottoms out of them, cut the side-seam of the rectangular tins, re-formed them into circular tubes, then joined them together to make a pipe. So cramped was the available space that the pipe had to be sunk into the floor along the full length of the tunnel, further delaying the work of driving it forward.

A pair of bellows was improvised from an RAF pilot's leather flying coat, and some pieces of wood screwed to a pair of wooden uprights. These were embedded in the clay floor and ceiling of a chamber cut out of the tunnel wall about six feet from the mouth. From then on, all the time that a tunneller was working at the face, another worked the bellows in the pump chamber, sitting on the floor facing along the tunnel and operating the pump with his left hand. As the tunnel face advanced, more biscuit-tin sections were added to lengthen the air pipe, but the air remained foul; they 'sucked air' from the pipe, but 'it was suffocating work'.

One other unpleasant hazard often confronted them as they worked: 'There were many rats living in the tunnel, and meeting one of them and seeing the glitter of beady eyes in the semi-darkness, was a feeling of revulsion only surpassed when one of the vile and foul creatures scurried over you.' As the tunneller crawled closer to the face, there was nowhere for the rat to retreat and the only solution for the man was either to kill it – no easy matter in the cramped confines of the tunnel – or to lower his head, flatten himself against the floor of the tunnel and wait for the cornered rat to clamber over him and make its escape.

CHAPTER 8
THE BLACK BOOK
Hidden Contraband

'*Licht Aus*' – Lights Out at ten p.m. every night was strictly enforced by the guards.

IN MAY 1918, there were claims in the German press that, despite the agreement between the warring powers that had been brokered by the Dutch the previous year, German PoWs in Britain were still being subjected to reprisals. Both sides had been guilty of reprisals at various stages of the war, a practice probably initiated by the first lord of the Admiralty, Winston Churchill, in early 1915, when he ordered captured German U-boat crews to be imprisoned in the Naval Detention Barracks at Chatham and Devonport. The policy was immediately abandoned when Arthur Balfour replaced Churchill in May 1915, but other reprisals by both sides continued, in particular the policy of stationing PoWs in areas subject to air attack. During 1917 British prisoners were moved to camps near the centre of Karlsruhe, Freiburg and Stuttgart, so that, as one newspaper claimed, 'they might share . . . the dangers of air attack'. On 5 February 1918, the under-secretary of state for war, Ian Macpherson, told the House of Commons that the German authorities had also 'placed officer prisoners of war in localities which are specially subject to air raids. Similar action is contemplated in this country,' and by May of that year German officers had been imprisoned in requisitioned buildings in Ramsgate, Margate and Southend, which had all suffered attacks by German bombers.

Britain had also submitted well-documented complaints of brutality and mistreatment in the German PoW camps administered by the Tenth Army Corps, Holzminden and Clausthal in particular, the domains of the now infamous Niemeyer twins. When these complaints were ignored, the British authorities imposed reprisals on German prisoners from the constituent regiments of the Tenth Army Corps, transferring them to the same PoW camp and stripping them of all privileges.

In retaliation, beginning in mid-May 1918, Niemeyer ordered immediate month-long counter-reprisals against the British prisoners under his command. No music, theatricals, games or walks on parole were allowed and the number of daily *Appels* was doubled. They were now held at nine and eleven thirty a.m., three thirty and six p.m., a very serious setback to the escapers, for it was possible only to work on the tunnel in the brief period between the late-morning and mid-afternoon roll-calls. Having ordered the reprisals, Niemeyer even encouraged the prisoners to write letters home about them, offering them the chance to send an extra letter in which to do so (PoWs were normally restricted to two letters a month). He told them that the additional letter would not even be subject to censorship, provided that it explained why Niemeyer had imposed the reprisals. However, his attempt to manipulate British public opinion was a dismal failure: not a single PoW availed himself of the opportunity to write such a letter.

Just before the reprisals were lifted in mid-June, there was a near-catastrophe for the tunnellers when, while he was making his way back to his quarters still wearing orderlies' clothes, one man was recognized as an officer by a sentry. The one piece of good news for the escapers was that, though the sentry reported it to Niemeyer at once and was insistent that the man had been an officer, he could not name him. Niemeyer called an immediate *Appel* and cross-examined several prisoners while the rest of them remained standing at attention on the parade-ground, but he gleaned no clues as to the identity of the officer. It was typical of Niemeyer's perverse and capricious rule of Holzminden that he did not carry out an identity parade, and when no further suspicious incidents were reported over the next couple of days, he had the hapless sentry hauled in front of him again and sentenced him to eight days in the punishment cells for making a false report. Apart from increasing the already strong dislike his men felt for him, the punishment that Niemeyer had imposed also made it much less likely that other sentries would report suspicious occurrences in the future.

Despite a search in the wake of the sentry's report, the tunnel had remained undiscovered, but in a further tightening of camp security, Niemeyer ordered the attic floor of the building to be evacuated and sealed off, and an additional guard was permanently posted by the door to the orderlies' quarters. Although the secret door to the tunnel chamber was still out of the guard's sight, his presence made it impossible for the officers to continue reaching the tunnel workings in the same way. As a result, out of dire necessity, a new access route was made. The tunnellers first attempted to break through into the tunnel chamber by making a concealed hole through the floor at the foot of the wall of Room 34, the large ground-floor room that adjoined it. All the occupants of the room – fourteen men – had to be let into the secret and all took their places on the ever-expanding unofficial 'waiting list' of those who might use the tunnel as soon as the working party had made good their own escape. The list eventually included eighty-six names and there were frequent, often heated, arguments between the tunnellers about the merits and capabilities of the various people and the places they deserved to occupy on the waiting list.

While some of the tunnellers went to work on the wall, others took it in turns to sit in a deck-chair in the corridor, pretending to read while keeping a wary eye open for guards. However, when they had removed an area of plaster and begun trying to break through the wall, they discovered that it was concrete. The difficulties of breaking through it at all and of concealing the evidence that they had done so were felt to be insuperable and the attempt was abandoned. Instead, the working party turned their attention to the attic of the building. As the top floor had been placed out of bounds by Niemeyer, the swing doors at the head of the stairs had been permanently secured with a thick chain looped through the handles and then padlocked. However, the handles were fixed to the doors by six screws and it had evidently occurred neither to Niemeyer nor to any of his guards that it would be possible to gain access to the attic by leaving the chain and padlock untouched and simply removing the screws. They had to be removed and replaced every time the escapers went in and out, but whenever the Germans checked the attic, they merely examined the chain and lock on the doors and then, satisfied, went back downstairs.

Having gained access to the attic, the escapers began breaching the thin partition separating one of the attic rooms from the eaves. Cutting the hole behind a bed 'with infinite care' and removing plaster and wood until 'only the thinnest shell remained', they made a removable panel that, with the joins suitably disguised under a mixture of dirt and cornflour to match the surrounding plasterwork, they hoped would be good enough to fool a casual inspection, though it was unlikely to survive a thorough search undetected. Having made the opening, the tunnellers could then make their way along the eaves and exit through an existing trapdoor in the wall of the attic in the orderlies' quarters. They could then go down the stairs to the secret door in the cellar, while an orderly kept watch on the guard outside. The tunnellers now had a huge advantage, for work could continue by day and night, only ceasing for the morning and afternoon roll-calls.

Even when the reprisals ended and Niemeyer removed the extra guard outside the orderlies' quarters, the tunnellers continued to use the new access route because it allowed them much longer working shifts. The lifting of restrictions also meant they could take walks outside the camp under parole, and all the escapers, overcoming their earlier reservations about signing the parole cards, took the chance to build up their fitness for the long route march to the Dutch border that would follow the break-out from the tunnel. Previously they had only been able to get fit for escape attempts by taking 'vigorous exercise' within the narrow confines of the camp itself. Five circuits of the *Spielplatz* was roughly equivalent to a mile, and they would endlessly circle it, 'keeping their strength up and their muscles supple'.

Having given their parole, they could now take more strenuous exercise in the country around the camp. On those walks the guards accompanying them were unarmed – 'at least they seemed to be and probably were' – and, although the officers were 'in honour bound not to attempt to escape', they were able to stride out over long distances and different terrain. Although it was forbidden, the prisoners also availed themselves of the chance to bathe in the River Weser, after bribing the *Feldwebel* who was escorting them to look the other way. During their swim the escapers took care to identify a point at which the river was fordable: their honour forbade them to attempt an escape while under parole but, said one prisoner, there was nothing in their parole cards telling them 'not to notice things'. On returning to the camp they handed in their parole cards and were then once more 'perfectly justified in endeavouring to escape'.

If they were to make a successful escape, they not only had to complete the tunnel, but also needed civilian clothes, rations to sustain them, and compasses and maps to guide them on the march of more than 150 miles to the Dutch border, travelling only at night to reduce the risk of discovery. All Germans had to carry a school certificate as well as an identity card issued by a local authority with a photo and an official stamp, sometimes in different colours, and a permit to travel when away from their home area. As well as these forged documents, escaping prisoners also needed money for bribes, although cigarettes and tobacco often proved as effective as cash: one prisoner spoke of instances when 'the Germans while on sentry duty refused money, but let a man out of camp for a few cigarettes'.

The prisoners displayed astonishing ingenuity in obtaining, manufacturing or improvising the items they needed, including authentic-looking rubber stamps made with 'the lid of a round tin, a 2-Mark silver piece and a child's printing outfit bought in the canteen'; 'we got a German two-mark piece with the cross and eagle and made a rubber stamp [and] beautiful identity cards'. They also fashioned skeleton keys, wire-cutters, saws, officers' swords, cap badges, insignia and compasses. Many years later, one prisoner still had the compass he made out of 'a pickle jar cork and a magnetic needle, and it still works!'

A group of Canadian prisoners made compasses with used razor blades, de-tempering the steel by heating it so that it could be cut easily, then re-tempering it by heating it and dipping it at once in water. The needle was magnetized, balanced on a collar stud and housed in a case like a small pill-box, carved out of a piece of solid wood. The face of the compass was made from a circle of window glass. They had no diamond to cut it but discovered by trial and error that if they placed the glass under water they could cut it with the point of a pair of scissors without breaking it. Another prisoner, Stanley Purves, a Scottish pilot who had been shot down in early 1918, made a compass using a pair of magnetized needles threaded end-to-end through two pieces of paper. Suspended from a piece of thread attached to a sliver of wood between the two papers, which allowed it to spin freely, it could be relied on to point to magnetic north. The whole thing was almost as slim as a razor blade and, in fact, was hidden in a Canadian-made paper wrapper for a Gillette safety blade.

The manufacture of plausible-looking civilian clothes or German uniforms occupied much of the tunnellers' spare time and many of them discovered hitherto unknown skills with needle, thread and thimble. Believing that 'the hat is the most important item in a civilian disguise', Captain Edward Wilmer Leggatt, formerly of the Wiltshire Regiment but attached to the Royal Flying Corps as a pilot, who had been shot down and taken prisoner on 9 August 1916, went to considerable lengths to obtain a white Panama hat with a black band – the least military-looking hat he could think of – to aid his disguise when travelling across Germany to the Dutch border. He also made a pair of leather moccasins 'worn for silent travelling at night', and had a compass fixed to a lanyard to be 'attached to his braces for safety'. The resourceful Leggatt also obtained a battery-operated German electric torch by the simple expedient of bribing one of the camp guards. An inveterate escapee, he had already passed through the camps at Gütersloh, Osnabrück, Clausthal, Ströhen, Neunkirchen and Saarlouis, before arriving at Holzminden in May 1918. If trying to pass as a civilian, good grooming was probably even more important than a good hat, for an unkempt and unshaven person was bound to attract attention. Jack Shaw's escape kit included a miniature brush and comb set, and a shaving brush, and he and several tunnellers included razors in their equipment, though it was uncertain whether there would be much opportunity to make use of them.

Genuine passes and identity cards were obtained by picking the pockets of guards or civilian workers. 'People used to come into the camps and do odd jobs and some of them were bribable and some of them didn't look after their identity documents very well, and they were "borrowed" from their pockets and copied and sometimes put back.' To avoid discovery, after copying the passes and identity cards, they were usually returned to the guards' pockets, an essential but even riskier business than removing them, but it was done with such consummate skill and sleight-of-hand that the guards remained blissfully unaware that their passes had ever been missing.

'The amount of illegal goods in the camp was astonishing,' another prisoner recalled. There were 'gold sovereigns galore, stitched under the stars on uniforms, cameras with film developers, chunks of rubber from which we made stamps of many varieties needed on documents of identity. Someone had a typewriter, maps galore, and instructions on routes of escape, plus all sorts of other things.' Some items of escape equipment were also improvised from things obtained quite openly from the camp canteen. A friend of one of the escapers was in the canteen when he saw on sale a large manicure set that contained 'an enormous pair of nail-clippers'. He bought it at once, even though the price – about forty marks – was stiff, and later, on trying out the nail-clippers on a piece of wire, he found that they 'cut it like butter!'

Other prisoners ordered escape equipment by mail order from British suppliers. When the parcels were delivered to the camp, the recipients either resorted to bribery or relied on their sleight-of-hand to sneak the contraband away from the guards. One prisoner, Tom Mapplebeck, wrote to the Army & Navy Stores asking for a copy of their catalogue; from it he ordered

escape material, compasses and all that sort of thing, [and] tinned pheasant and things from Fortnum & Mason. My Fortnum & Mason parcels were duly opened and put in lockers . . . but the parcels from the Army & Navy Stores used to be shuffled under a sack and then collected later. I had my own key to the parcel room and I'd remove and distribute [the escape material]. I was in solitary confinement for three days when a parcel arrived with six lovely hats. When I was released the German warrant officer said to me, 'There's a parcel for you,' so I had to open it in front of him. He said, 'This is escape material.' I said, 'Oh, no, we need them to shade our eyes when we're playing tennis.'

The guard insisted that the hats were contraband and confiscated them, but [I] needed those damn hats, so at midday I went in and removed the hats and put in makeweights. I put the hats under my pillow and sent a round robin saying, 'Remove them and don't tell me where they're hidden,' because I knew I'd be called in if the loss was discovered. The next day I was called in and they said, 'Where are the hats?'

I said, 'I don't know.'

'Can you swear on the Bible?'

I said, 'Yes.'

They told me, 'Court martial in Hannover.'

Mapplebeck was duly tried and sentenced to six months' solitary confinement or a sixty-mark fine, but he refused to pay the fine, saying, 'Pay sixty marks and go back to England after the war and be court-martialled for financing the German war effort?' As a result of his refusal, he was sent to the cells and spent five and a half months in solitary confinement before being released.

Other escape material was brought in by a guard who had been bribed. Jack Shaw's brother Wilfred played no part in the digging of the tunnel, for it was 'well under way, about half done, I should think', by the time he arrived at Holzminden, but he was deputed to act as go-between with the bribed guard. 'Some bloke in London used to send things like German maps and money into Germany and somehow they got into the canteen and a certain German there was in the pay of our chaps, so that all I had to do was go in there when a certain bloke was on duty and draw the stuff out as food.' Wilfred delivered it to his brother who hid it under the floor of his room. During searches, 'Old Gerry [the Germans] used to go and bang on the walls and everything,' Wilfred later said, 'but he never thought of banging the bally floor.'

There was a remarkable array of occupations and talents among the prisoners, 'lawyers, businessmen, engineers and craftsmen of all kinds, including a very expert burglar, who went through into German quarters nightly "borrowing" all sorts of things and clothes and other equipment'. Captain Jack Shaw, who had been temporarily transferred from *Kaserne* B to A, decided to go to the very top. 'One of the guiding principles of an escaper was that he would never learn too much about his surroundings and, with the object of improving my knowledge, I decided to have a look at "Milwaukee's" office.' He scrutinized the wooden partition separating the prisoner's half of the first-floor corridor from the *Kommandantur*, then 'walked up and down this corridor most of the day, a wet one'. Pausing each time he reached the partition, he managed surreptitiously to loosen three boards, and then carefully placed them back in position.

About one thirty the following morning, he left his bed 'and got through the gap. One board dropped, but I managed to catch it without making much noise.' He made his way along the corridor and, to his surprise, found the door to the commandant's office wide open. Using his electric torch, shaded by his hand, he searched the office. He had pocketed three compasses and some papers that were on the desk when he heard footsteps. He hid behind the door as, alerted either by the noise he had made or the dim light from his torch, 'in walked three German soldiers with rifles and bayonets at the ready, and behind them came Feldwebel Caston with a flash-lamp. Anything might have happened had I waited but Caston luckily went a little way past the door, so I charged into him and hit him in the face at the same time. He was a large man and fell into an upright stove, his flash-lamp also very luckily going out on dropping to the floor.' In the darkness and confusion, Shaw sprinted out of the office, along the corridor and back through the partition. He had just got into bed when all the lights went on and the guards began searching every room, but could not identify the culprit. Had they noticed the sheen of sweat on Shaw's forehead or taken his pulse, they would have known it was him, because his heart was still pounding from the exertion and the excitement.

Undaunted, Shaw carried on his escape preparations,

making use of both his own efforts and the skills of his fellow prisoners. 'There were always people in prisoner-of-war camps who could do anything. If you said to a man, "I want somebody that can pick a lock," well, somebody was there who could pick a lock.' Some men fashioned lock picks from thin pieces of metal and one swore that 'there is nothing better for this purpose than the thin strong steel wire used for stiffening an officer's cap'. Others used sardine-tin openers, which 'when bent over to certain lengths, made good lock-picks for certain types of lock . . . They eased the situation when raiding the German potato cellar, but eventually a lock was substituted which beat me.' There were men who could make 'a pair of wire-cutters out of a safety razor, a metal saw out of an officer's epaulette, or a complete German uniform out of a Russian greatcoat and a Frenchman's breeches'. Some of the orderlies had been tailors in civilian life and 'they could dye cloth too. There didn't seem to be anything that someone couldn't do.' Thrown back on their own resources, many prisoners discovered that they possessed hitherto unimagined skills, and older officers remarked that being imprisoned at Holzminden was 'working wonders for some of the young ones here. They are learning to do things for themselves, to be independent, in fact to stand on their own legs.'

The safest location for hiding escape materials was often the quartermaster's stores or the parcel room which, being manned by camp personnel, was never searched. Even though searches of the PoWs' quarters sometimes revealed contraband, the items were often stolen back, sometimes over and over again, in the course of the search, and then hidden again to be rediscovered by the guards. As a result the meticulous records they always kept might show that, for example, three civilian hats had been confiscated, even though there was only one, and by the end of the search it was once more in the prisoners' hands.

Prisoners were also 'terribly ingenious in the way things were hidden . . . There were carpenters and cabinet makers who could make secret places in which things were hidden and you couldn't see there was a concealed entrance.' Much of the escape material at Holzminden was hidden in Room 83 in the attic of *Kaserne* A. At a casual glance 'there was not a more innocent-looking room in the whole of the two buildings', but appearances could be deceptive. The floor was of straight-edged planks, and once the nails had been removed and one plank lifted, the remainder could be slid up and down to give access to the whole area between the joists, in which any amount of 'treasure' could be concealed. Room 83 was riddled with hiding places: it also contained sliding panels in the walls, fake partitions in the cupboards and false bottoms in the drawers. It was 'as full of moving panels, planks which lifted and sills which slid, as any medieval castle. It was simply honeycombed with hiding places and half the escaping kit in the barrack was stored there, if only the Huns had known.' It also served as the manufactory for dummy keys, fake German insignia and cap badges, and any other improvised kit and equipment that the escapers might need.

The techniques of hiding contraband were copied and steadily extended to the other rooms in the barrack blocks until there was scarcely one that did not contain secret caches of escape materials beneath its floor. Jack Shaw loosened a board in his room, 704 in *Kaserne* B, 'discovering underneath a useful space in which to hide *verboten* goods, and in this I had chocolate, pemmican [a concentrated mixture of protein and fat], a compass and a set of British Ordnance Survey maps covering the ground between Holzminden and the Dutch frontier . . . There were also my newly made rucksack and an almost complete civilian suit, obtained through the offices of a German scavenger in return for some 80 marks contained in the handle of a tennis racket.'

The prisoners in Room 14 of *Kaserne* B cached their escape kit in the air shaft between the wall of their room and the adjoining one. They stripped away the plaster, removed several bricks, fixed a stick across the gap between the two walls and left 'several contraband articles suspended from it' on strings. After the bricks had been replaced, they covered them with a mixture of flour, water and dirt so that they were indistinguishable from the surrounding plasterwork. Another escaper made a false piece of wall to match the surrounding brickwork by stealing a broad piece of plank from the Germans and cutting it to size. 'On this plank I nailed squares of wood to resemble bricks, filled the spaces with cement and then whitewashed the whole thing.' He obtained some lime from an orderly and mixed it with sand 'sifted through a loofah sponge, thus making a splendid cement with which we were able to fix our dummy wall in place'.

The orderlies' uniforms that the tunnellers used were concealed in Room 24, the tiny ground-floor room where they changed. Since they were used so regularly, the tunnellers were unwilling to go through the laborious process of having to retrieve them from a hiding place under the floorboards every time they were needed, and instead simply hid them beneath a few officers' uniforms in an unlocked wooden box. They would have been found in a thorough search, but the 'Purloined Letter' technique of leaving them in the open, within easy reach, proved successful and the box was never searched by the guards. Rather better concealed in Room 24 was the 'Black Book', a meticulously documented compilation of the crimes and misdemeanours committed by Niemeyer at Holzminden up to 9 January 1918, when Major Haig, the latest senior British officer, decided to close it, 'as it appeared unnecessary to go on reporting similar and recurring incidents ... [when] a complete case had already been made out' against the commandant. It had been intended to hand it to the representative of the Netherlands Legation when he was inspecting Holzminden, but he told the senior British officer that he was not permitted to take any documents away with him. As a result, the Black Book was kept hidden throughout the remainder of the war and was then taken home to Britain with the returning PoWs after the Armistice and handed to the government as evidence of German war crimes.

Simple codes were also devised to evade censorship and send hidden messages asking for items of escape equipment in the prisoners' letters to their families. 'Lemon juice, spittle or, on a certain kind of paper, even plain water were used as invisible inks, or certain letters could be written above the line and those letters used as a code. In case the German censor noticed the raised letters, there was a further refinement: 'If a capital letter was raised above the line, the next raised letter was to be ignored.' Prisoners taught each other the code and were able to send concealed messages. Others, like Cecil Blain, David Gray and Caspar Kennard, chose 'invisible writing with milk inside the envelope of our letters'. Blain later explained that 'to teach people at home what to do, my first letter ran something like this: "My dearest Mother, I am so sorry I am unable to account for the los of my letters home to you, but I hop that this one will rive soon, telling you that I am very fit and well. I cannot tell you how I long to be home again, etc., etc." ' The missing or duplicate letters spelled out 'Search all envelopes', and the items he wanted were then listed in invisible writing on the flap. To his relief, the German censors failed to detect anything other than bad spelling, and in due course the first requested item arrived: a map hidden in the bottom of a box of chocolates.

Blain's brother Harry, also a pilot, then wrote a bizarre

letter to him, describing a flight in which his compass had broken, forcing him to buy a new one. Harry said he had crash-landed his aircraft in a duck-pond and come out smothered in mud and algae-like green jelly. He concluded his letter with the news that their mother would be sending him a new uniform and had promised to send a tin of sweets to Blain at the same time. Blain was still puzzling over this when the parcel arrived. There were a few bags of sweets and a tin of Pascal's Crème de Menthe drops, which Blain never ate. He was still puzzling over this when he remembered his brother's curious letter about the compass, the green jelly and the tin of sweets. Trying to conceal his excitement and praying that the parcel-room attendant would not be too zealous, Blain offered him the tin for inspection. He turned it over in his hands for a few moments, then passed it back. When he got to his room, Blain opened the tin and tipped out the sweets; concealed among them was a square of oil-skin cloth containing a little brass compass. By similar means, Caspar Kennard received a small electric torch and a file from his family. Relatives could also write back in code and if a prisoner knew that a certain tin in a parcel contained contraband he could distract the attendant by offering him a different tin of food for inspection, or arguing about the number of tins in the parcel, or persuading the German on the other side of the counter that a tin had dropped by his feet. The prisoner could then either slip the crucial tin into his own pocket, or pass it to a confederate who could 'nip off with the treasure'.

At one camp, the attendant always cut cakes of soap in half until a prisoner demonstrated to him by holding one up to the light that he could see right through it and tell if anything was concealed inside it. From then on, the attendant held every cake of soap to the light and never cut them open, evidently not realizing that ordinary soap differed in one important respect from the transparent Pears' soap he had been given in the original demonstration. If such deceit or sleight-of-hand failed, there was always bribery: one tin-room attendant at Holzminden would often let a prisoner take away a tin unopened in return for 'a cake of decent soap or chocolate'.

Codes were normally used to request contraband items but Captain Jack Shaw perfected a code by which he sent messages to the British Secret Service. Ostensibly about his home town of Marlow and his family, they actually informed the government that the great mole at Zeebrugge was not bomb-proof, as had previously been believed. Not all codes were as successful. Norman Insoll had told his family that any letter containing a hidden message would be addressed to 'C. Insoll'. When it arrived his parents duly discovered the hidden message but Insoll's code was so fiendishly complicated that they were unable to decipher it.

As the brother of another prisoner, Robert Paddison, later recounted, his family received a letter from Robert asking for '"an illuminated photograph of [here a list of family nicknames] behind a donkey and a picture of Granny". This did not make sense, but by taking the first letter of the Christian names on the list my mother got COMP behind ASS [donkey] and my grandmother's initials were M.A.P.' The luminous compass was put in a hollowed-out walnut and the two halves of the shell were then carefully glued together again and sent to him in a parcel of mixed nuts. The map was stuck on to the inside of the lining of a fancy waistcoat. Both parcels arrived safely and their illicit contents were undetected by the Holzminden guards. By using the nicknames of family members, schoolfriends and schoolmasters, Robert Paddison and his mother managed to communicate with each other without the knowledge of the camp censor throughout the whole time he was a prisoner.

There were other ways to fool the censor. One prisoner sent a letter home requesting a tin of 'Magnapole Cream'. There was no such brand but Magnapole did make compasses and one duly arrived for him, hidden beneath the false bottom of a tin of cream. Another prisoner, Lieutenant James Bennett, wrote a letter to his brother in England, saying, 'I should like to have a picture of my Rolls-Royce to look at while I'm here. Could you go along to Stanford's in Long Acre and get me one?' The German censor saw nothing wrong in that and allowed the letter through: he didn't know that the prisoner did not own a Rolls-Royce, or that Stanford's was not a photographer but a map seller. Bennett's brother was also baffled by the letter and asked the manager of Stanford's if he could throw any light on his brother's strange request. The manager, who was rather quicker on the uptake, suggested that the letter be forwarded to the War Office, where officials understood at once what was being asked for. Compasses and escape maps on silk were dispatched to that officer and others, concealed in the handles of tennis racquets and other apparently harmless items of sporting equipment that were often sent to prisoners. The officer noticed that the balance of the handles of the racquets was not true, and when he took off the caps on the ends, he found the maps. However, the use of tennis racquets had to be discontinued after the commandant of another camp informed Niemeyer that they were being used for contraband; 'After that about 14 rackets [sic] coming into the camp were found to contain articles in the hollow handle.'

A case of badminton shuttlecocks sent from England also contained one that had 'a very minute compass in its base instead of the usual cork', and another prisoner received maps rolled inside ham bones with the ends sealed with bone marrow. Captain Jack Shaw had a timetable of trains from Holzminden to Aachen, a town a couple of miles from the Dutch border, and a silk map showing the area between the town and the border that had been sent to him hidden inside prune stones and was now concealed in the handle of his shaving brush.

Having established his channel of communications with the British Secret Service, using letters sent to his mother at Bourne End in Buckinghamshire, Shaw also sent coded requests for items of escape equipment for various other prisoners. They were packed by the Secret Service into tins of

'Halford's Curry Powder' and other widely available brands of tinned food, then delivered to Shaw's mother to be sent out as part of her regular food parcels to her son. A coded letter would go ahead, warning Shaw which tin would contain the contraband and, with the help of one or more of his comrades, he would obtain it from the tin room uexamined, either by paying a bribe or using sleight-of-hand. At one point, parcels for Shaw were arriving with such frequency and on such a scale that he was 'receiving whole tins of maps, wire-cutters and compasses'. A single tin of 'Armour Tongue' contained an astonishing range of equipment: several compasses, two pairs of wire-cutters, two sets of Ordnance Survey maps covering the area from Holzminden to the Dutch frontier, a list of the names of prisoners for whom the equipment was intended and a lead weight to ensure that the tin was the same weight as that stated on the label.

Such contraband items were only ever sent in parcels genuinely or ostensibly from the friends and family of prisoners. There was an absolute taboo against using parcels originating with the Red Cross to smuggle contraband: had any been found, whether or not Red Cross officials had any knowledge of it, the system of food parcels that kept thousands of prisoners from malnutrition would have been placed in jeopardy.

Once received, escape equipment had to be well enough hidden to evade the fortnightly searches of officers' bodies and belongings. These searches, 'ruthlessly made', saw prisoners' possessions strewn all over their rooms. Personal items and food were sometimes stolen by the guards while the prisoners remained locked up for hours at a time. However, the traffic was not all one way. Despite the often-executed threat of instant arrest for disobeying the guards' orders to remain still during searches of their persons and possessions, the prisoners made life as difficult as possible for the searchers by continually moving around and pushing past the guards and each other, affording endless opportunities for contraband to be slipped from hand to hand or be spirited away. The resultant confusion meant that some prisoners were searched more than once, while others were not searched at all.

Other prisoners would enthusiastically join in with the search, adding armfuls of already searched items to the mounds of property that the guards were examining, upsetting tables and chairs and, even less helpfully, removing other items while the guards were distracted. One search of Room 14 in *Kaserne* B unearthed one of the prisoners' two caches of escape kit and contraband, but not the other, though it was a close-run thing: the guards were bracing their crowbar against the floorboard that hid the cache while trying to prise up the undisturbed board next to it. Among the equipment they did find was 'a small dynamo useful for making light when necessary'. This was added to a sackful of contraband material that the guards had already found elsewhere in the building and which they left just inside the door while they searched the room. When the officer in charge arrived, he was told 'in very gleeful tones', about the find, but when they went to the sack to produce the dynamo, it had disappeared. 'So neatly had an officer in the room managed to get it out of the sack and out of the room that not one of us, English or German, had seen his action. They gave us five minutes to produce the dynamo, but as we decided the room needed a spring-clean, we allowed them to do it for us. They turned everything upside down, but never saw the dynamo again.'

After a further search a fortnight later, their sack was once more nearly full of contraband and this time was kept outside the room in which the search was being conducted with one of the guards watching over it. Seeing this, two prisoners started a fight further along the corridor. It was 'a real thriller' and the sentry was so enjoying seeing two British officers 'scrapping like any Tom, Dick or Harry' that as the action moved out of his sight, he followed, desperate to see the outcome. It ended in anticlimax, with the two officers agreeing to shake hands and walk away without either landing a knockout blow. When the guard returned to his post a few moments later, he discovered another cause for disappointment: the sack of contraband goods was now 'all but empty'.

As well as searches by the camp guards, the inmates also had to hide their escape equipment from teams of civilian detectives from Hannover or Berlin who were brought in to make periodic searches of the camp. The first took place on the morning of 26 January 1918 when, as the prisoners paraded for *Appel* in the normal way, there appeared on the scene a number of uniformed policemen and some 'quaint little spectacled civilians': a group of plainclothes detectives from Berlin. 'We took it as a compliment when the Commandant admitted his inability to find our secret stores and called in a number of Berlin detectives to unravel the mystery. The occasion was regarded as a welcome diversion from the monotony of camp routine.' Soldiers poured into the two barrack blocks and sentries stationed themselves at the door of each room. The prisoners were then sent back into the buildings but had to remain in the corridors until it was their turn for their room to be searched, no one being allowed out of doors. 'It was far from comfortable,' one said, 'being very overcrowded; however, it was better than the Black Hole of Calcutta and they found nothing in our room.'

While the search went on, the prisoners 'had a right royal time of it'. The detectives 'hunted high and low, and turned over everything we had. Not content with that [they] stripped us and searched our clothing and uniform. To make things worse we got practically no food all day, as they did not finish until 7.30 p.m. . . . On the whole this was one of the most miserable days I spent in captivity.' The detectives had 'under their noses, hundreds of small items they would have loved to find', and they were 'full of zeal for their duties for an hour or so, but tiring rapidly as the same ritual was gone through in room after room', and although they went about their work systematically, [they were] not equal to the job. Hours of thought and careful preparation had been spent in selecting suitable hiding places, so . . . we had little to fear from the brains of the German police force. It would, however, have been unwise to have left them nothing to 'find', for they were determined to protect their professional prestige and might have become dangerous if entirely thwarted. Accordingly, a few articles of doubtful value were 'hidden' in comparatively conspicuous places – with which these sleuths had to be content.

The detectives spent the entire day minutely searching the officers' quarters and 'obtained heaps of stuff, wire-cutters, maps, German money, tinned foods and plain clothes'. Large numbers of books were also temporarily confiscated and removed to the parcel room for close examination, with maps that had been 'carelessly left uncovered', but despite the size of their haul, the searchers missed the vast majority of escape materials that were concealed in the two *Kasernen*. Maps, compasses, forged papers, German currency, stores of chocolate, potted meat, biscuits, raisins, oats or barley, Oxo cubes, 'Bivouac' cocoa and biltong (dried meat), and even pairs of wire-cutters, made from steel bed-rails, remained undiscovered.

Lieutenant James Bennett hid all his escape equipment in a dummy beam on the ceiling, made from cardboard and whitened with cornflour to match the genuine whitewashed beams on either side of it. It was enough to fool the guards and the detectives, whose enthusiasm for the search had abated long before they reached the attic where most of the contraband was hidden. They even failed to find a complete escape kit hidden under one prisoner's bed. At the foot he had a large black wooden box with a false bottom, which became the object of great interest and 'frenzied argument' among the detectives. After half an hour of measuring and probing, a detective put his foot through the false bottom to reveal a couple of books and 'some private papers of no particular interest'. These were carried off in triumph and every German present shook the detective's hand, 'as if he had scored a goal for Blackburn Rovers. They were so pleased that they forgot to look under the bed' before departing.

The prisoners were also aided and abetted by a few of the more corruptible camp guards, who, for the usual few marks, a bottle of wine, a cake of soap or a bar of chocolate, were willing to hide or move pieces of escape kit or act as 'bankers' for large amounts of illicit currency. 'We used wine and soap,' one prisoner recalled, 'the latter very valuable, worth as much as 14 marks a cake, I believe. We had a stock of both in our room, also some maps and compasses; we told the *Feldwebel* in charge of us where to find all these and said that if he would go and bring us the maps and compasses he could keep the wine and soap for himself, which he did.' The guards also escorted a constant procession of prisoners to the latrines, well knowing that the visit was required not to answer a call of nature but to deposit some forbidden items until the search of the barrack blocks was over.

While prisoners and detectives were occupied in the

search of the prisoners' quarters, some of the guards also availed themselves of the distraction by stealing some of the contents of the prisoners' Red Cross parcels from the dining rooms. In 'an amusing climax to the whole day's sport', those guards were then marched off to the parcel room to be searched in their turn, 'the delinquents making frantic efforts to eat a two days' supply in two minutes and incur the penalty of indigestion rather than that of nine days' cells for being found in possession of stolen goods'.

In addition to failing to find most of the hidden escape equipment, some of the visiting detectives even contributed items to it during the search as 'an umbrella ... or some other object of civilian attire useful for escapes' went missing. Some had their pockets picked and their identity cards stolen; others merely suffered a loss of dignity, like the 'German Sherlock' who, unknowing, had a placard surreptitiously fixed to his coat-tail, reading, 'You know my methods, Watson.' It was still in place as he made his way out of the camp gates. One detective 'lost his hat ... and another his watch'. A third was wearing a pair of detachable starched white cuffs with gold cufflinks and took them off to avoid dirtying them during the search. When he came to put them on again, they had disappeared. 'Mardock pinched the cuffs; they were standing right beside him when he pinched them.' A feverish and furious search in which the detectives 'even examined our hair and mouths' failed to unearth either the cuffs or the gold links, and after the disgruntled detectives had departed, the cuffs and links were added to the escape kit.

'They couldn't find them – never found them again.' 'So we were not the only losers,' as one prisoner noted with satisfaction, 'and if they had had any inkling of what was going to occur, they would not have had what they did.'

Although the searches yielded some returns, Niemeyer must have realized that the goods impounded were no more than a fraction of the total escape equipment hidden in the camp because his paranoia about further escape attempts deepened: he began to order the confiscation of anything that might be converted to improper use, however implausible that might be. As one prisoner complained, 'For the past few weeks we have not been allowed to take our cardboard boxes from the parcel room when drawing parcels and now we are not allowed to take the paper. What next? Probably they'll bag our parcels, but many of these are on the missing list already.'

CHAPTER 9

ZERO DAY

Breaking Out of the Tunnel

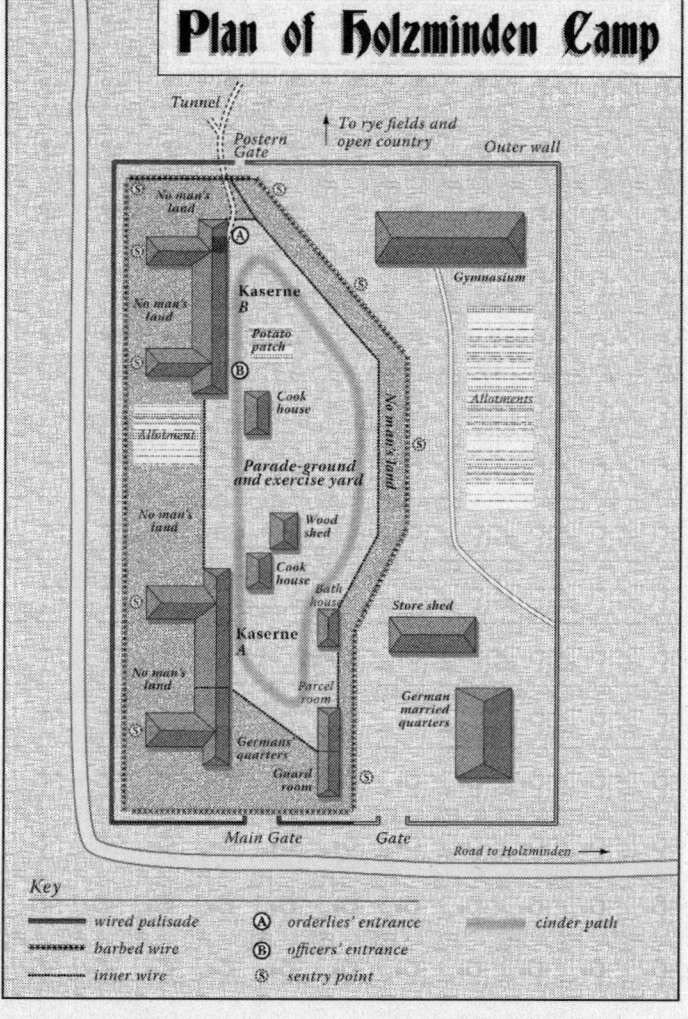

Plan of Holzminden Camp

Tunnel

Postern Gate

To rye fields and open country

Outer wall

No man's land

Gymnasium

Kaserne B

Potato patch

Cook house

No man's land

Allotment

Allotments

Parade-ground and exercise yard

No man's land

Wood shed

Cook house

Bath house

Store shed

Kaserne A

No man's land

Parcel room

German married quarters

Germans quarters

Guard room

Main Gate

Gate

Road to Holzminden →

Key

—— wired palisade	Ⓐ orderlies' entrance	cinder path
✕✕✕✕ barbed wire	Ⓑ officers' entrance	
- - - inner wire	Ⓢ sentry point	

THE TUNNELLERS' FEAR of discovery was increasing the nearer the tunnel came to completion: nine months of work was in jeopardy and every unexpected sound or footfall in the hallway of the orderlies' quarters above their heads was enough to provoke a frisson of fear. Despite their best efforts to maintain total secrecy, knowledge of the existence of a tunnel, though not its location, was also growing more widespread. An indiscreet officer or orderly might have dropped a hint to a friend, 'in the strictest confidence', or the sight of officers wearing orderlies' uniforms disappearing into the orderlies' quarters and then not reappearing for hours might alone have been enough to set tongues wagging. One newly captured officer was heard to ask a friend whether he had also noticed 'these officers walking about in orderlies' clothes'. Whatever the cause, it was increasingly being whispered around the camp that 'something was up' and that that something might well be a tunnel. Those looking to escape – and that was a large number of prisoners – were eager to find out more and anyone thought to be involved was subject to a number of more or less subtle approaches.

Despite an order from the senior British officer requiring all prisoners to maintain absolute secrecy about any escape attempt – a stricture reinforced by personal harangues delivered to the occupants of each barrack block, including dire threats of courts of inquiry and post-war reprisals – there were always one or two men too indiscreet, too selfish or too stupid to appreciate the need for secrecy. The chances of discovery or betrayal were greatly increased as a result, never more so than when a padre – one of a large intake of new prisoners following the great German offensive in March 1918 – turned to his neighbour at a 'show' in the dining room of *Kaserne* B and asked him, 'Are you in the tunnel?' The query on its own was bad enough, but it was made infinitely more dangerous because not only had the padre spoken in the high, penetrating tones peculiar to parsons, but the word 'tunnel' was the same in English and German. In any event, in addition to the guards in the room, two German interpreters, who spoke excellent English, were sitting within two yards of him. Only by sheer luck did they fail to hear his gaffe.

The need for all those who would be making the escape attempt to be housed in *Kaserne* B also had the potential to arouse suspicion, but it was essential, since the break-out would occur during the night when the outer doors of the barrack blocks were locked and closely watched. Most of the working party were already in *Kaserne* B, but three – the inveterate escapees in Room 83, Blain, Kennard and Gray – were not. In early June 1918 they suddenly applied to swap their relatively comfortable three-man room in *Kaserne* A for a share of a twelve-man room in the other block. The excuses they proffered would not have withstood much scrutiny, but neither the *Feldwebels* in charge of the two blocks nor Niemeyer thought to question their motives. The changes were allowed and all the potential escapers were now housed in *Kaserne* B.

Had Niemeyer's antennae been more finely tuned, he might have detected some of the undercurrents, hints and rumours about an escape attempt but, solid in his belief that the security of his camp could not now be breached, he remained ignorant of what was going on literally under his feet. To ensure that he remained in ignorance, the senior British officer, Colonel Charles E. H. Rathborne, who was not an entirely disinterested spectator since he was scheduled to be the next man out of the tunnel once the thirteen-strong working party had gone through, issued fresh strict orders that no provocations were to be offered to the Germans. When a hammer went missing from a civilian carpenter's toolbag and Feldwebel Leutnant Welman demanded its immediate return or a general search of the camp would be made, the hammer was restored to its owner at once. When a hat was whipped from the head of one of the tin-room attendants and whisked away, it was also swiftly restored. Once more, if Welman or any of the other guards had paused to wonder why the British had suddenly become so cooperative, they kept their suspicions to themselves.

One of the problems that Niemeyer and every other prison-camp commandant faced was that the calibre of man available for prison-camp duty had progressively declined as the war continued. With manpower shortages becoming acute, the guards at Holzminden were 'always being weeded out' and sent on active service, as every able-bodied man was transferred to shore up the creaking armies in the front lines. Those who remained were 'mostly old men and boys'. By June 1918, even the febrile old bathman at Holzminden had been taken for sentry duty.

Despite Colonel Rathborne's strictures, the risk of discovery of the tunnel was further heightened after a quite separate escape attempt was made in early July 1918. Two young officers, Lieutenants Brean and Sutcliffe, had devised a plan of breathtaking audacity, which involved Brean walking straight out of the prison gates dressed in a German private's uniform, and accompanied by his 'girlfriend', wearing makeup and dressed in women's clothes. To aid his disguise, 'Fluffy' Sutcliffe – 'a fine little sport and the chief female impersonator in our plays and sketches at Holzminden' – had been growing his hair for several months, concealing its length when on *Appel* by tucking it down the back of his collar. Phase One of the plan had worked perfectly. During the lunch-hour, when the *Kommandantur* was largely deserted, the two escapers had broken through from the officers' quarters into a passageway in the *Kommandantur*, walked down the stairs and strolled towards the outer gate. Fluffy Sutcliffe, 'a most seductive little flapper typist', was waved through and Brean also passed the duty guard without challenge, but one of the other men in the guardroom happened to be glancing out of the window and recognized Brean as a British officer. He gave the alarm and the two were apprehended and led away to the cells. The Germans' volubly expressed admiration for Sutcliffe's disguise was no consolation.

Although the timing had been coincidental – Sutcliffe and Brean had no knowledge of the tunnel, let alone any idea of how close it was to completion – the result of their escape attempt was to put Niemeyer and his guards on heightened alert. A full-scale search of the camp was a real possibility and the tunnellers spent the next few days and nights in a state of gut-gnawing tension. They suffered a further blow when one of their number, Captain David Gray, was suddenly removed from Holzminden and sent to Hannover to be court-martialled on a charge of attempted murder. A few weeks earlier, in the middle of a furious argument with a parcel-room attendant, Gray had handled a large knife lying on the parcel-room counter. The attendant said that Gray had threatened him with it, a charge that Gray denied, but his fellows were not optimistic about his fate in front of a German court martial.

Blain and Kennard, who were planning to travel to the Dutch border with Gray after the escape, were distraught at this blow to their long-laid plans. However, to their surprise and delight, the Hannover court martial found the parcel-room attendant such a dubious witness that they sentenced

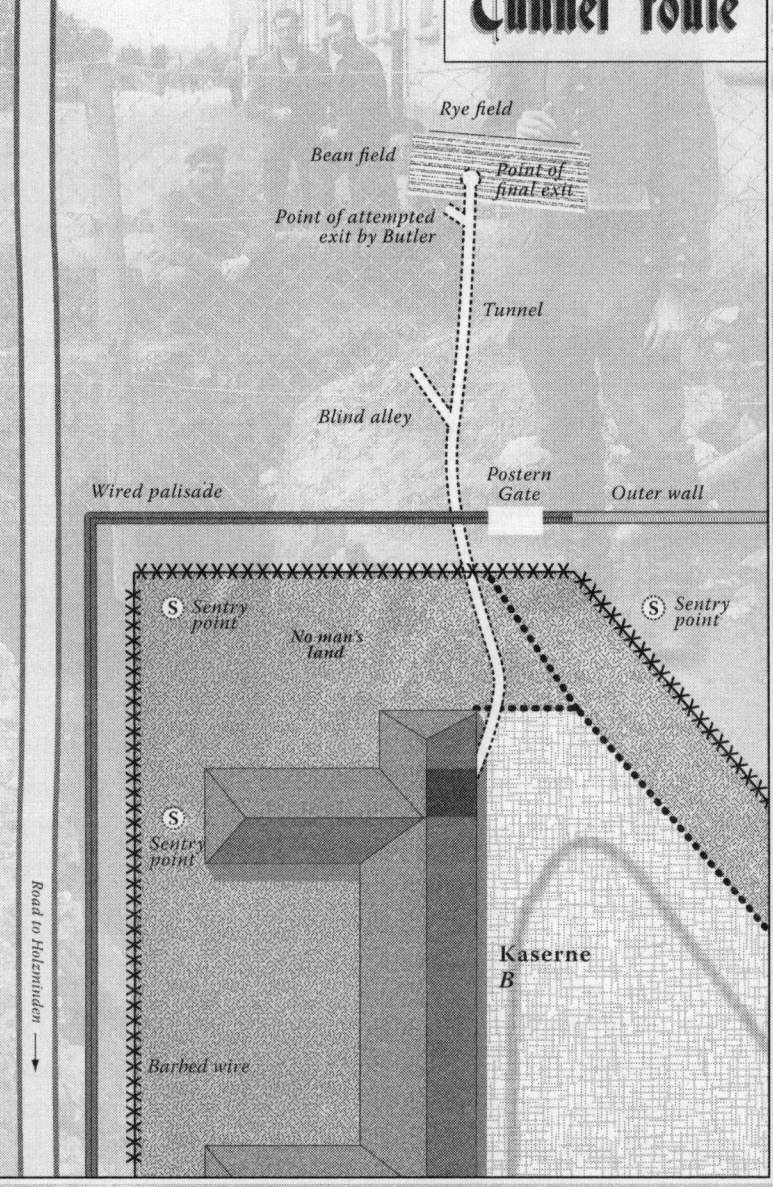

Tunnel route

Rye field

Bean field

Point of final exit

Point of attempted exit by Butler

Tunnel

Blind alley

Wired palisade

Postern Gate

Outer wall

(S) Sentry point

(S) Sentry point

No man's land

(S) Sentry point

Road to Holzminden →

Kaserne B

Barbed wire

Gray to a mere fourteen days' solitary confinement, to be served in the cells back at Holzminden. The camp adjutant Hugh Durnford's room was directly above the cell and since, as another ex-Indian Army officer, he also spoke Hindustani, he was even able to keep Gray informed of the tunnel's progress in a language that none of the German guards could understand.

By now the tunnel was at least 150 feet long, passing though the foundations of the barracks, under the *Spielplatz*, the wall, the barbed-wire fences and the cultivated ground beyond. Hoping that they had now reached the edge of the rye crop, the tunnellers had begun to incline the tunnel upwards again towards the surface, but they made very slow progress through the stubborn layers of stones and glutinous clay. 'Came the great day when, full of joy, they calculated that the tunnel must at least be long enough', but its twisting, undulating course made it impossible to be sure exactly how far from the wire and how deep beneath the surface they were, and a test was therefore carried out. While several of the tunnellers crowded round a fourth-floor window in the officers' quarters and stared out towards the cultivated land, Lieutenant Walter Butler wormed his way to the face of the tunnel, and carefully bored a hole above his head.

The first dispiriting discovery he made was that there still remained a further six feet of soil above him that would have to be excavated before they could break surface. He then pushed up a long stick through the hole with a small 'bit of white rag tied firmly to the end' as a flag and waggled it from side to side for two seconds.

> The little flag, so pregnant with meaning, stayed above ground for a brief moment and then was withdrawn again.' His comrades had seen it at once, but to their horror it was not waving in the field of rye but out on the open ground, still four yards from the row of beans and eight or nine yards short of the rye crop. 'A nearby sentry was looking in that direction at the time and rubbed his eyes, but carried on. We thanked our lucky stars that he must have thought it was a butterfly.

Although the tunnel remained undiscovered, it was dispiriting for the prisoners to realize that at least another month's digging was still required to reach the rye, and with high summer now upon them, the crop might be harvested any day. However, the row of bean plants was four yards nearer than the rye and, after heated discussions, they decided to dig flat out for one more week, aiming to reach a point just beyond the row of beans, where they could bring the tunnel to the surface and use the plants as partial cover when they broke ground, then made their way into the rye field. There was some risk of discovery, since the arc lights on the perimeter fence also illuminated the fields at night, but that was better than finding all their work undone because the rye had been harvested, leaving them to emerge into open ground, unprotected by any cover at all.

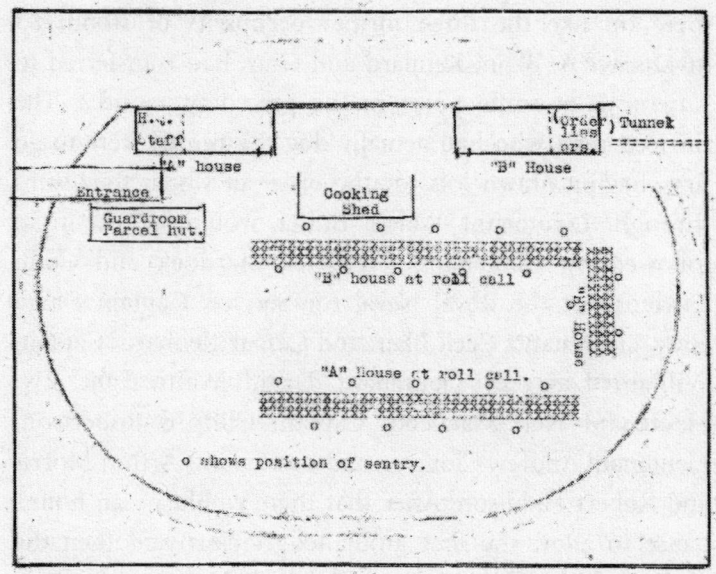

Sketch plan of the camp and the positions taken by the prisoners at *Appel* (roll-call).

One week later, on the night of 23–24 July 1918, immediately after the tunnellers had completed digging out the chamber to receive the excavated soil from the last push to the surface, the break-out was made. Only two days beforehand, a jocular Niemeyer had told the assembled prisoners while on *Appel*, 'Well, gentlemen, I guess you know if you want to escape you must give me a couple of days' notice.' Notice was not given and the escape went ahead without advance publicity.

It was to be made from *Kaserne* B, and all of the people involved in making the attempt were either already resident there or, like the three former occupants of Room 83 in *Kaserne* A, Blain, Kennard and Gray, had transferred to *Kaserne* B at some point in the preceding months. The thirteen men who had actually dug the tunnel were to go first, having drawn lots for the order in which they went through. Lieutenant Walter Butler would be the first, followed by Lieutenants Frederick Mardock and Colin Lawrence of the Royal Naval Air Service, Captain David Gray, Lieutenants Cecil Blain and Caspar Kennard, Captain William Langren, Lieutenant David Wainwright RN, Lieutenant Neil MacLeod, Captain Clifford Robertson, Lieutenant Andrew Clouston and Lieutenants Arthur Morris and Robert Paddison. After that there would be an hour's pause to allow the first group to get clear and then the senior British officer, Colonel Charles E. H. Rathborne, and six other officers from the supplementary work party who had helped with the tunnel project, including Major John Morrogh, Captain Edward Wilmer Leggatt, the Australian Captain Peter Lyon, and Lieutenants J. K. Bousfield and James Bennett would make their escape. Bennett had the unusual distinction of being a pilot who had been captured by a U-boat. With his navigator, Colin Lawrence, he had been taken prisoner by the crew of the submarine after their aircraft developed engine trouble and they were forced to ditch in the sea. Colonel Rathborne, 'who was somewhat square-rigged in shape', had even been given a trial run through the tunnel to ensure he could fit through it. After a struggle, he had succeeded in reaching the face, though it had taken him an hour to make his way back again.

After the first two groups were clear of the tunnel, 'the ruck' – all other prisoners who wished to try their luck, another sixty-six men – could avail themselves of it in the remaining time before dawn broke. In all, eighty-six men were waiting that night for the signal to go. Apart from those already 'in the know', the other escapers were only alerted after the evening roll-call that the attempt was about to be made, ensuring that there was no chance of betrayal, whether deliberate or accidental. Nonetheless, if only through the general air of suppressed excitement, many of the prisoners came to realize that 'Zero Day' had arrived. Civilian clothes, maps, compasses and other items of escape equipment were taken from their hiding places and readied, and 'more risks of detection were run . . . in a day than had been run before in a whole month'.

Hearing rumours, or guessing that the moment had arrived, two other officers in *Kaserne* A also made a last-minute attempt to obtain a transfer to the other block, which was hastily squashed after the intervention of Colonel Rathborne. A further group of officers in *Kaserne* A, fearing that the inevitable restrictions in the wake of the tunnel escape would jeopardize their own plan, then tried to get in first with a scheme to fuse the camp lights, drop a dummy from a window at one end of the block, then escape from the other and climb over the wire in the confusion. In other circumstances it would probably have received the senior British officer's blessing, but with the tunnel scheme so close to fruition – and with his own place high up the list of those planning to use it – Colonel Rathborne again intervened, forbidding the attempt. At other camps like Clausthal, there was an Escape Committee that approved and co-ordinated escape attempts so that two were never taking place at once, but at Holzminden there was none and the risk of the tunnel being jeopardized by some maverick scheme remained very real.

Even on the night chosen for the escape, none of the men on the waiting list had been told their allotted number in the sequence of escapers in order to prevent 'unnecessary heart-burning and traffic'; all were merely told to go to bed fully dressed and ready, and they would be roused when their turn had come. The escape would have been made the previous night, but was aborted at the very last moment when one of the dissident officers from *Kaserne* A was discovered to have sneaked into *Kaserne* B just before the lockdown for the night. The risk of his absence being discovered and the alarm raised forced the tunnellers to delay their escape for twenty-four hours and the officer was politely but firmly evicted and told to make his excuses to the *Feldwebel* in charge of his own block as best he could. To prevent any repetition the following night, the officer was also persuaded that the rumours he had heard were false and the tunnel was not yet complete.

After that alarm the escapers prepared themselves again the following night, keeping a close watch for further intruders from *Kaserne* A until the doors of both barrack blocks were locked for the night at nine p.m. The final tour of inspection of the day was made by a sentry around ten p.m. He closed all the corridor windows that had been left open but made no formal check of the rooms before leaving the block and locking the doors behind him. The only people moving about in *Kaserne* B after that were the officer given the job of rousing each man as his turn came and the other officers and orderlies needed to guide the escapers to the tunnel and conceal any visible evidence of the escape afterwards. To protect the orderlies from reprisals as far as was possible, they were to disappear to their beds at once if the alarm was raised, then deny all knowledge of the escape attempt when interrogated.

The external doors of their quarters were locked for the night and under constant surveillance by guards, so all the escapers had to make their way through the hole cut in the attic of the officers' quarters, and along the eaves to the trapdoor in the orderlies' section. A powerfully built Australian, Lieutenant Louis Grieve from Sydney, was assigned to work as 'doorman' at the hole in the attic, with orders to permit the next man to pass through only when he received word from the orderlies that the previous one had cleared the tunnel entrance. There was little chance of anyone barging past him: he was 'about five foot nine and I reckon he had a chest of about fifty-one inches'. One orderly guarded the other side of the hole in the attic wall, another was on hand to guide the escapers down the stairs to the tunnel entrance, where two more orderlies were waiting to help them through. To avoid any noise, everyone was instructed to move through the building and down the stairs in the orderlies' quarters in their socks, carrying their boots, and not to put them on until just before entering the tunnel.

The first man through the tunnel was the 'break-out man', Lieutenant Walter Butler, who, with the next two to go through, his 'travelling companions', Captain William Langren, and Lieutenant Andrew Clouston from the Royal Newfoundland Regiment, 'a big, coarse-featured and red-faced man with beetling brows and a dark moustache', left their room at ten fifteen, as soon as the ten o'clock check on the rooms had been completed. They had taken their escape kit down to the tunnel chamber earlier in the day, and within ten minutes Butler was worming his way 'along the hole for the last time, noting all the old familiar ups and downs and bends, and bumping my head against the same old stones'. When he reached the face, he knelt in the pit they had dug to take the remaining earth excavated as he cut his way out and, working in pitch darkness, 'got to work with a large bread knife' on the roof of the tunnel above him. 'The earth fell into my hair, eyes and ears, and down my neck.'

By eleven that night he had cut a six-inch-diameter hole through to the surface. 'It was raining but the arc lamps made it look very light outside.' As he peered through the hole, he discovered to his delight and relief that he had come up just beyond the row of beans, which screened the tunnel mouth and the emerging escapers from the sentry in the open ground behind them. He spent another forty minutes widening the hole he had made and then, at twenty minutes to midnight, pushing his kit ahead of him, he emerged into the field; 'the night air, how good it was'. The nearest sentry had a cough, enabling Butler to locate him, but he was standing in the shadow of the wall, not the glare of the arc lamps, and Butler could not see whether the man was looking in his direction or away from him. However, he crawled out of the tunnel and, after waiting crouched for thirty seconds – as he had agreed with the orderly who would give the all-clear for the remainder of the escapers to start making their way through the tunnel – he crept to the edge of the rye crop. When one of the later escapers emerged from the tunnel, the sentry, armed with a rifle, had moved to a point no more than a few yards away from him, but he posed no threat. 'I had to laugh,' the escaper said. 'He was fast asleep.'

Back in *Kaserne* B, one of the orderlies, Private Ernest Collinson, had been peering through the window in the entrance door to the orderlies' quarters for some time, straining his eyes into the night as he waited for Butler to emerge. The rain and the darkness beyond the fierce glare of the arc lights made it hard to see anything and Collinson had just convinced himself that Butler must already have left the tunnel and begun his long journey to the Netherlands when he saw the faint shape of a crouching figure.

At once, he turned and, silent in his socks, ran up the stairs to the attic. He made his way through the trapdoor and along the eaves to the secret panel into the officers' quarters. As soon as he gave a gentle tap on the wall, Lieutenant Grieve opened it and, after a couple of whispered words, allowed the first of the remaining escapers to make his way through. At intervals, man after man passed through the attic and was guided down the stairs. Each one tapped on the wooden partition and was admitted to the chamber beneath the stairs where two orderlies were waiting to help him through the chamber and into the tunnel entrance. He then worked his way forward, guided by the light of the series of candles that Butler had left along the tunnel to illuminate the way. Each man wriggled past them, pushing his heavy bag in front of him, shortly followed by the next escaper.

As Butler waited for Langren and Clouston to join him, he glanced at his watch. It was eleven forty-five p.m. At that moment the rain stopped, and the light of the full moon broke through the clouds. There was absolute silence and the rye was so ripe, and very dry, that it made a loud crackling noise when it was touched. After a whispered consultation with his fellow escapers, Butler led the way along the edge of the crop, still using the cover of the beans. That limited cover gave out before the edge of the field and they were again engaged in a whispered debate about how to cross the open ground when it began to rain again. The noise of the raindrops pattering on the rye was now loud enough to cover the sound of their own movements, so they crawled into it and made their way across the field.

At the far side, they paused for a moment to put on their rucksacks and take what they hoped would be their last look at Holzminden, then made for the banks of the River Weser.

There they had a stroke of good luck: they found four or five large wooden hurdles and, by piling them on top of each other, they made a raft strong enough to ferry first their kit and then their clothes across the river while they swam alongside; the water felt warm but the wind was bitingly cold. It was now two o'clock. As they dressed on the far side of the river, Clouston thought he heard a shot and they were at once afraid that the German guards had seen someone getting out of the tunnel and raised the alarm. If so, there was nothing they could do, and they hurried away from the river, steering a north-westerly course towards the distant Dutch frontier.

While the first three were making good their escape, the rest of their comrades were working their way through the tunnel, and 'figures with big bags streamed out as in one huge crocodile – heads and feet all touching, to crawl behind beans, peas and through high-standing corn [*sic* – rye], to break away each party for itself and its own special direction'. To increase the chances of the maximum possible number making a successful escape, the men were travelling either solo or in groups of no more than two or three, and each group was taking a different course. Some were heading due west, the shortest route to the Dutch border, but others were heading north or south, or even east – the opposite direction to the one they would have been expected to take, and therefore the least likely to be searched – before striking out for the frontier. Most were planning to walk all the way but a small number whose command of German was good enough were aiming to use the railway to speed them to the frontier, although, once more, they had chosen different routes and different stations at which to board the trains.

When Cecil Blain went through, with Caspar Kennard and David Gray at his heels, he saw again the familiar sinister glitter of a rat's eyes in the darkness ahead of him, but this time there was no need to lie flat and stifle his revulsion while the rat clambered over him. The far end of the tunnel was now open and the rat simply retreated in front of him until it emerged into the open air. A mixture of impatience to be out and fear of discovery on the very brink of freedom made the journey through the tunnel seem interminable, but at last Blain banged his head on a particularly stubborn boulder that had delayed them as they dug the last few yards of the tunnel and knew that he was almost out. The last candle was already behind him, but as he rounded the final bend, he was brought up short by the bright light pouring through the tunnel mouth. For a moment he lay motionless, convinced that the Germans had found the tunnel, mounted a searchlight over it and were waiting for each man to emerge so that he could be shot in the act of escaping. Behind him Kennard's bag bumped into the soles of Blain's boots and, in a fierce whisper, Kennard demanded to know why the hell they had stopped.

Blain forced himself on and, as his eyes grew more accustomed to the light, he realized it was only the glow of the arc lights from the camp perimeter. He had to steel himself again to climb out of the tunnel mouth, still half expecting to be shot as he emerged, but though the brightness of the arc lights after the darkness of the tunnel made him feel even more conspicuous, there was no challenge and no shot and, like Butler, Langren and Clouston before them, one by one Blain, Kennard and Gray slipped away into the night.

The last member of the original thirteen-man working party, Lieutenant Robert Paddison, left *Kaserne* B at eleven thirty, and entered the tunnel ten to fifteen minutes later. As arranged, there was a one-hour pause before the senior British officer, Colonel Rathborne, made his way into the tunnel at twelve thirty, followed at intervals of a few minutes by the other six men on the supplementary list. Even for the thirteen-man working party, familiar with the claustrophobic tunnel, and strengthened and hardened by the months of gruelling digging underground, the effort of pushing their heavy packs before them through the tunnel was punishing work. For men like the portly Colonel Rathborne and the other non-tunnellers, it was a back-breaking trial by ordeal.

The last man on the supplementary list, James Bennett, had cleared the far end of the tunnel by one fifteen a.m. and five minutes before that, the orderlies had begun sending through the first of the more than sixty men on the extra list. However, only two or three had gone through before there was a hitch when one man became stuck in the tunnel, unable to go forward or back, either because he fainted, or became claustrophobic and lost his nerve, or because he was carrying too much bulky escape kit with him, all of which had to be pushed along the tunnel in front of him. According to Caspar Kennard, the man was Lieutenant Leonard Pearson, who was unable to swim: to ensure that he made it across the River Weser he had constructed a pair of bulky water-wings out of old oilskins. He'd tied them around his waist and this was what had caused the blockage in the tunnel. Whatever the true cause, Captain Edgar Garland, a New Zealander who was small and wiry, but very strong, and was awaiting his own turn to go through the tunnel, was then sent down to haul the man back. Garland took hold of the man's heels and gradually managed to pull him clear.

Ignoring instructions, the next man due to go through had clattered up the stairs of *Kaserne* B in his hobnailed boots and his pack was so bulky that it was feared he would become stuck in the tunnel as well. He was stopped at the attic entrance by Lieutenant Grieve and told to take off his boots, then sent back to his room to discard the stick he was carrying and remove a dozen or so tins from his pack. Amid mounting tension, like all the other escapers, he then had to wait in the darkened barrack block for the all-clear from the orderlies. For some reason that was never subsequently explained, the signal was not given, but when Captain Frank Sharpe, who was among those waiting his turn, finally lost patience and went to reconnoitre, he reported that there was no sign of the orderlies and the tunnel was empty of people. The delay might have been deliberate, a further attempt to give the first men through the tunnel – who, after all, had done the work to make it possible – a better chance of making good their escape, or simply the selfish action of one individual. One of the frustrated would-be escapees, Flight Lieutenant Leslie Nixon, later offered support for that belief, claiming that Major John Morrogh had told the orderlies to shut down the tunnel and go to bed as soon as he had passed through it. Whatever the cause, it was after three a.m. when the orderlies had again been roused and returned to their stations, and the flow of men through the tunnel resumed.

Escapers kept going through slowly until four thirty a.m., and by then, twenty-nine men, including Lieutenants Thomas Burrill, Douglas Birch, Frederick Illingworth, Bernard Luscombe and Alan Shipwright, and Captains Philip Smith and Frank Sharpe, had already made it safely through the tunnel and past the dozing sentry before disappearing into the night. Another five men were on their way through when there was a roof-fall 'on Lee, the thirtieth man to go'. Immediately behind him was Captain Jack Shaw, who was thirty-first in the queue, and now saw his hopes of freedom dashed once more. Partially trapped by fallen earth, struggling for air in the pitch darkness of the cramped and now blocked tunnel, those five must have come close to complete panic. There were 'groans, curses and cries of encouragement' from those waiting their turn behind, but they were in vain. The rearmost man of the five in the tunnel, Captain Gardiner of the AIF (Australian Imperial Force), struggled back and reported that any further escapes that night were now impossible. The tunnel had become blocked at the bottom of the final slope up towards the surface. As each of the previous twenty-nine men, including the 'square-rigged' Colonel Rathborne, had fought his way through the tunnel, pushing his pack in front of him, a steady stream of small stones and rivulets of loose earth had been dislodged from the walls and roof of the newly dug final section where there were no wooden boards to revet the roof and sides. All the fallen earth and stones from that section had rolled to the foot of the slope, where so much material had eventually accumulated that it had now become impossible to force a way past it. In trying to do so, the men had dislodged yet more debris, completely blocking the tunnel.

With dawn breaking, there was no hope now of more men making their escape, and the agonizing decision was made to evacuate the tunnel at once to avoid the risk of a premature discovery by the guards. Heartsick, the remainder waiting their turn – more than fifty men – stood down, concealed their escape kit and went back to bed to await the nine o'clock roll-call, with the inevitable searches and reprisals that would follow. Captain Edgar Garland was one of the many prevented from escaping by the tunnel collapse.

It was still essential to conceal all evidence of the break-out before the guard came to unlock the doors of the building at six a.m.: if the alarm was not raised then, the men already through the tunnel would have an additional three hours to make good their escape before their absence was discovered at the nine o'clock *Appel*. However, such was the difficulty in reaching and bringing back the men trapped in the tunnel that only three had been extricated as six o'clock approached. The other two had to be left in the tunnel while the orderlies and two officers hid any visible evidence of the escape and bolted the concealed door to the cellar. The officers then raced up the stairs, back through the eaves and the hole in the attic and got into their beds, just before six, so that all was quiet as the guard unlocked the doors and made his first inspection of the day.

After the guard had completed his rounds, the officers and orderlies returned to the cellar and managed to get the last two men out of the tunnel. However, these two, whether merely careless or disoriented by their ordeal, did not return to their quarters via the attic, but went out of the orderlies' entrance instead. As they did so, they ran straight into Niemeyer, who was making one of his impromptu early-morning tours of inspection. He questioned them about what they were doing, but even though their clothes were stained with mud, he did not 'tumble to' the escape until a few minutes later, when some excited farmers appeared at the postern gate.

They had been on their way to their work in the fields when they had seen tracks through the rye. It was a heinous crime to trample crops at a time of severe food shortages and the irate farmers had at once run to the camp to report it. Niemeyer himself tracked the footprints back through the rye field and found the tunnel mouth. He ordered a soldier to go down and follow the tunnel back to its source, but the soldier refused: although he was terrified of Niemeyer, he was even more frightened of going alone into that dark tunnel where prisoners might still be lurking.

Since he also believed that British officers might be down there, Niemeyer posted an armed guard over the tunnel mouth, then returned to the *Kommandantur* to report the break-out to the Holzminden police and to the Tenth Army Corps headquarters in Hannover. Having raised the alarm, his next question was 'How many?' A 'fat *Feldwebel*', Mandelbrot, was dispatched to *Kaserne* B to complete a count of the prisoners. He found those present 'unusually wide awake and good-humoured for that hour of the morning', and rushed back to report twenty-six men missing, having in his haste and excitement forgotten to count the vanished occupants of one three-bed room in the officers' quarters.

Until this point, the commandant's reaction to the escape had been surprisingly muted, but as the *Feldwebel* made his report, Niemeyer's 'jaw dropped, his moustachios for a brief instant lost their twirl, his solid stomach swelled less impressively against his overcoat. Just for a moment he became grey and looked very old.' Niemeyer had always prided himself that his was a camp where no escapes could take place and he was now 'thoroughly deflated and absolutely mad'. 'For a second we thought he was going to fall but he just managed to bear up and then began gesticulating in such a furious way' that roars of laughter could be heard from every room in the two *Kasernen*, though the prisoners took the precaution of ducking first, in case the incandescent Niemeyer ordered his guards to fire at the windows. He then 'went dashing across to an imaginary opening in the wire, only to be greeted with most derisive cheers again'.

Niemeyer gave full vent to his fury. He ordered all the outer doors of the barrack blocks to be locked, issued 'Safety of Camp' orders confining all prisoners to their own rooms and forbidding them to speak to anyone in another room, and he also warned the officers that if they looked out of the windows they would be shot. A few minutes later he saw an officer near a third-floor window and ordered a guard to shoot at him. The bullet shattered the window and narrowly missed killing the officer. 'One fellow was slightly struck by a bayonet and shots were fired at the building; in fact there was general pandemonium.' One prisoner, known as Bobbie, rigged up a life-like dummy, which could be made to move up and down by pulling on a string. He placed it at one of the windows and there was much 'splintering and smashing of glass' as shots were fired at it on the orders of the furious Niemeyer, while the prisoners, crawling around on their hands and knees, safely out of sight, 'were laughing until we could hardly move, but Bobbie was just absorbed and proud, like a child with a new toy'.

By coincidence, a tunnel at Clausthal, the camp run by Karl Niemeyer's twin, was also nearing completion, but the general alert after the Holzminden 'Great Escape' persuaded Heinrich to order an immediate thorough search of his own camp and the Clausthal tunnel was discovered. It was cruel luck for those who had laboured so long and were within days of making their own escape.

Back at Holzminden, Niemeyer accompanied the guards as they roused the prisoners the following morning. They dragged some out of bed and turned the beds of others over on their occupants, while Niemeyer stood 'rapping his stick on the table as hard as he could, telling us that those days were over, meaning the days when he had left us more or less alone'. There was 'much strafing [punishment], indiscriminate shootings, confinements, searches, roll-calls and nearly an apoplectic fit by Niemeyer'. Prisoners were arrested 'for no offences whatever. In two days sixteen or seventeen officers were sent into the cells for doing absolutely nothing. Niemeyer simply went off his head.' As Vernon Coombs remarked, Niemeyer 'broadly permitted us only to eat, sleep and breathe, and all the camp cells were quickly filled. But his Prussian arrogance had been punctured.'

Although there was 'a lot of shooting . . . nobody was actually shot', but one incident, in which a British officer called Phelan received a brutal kicking from a sentry, 'under the approving eye of a particularly odious *Feldwebel*', led the new senior British officer, Colonel Stokes Roberts, who had replaced the recently departed Colonel Rathborne, to demand redress from Niemeyer for this and other British grievances. When it was not forthcoming, he ordered a policy of passive resistance. One prisoner's loose interpretation of 'passive' led him to throw at Niemeyer, from an upstairs window of *Kaserne* B, what was variously described by one prisoner as 'a large piece of black bread' that hit him, or by another as 'a great log' that narrowly missed him. Boiling with rage, Niemeyer sent one of the sentries inside 'to go and shoot somebody'. A lame flying officer was unfortunate enough to be limping up the stairs at that moment and the reluctant sentry 'came up and fired off his rifle just behind me. He wasn't trying to hit me – the bullet went out of the window – he just had to make a noise, but it frightened me to death. I came down quickly and went back to my room.'

Holzminden had always been something of an attraction to the citizens of the town, who regularly took evening strolls along the road outside and peered through the barbed wire at the British prisoners of war. As one prisoner remarked, German civilians near several prison camps were 'rather given to taking their constitutionals in this direction and gazing at our windows as one would gaze at strange animals in the zoo, while the small boys amuse themselves by singing various hymns of hate'. To Niemeyer's redoubled fury, as news of the escape spread, the numbers of spectators outside Holzminden's perimeter fence now grew so large that he put the whole area surrounding the camp out of bounds to all civilians.

The commandant 'got very nasty', and life inside the camp continued to be 'made hell' for the remaining prisoners over the next few weeks. Most of them were too happy at the success of the escape to worry overmuch about that, though prices in the thriving black market at Holzminden in

'Sausages, Meat, Butter, Dripping, Peas, Jam, Tinned fruit, Boots, Nails, Tennis Balls and Trousers' all showed a marked increase, as a result of the shortages caused by the reprisals Niemeyer had ordered. Prisoners were forbidden to congregate or move about in groups of more than two people, the tin room and parcel room were closed, and the orderlies taken off all duties to the officers to begin excavating the course of the tunnel. The already tiny windows in the punishment cells were now boarded up to complete the isolation of the inmates. A number of prisoners were transferred to other camps, and to prevent the possibility of any further escapes by the remainder, Niemeyer ordered every member of the camp personnel on to sentry duty and instituted regular patrols of the barrack-block corridors during the night. Those who had attempted escapes in the past were moved into the ground-floor rooms of the block, where the lower windows were kept locked and the heat and flies were correspondingly oppressive. The prisoners' sleep was also disturbed three times a night as the sentries entered their rooms, checked that all the occupants were present and deliberately woke them up by shining a torch into the face of each man in turn.

Still trying to discover the starting point of the tunnel, Niemeyer 'endeavoured to get the police dogs to burrow, then the Germans, and lastly offered a reward to the orderlies if they would show him where it began'. 'They sent a boy down with a piece of string, but he became afraid and had to come back. Then they sent a dog. It didn't like it and came up.' Niemeyer's blushes were at least partly spared after a special investigator from Berlin arrived to inspect the tunnel and unearth its source, but having also failed to detect the door in the partition, he too could not find the starting point and 'all he could advise was to dig it up'.

Although the camp was turned upside-down, the tunnel entrance was only found after Niemeyer accepted the special investigator's advice and forced British orderlies under armed guard to dig down from the exit hole of the tunnel in the rye field and excavate it along its entire length, tracking its course all the way back into the camp and up to the doorway of the orderlies' quarters. The wooden barrier was then at last breached, revealing the concealed door, the tunnel entrance and the cellar full of excavated earth. Even though Niemeyer and his men 'interrogated the orderlies, cross-questioned the officers, grilled the sentries, they never found out exactly how it was done'. The hidden panel in the attic remained undiscovered and Niemeyer was unable to work out exactly how the tunnellers had managed to avoid detection for so long. Having excavated tons of soil to expose the tunnel, the orderlies were then set to work by Niemeyer on filling it all in again, lest any more prisoners managed to find a way to use it to escape.

The special investigator had departed after taking numerous photographs of the crime scene, but neither he nor a staff officer from General von Hanisch's headquarters, who also arrived on a tour of inspection, appeared to find much, if any, fault with Niemeyer's conduct. To the despair of the remaining prisoners, he continued in charge of Holzminden, where their misery was deepened by the onset of the influenza pandemic sweeping the world. It claimed several victims at Holzminden, though there were far more fatalities at other camps. One inmate at Parchim camp recorded that 'About 1,000 of the blokes died in a fortnight – some of the poor devils had been prisoners for four years. I remember we buried thirty in one day in a mass grave.' Niemeyer also fell prey to the disease, but to the considerable disappointment of his captives, he made a rapid recovery. His recuperation would have been in jeopardy had he known that the remaining prisoners, frustrated in their previous attempt by the collapse of the old tunnel, had begun a new one from a different part of the cellars of *Kaserne* B, 'in a disused lavatory', within a fortnight of the first one having been uncovered.

Other escape attempts continued and, despite all Niemeyer's precautions, some were still successful. Lieutenant Hector Fraser Dougall, a Royal Flying Corps pilot from Winnipeg in Canada, who had been shot down behind enemy lines in February 1918, was a 'difficult prisoner', who made repeated attempts to escape. On two separate occasions he had the demoralizing experience of being part of a two-man break that got within a short distance of the frontier, but on each occasion his companion eluded the pursuers and crossed into Holland while the unfortunate Dougall was recaptured.

On the first escape, he and Sedley Williams evaded their

guards and jumped from the train while being transferred to Holzminden. They were free for more than two weeks before German soldiers caught up with them close to the frontier. They spotted Williams and were about to fire when Dougall broke cover and distracted their attention. Williams made good his escape but Dougall was captured, taken to Holzminden and placed in solitary confinement. Dougall was still in the punishment cells and unable to take part in the Great Escape, but with another pilot from Winnipeg, William Stephenson, he escaped from the camp in mid-October and set off again on 'a hike to the frontier'. Although Dougall was once more captured almost within sight of the frontier, Stephenson crossed it safely and later admitted that, like Williams, he owed the success of his 'home run' to Dougall who, even at the cost of his own freedom, had again staged a diversion to draw off the German soldiers tracking them down.

CHAPTER 10

DEAD OR ALIVE

The Search for the Escapees

Lieutenant Cecil Blain, Captain David Gray and Lieutenant Caspar Kennard, still wearing the clothes in which they made their successful escape from Holzminden.

AS SOON AS Niemeyer had informed Corps Headquarters of the Great Escape, searches by mounted cavalry and dogs had begun, with a reward of 5,000 marks – around £250 – offered for each captive returned, dead or alive, but the escapees had had several hours' grace; time enough for most already to have crossed the River Weser. The majority waded or swam across, though others, braver or more foolhardy, used the bridge in the town before the signal shots were fired to raise the alarm and increase the guard mounted on the bridge. Some escapees travelled alone, but most were in pairs or threes and, walking at different speeds and following different routes, they were soon widely dispersed.

They knew that the Germans used bloodhounds to track escapees and some had garlic to rub on their heels in case they were chased by dogs and 'some pepper for the same purpose'. Pepper could also be used against German soldiers or border guards: 'If you hurl a handful of pepper in any-one's face, they don't see to shoot at you as you run away.' All of them were carrying dried food and, to save weight, most of them, with the exception of the hapless would-be escapee sent back to lighten his load, were carrying little or no tinned food. Most planned to forage for whatever vegetables or fruit they could find as they travelled, but in a country where many of the citizens were close to starvation, there was little food of any sort to be had.

Every German farmer was visited once a week by an official whose duty it was to check over his stock to see that none had been eaten or sold, and to make a note of the amount of produce growing in his garden. The farmers were also forbidden to thresh any grain unless these officials were present. Every farmer and every man who had any land was ordered to give up everything he grew, and if he did not, he was at once imprisoned, and his wife and family suffered. After the produce had been given up they received a slip of paper as a receipt, and were told they would be repaid as soon as Germany was victorious, but many Germans were privately beginning to wonder if they would ever be repaid and, rather than give it up, farmers often hid their produce for their own use. One pair of escaped prisoners noticed people in the fields acting furtively and saw several disappearing behind a haystack carrying sacks. When they investigated later they found potatoes buried in holes in the ground, and sacks of grain concealed under the haystack. Whenever they could find some potatoes or other vegetables, many of the escapees cooked them on their Tommy's stove with Oxo or biltong – if they had any – to flavour them; the psychological effects of the hot food were probably almost as important as the calories they were consuming. Two of them even came across some milk in a can outside a farm and drank it – the first fresh milk they had tasted in three years.

One of the frustrated would-be escapees, Captain Jack Shaw, had sent numerous coded messages to British Army Intelligence concealed in apparently innocuous letters and it is almost certain that intelligence officers knew about the planned escape before the event and that the tunnellers' aim was to cross into the Netherlands. As a result, in what must have been a pre-planned piece of disinformation, when news of the Great Escape began to filter out a couple of days after the break-out, and the escapees were making their way towards the Dutch border, British newspapers were reporting that 'It is believed that the officers made for the Danish frontier.'

Lieutenant James Bennett who was 'teamed with an Anglo-Indian officer', Lieutenant J. K. Bousfield, hid for twenty-one hours every day, walking only in the three hours of full darkness before the pre-dawn light began to strengthen again. As his disguise, Bennett was wearing his naval uniform 'with buttons and braid removed, and sporting a civilian cap'. On their first night out, the two men – perhaps having reconnoitred it on one of their walks on parole – found a place on the River Weser where the water was shallow enough for them to wade across. After fording the river, they had walked on for only another two or three miles before 'all hell broke loose' in the distance behind them, with what sounded like 'dogs barking and guards shouting'. They hid in a small field of maize and 'lay there until ten o'clock that night'.

The following night, and on most subsequent nights, they travelled on a further twelve to fifteen miles, then found cover in small patches of rye, often surrounded by low-growing root crops. However, 'we were always afraid the searchers would have dogs with them,' Bennett later said. 'But the dogs would have damaged the crop fields while searching, so they weren't allowed to take their dogs out there with them. Otherwise we'd never have got through.' Like most of the other escapees, they made it a rule to use the first good cover they found after three in the morning, avoiding the risk of being left exposed without a hiding place as dawn began to break, but there was very little cover on the route they had chosen and they sometimes had to perch in high tree branches throughout the day, 'almost fainting from cramp'. On another day they lay up in a small patch of rye, with farmers working so close to them that the escapees could hear them talking across their heads as they hid there. Later, surprised by a policeman in the centre of a small town, they escaped by out-running him – Bousfield was 'an old Cambridge 3-miler' – and then evaded a detachment of cavalry sent to hunt them down.

'Travelling only by night with the aid of a map and compass', they eventually crossed the Dutch frontier after ten days and nights on the run. The River Ems (now the Rhede), two miles before the border, was the last significant obstacle in their way. A solitary sentry was guarding their path, the only gap through the barbed-wire entanglements along the riverbank. The sentry 'knew there was someone out there, but was quivering with fear'. As they crept towards him, the guard heard them and shouted, 'Halt!' but they rushed past him and plunged into the river. The guard fired a shot after them but it went wide. They swam the river safely and crossed the border soon afterwards, though the Dutch frontier post was three-quarters of a mile beyond the border and it was another two and a half to three hours before they were safe, drinking coffee in a Dutch police station and regaling the duty policemen with the tale of their escape. Half an hour later, by complete chance, another of the escapees, Captain Edward Wilmer Leggatt, arrived at the same police station 'dead beat, face swollen, clothes torn' but free.

Even though few of the escapees could speak even one word of German and only one had genuine civilian clothes, the remainder using British officers' coats turned inside out or suits made out of blankets, ten of the twenty-nine eventually completed successful 'home runs'. Among them was Lieutenant Stanley Purves. He had with him two beautiful escape maps, perhaps among those sent in the tennis-racquet handles: they were hand-drawn and coloured on silk and assembled from a score of small rectangles to form a larger map. Good-quality maps were almost essential, for in a zone extending many miles back from the Dutch border, the German authorities had reversed all the signposts 'partly to obstruct escapers and partly to mislead deserters from the German Army'.

Most of the escapees carried photographic copies of the same escape map, provided by an Australian orderly, Private Dick Cash. A Sydney photographer in peacetime, Cash exchanged food from his Red Cross parcels with German civilians in return for wire-cutters, a map, a plate camera and photographic printing equipment with which to produce copies of the map, three hundred in all. Cash had been listed as missing in action on 3 May 1917, during the battle of Bullecourt, and several of his comrades claimed to have seen him die, but in fact he had been badly wounded in the shoulder and partially buried in a shell hole. Rescued and captured by German soldiers, Cash spent four months in German hospitals near Hannover and Celle before he was moved to a prisoner-of-war camp and then to Holzminden. As an orderly, Cash himself was not among the prisoners who escaped, and remained at Holzminden until the end of the war.

Of all the escapees, Gray, Blain and Kennard were perhaps the most ingenious. They had first thought of travelling disguised as German soldiers, but while Gray's command of the language was so good that he could pass for a native speaker, Blain's limited German and Kennard's inability to utter more than a couple of words made such a disguise impossible. After long thought, Gray hit on a brilliant solution: Kennard would pose as an escaped lunatic and Gray and Blain would be his keepers, returning him to the asylum at Vechta, a genuine asylum that Gray had discovered was only a few miles from the Dutch border. With Kennard dressed in the grey uniform that lunatics wore, most people would give him a wide berth and any failure to speak or eccentric behaviour on his part was likely to be attributed to his madness and not the fact that he was an escaped prisoner of war. Blain would take the role of a junior guard from the asylum, while Gray, acting the role of his superior officer, would naturally be the one to answer any questions put to them by police, soldiers or German civilians.

Gray's research – aided by bribes and his promises of help in returning Kurt Grau to India after the war – even established the name of the chief of police for the Vechta district, and his name and fake signature were on the forged document authorizing them to make the journey to bring back the recaptured lunatic. Grau might have been less than pleased had he known that, in a private joke, the escapees had given the fake lunatic the name 'Kurt Grau'. The forged document read: 'We hereby certify that the two guards, Karl Holzmann and Franz Vogel (Chief Guard) have the job of transporting the lunatic Kurt Grau to the asylum at Vechta. The above lunatic is forbidden to travel by rail or other public transport and may not meet other people. All policemen and officials are earnestly requested to give all possible help in transporting this lunatic to his destination.' The document was dated six days before that of the planned escape to help explain the dishevelled appearance the men were bound to exhibit after crawling through the tunnel and then living rough as they made their way towards the border. They also carried forged identity cards, though, in character as the chief guard, Gray was holding 'Kurt Grau's' along with his own.

On the night of the Great Escape, they reached the banks of the River Weser at two fifteen, about a quarter of an hour after Walter Butler, Andrew Clouston and William Langren had climbed up the far bank and moved on. There, Gray, Kennard and Blain also made a crude raft from wooden fencing posts and used it to keep their clothes and packs dry as they swam across, pushing the raft in front of them. Their packs contained their papers, dry food, like Oxo cubes and biscuits, a generous supply of Caley's Marching Chocolate, a bottle of cognac for medicinal use and some tins of food that they would have to eat almost at once, for they had been forced to open them by the tin-room attendant at the camp earlier that day. Having unloaded their makeshift raft, Kennard then swam back up-river with it, broke it up and threw the pieces of wood on to the bank, hoping to lay a false trail to fool searchers using tracker dogs. When he had swum back downstream and dressed, the three men set out at a brisk marching pace, using a road running roughly due north past the villages of Heinsen and Polle to Brevörde. By this time dawn was fast approaching, so they left the road and lay hidden in a nearby wood throughout the day, two men sleeping while the other remained awake and on watch. Although they had already covered ten miles, they were scarcely a step nearer the Dutch border than when they had started, for it lay due west of Holzminden, not north. However, the three had decided that there was less chance of pursuit if they avoided the most direct and obvious route to the border.

Like their fellow escapees, Blain, Gray and Kennard hid by day and travelled only at night, but they were sufficiently confident in their disguises, cover stories and in Gray's German to keep to the roads for the most part, rather than travelling across country or detouring round villages and towns. On their second night out, they were given an unexpected and unwelcome early test of their cover. They entered the village of Gellersen after midnight, expecting to find the inhabitants fast asleep, but instead the lamps and candles in every house were lit and the occupants had gathered in the street, talking excitedly. The three men felt that the cause of the excitement could only have been the news of the mass escape from Holzminden, but they had already been spotted approaching the village and any attempt to detour through the fields would merely have led to a chase and their probable arrest. So instead they carried straight on, acting out their agreed roles, with Gray and Blain on either side of Kennard, dragging him along.

Their arrival aroused much interest and suspicion among the villagers, but, followed by a growing crowd, Gray waited until they had almost reached the far end of the village before stopping and asking them what had roused them from their beds. He then produced his letters of authority and warned the villagers to keep well clear of 'the dangerous lunatic', whom they were moving by night to lessen the danger of him attacking someone. As he said this, several villagers took a few steps backwards. Gray then gilded the lily by demanding water because the lunatic was working himself up into one of his fits and would have to be given a 'quietening drug'. Kennard and Blain played their supporting roles in this tableau, with Kennard rolling his eyes and emitting strange gurgling noises, while Blain shook him roughly and hit him once or twice, eliciting a few cries and words of protest from some of the village women.

When a glass of water was produced, Gray rejected it because of the danger of the lunatic smashing the glass and attacking someone with the jagged pieces, and a pewter mug arrived instead. Kennard was then wrestled to the ground by his keepers and the quietening drug – an aspirin from Gray's pack – administered. Slowly his struggles subsided until he lay apparently unconscious. Gray assured the spectators that he would soon revive and would then be quite calm again. While they waited for Kennard to regain consciousness, Gray and Blain ate some bread and cheese and drank some wine provided by one of the villagers. During the idle conversation that ensued, Gray discovered that a large search party was in the area, hunting for Holzminden escapees, some of whom had been spotted near a neighbouring village and were being pursued. Their informant added the invaluable rider that the fugitives would have no chance of crossing the main road and the railway running between Barntrup and Hameln, which were being intensively patrolled. Their patient had now revived and, having said their goodbyes to the villagers, Gray and Blain hauled Kennard to his feet and frog-marched him out of the village and away into the night.

They could hardly believe how well their deception had worked but, deciding not to push their luck by braving the patrols on the road and railway line, they hid in a wood a mile or so down the road and remained there throughout the next day. As they set off the next night, they almost walked straight into a large group of German soldiers, but ducked back into the cover of the trees just in time and, as the soldiers passed them, Gray heard a couple celebrating the capture of one or more of the Holzminden escapees. If that was depressing news in one way, the departure of the soldiers also indicated that the patrols in the immediate area were now being discontinued. That night Gray, Blain and Kennard duly crossed the road and railway without incident, and over the next few nights moved steadily onwards, avoiding numerous patrols that were still searching the countryside for the escapees in an ever-widening net.

Conditions were poor, with continual drenching rain and numerous marshes that either took hours to cross or forced them into ever more time-consuming detours. Their filthy clothes and unshaven condition would now have made their cover story hard to sustain. By the twelfth day they had eaten the last scraps of their food and had nothing but an occasional raw turnip or cabbage that they found in the fields. Soaked to the skin, hollow-eyed with fatigue, and all suffering from heavy colds that only increased their misery, they struggled on. As they rested that twelfth night, they were less than ten miles from the frontier, but they faced two more natural barriers – another marsh and the River Ems – and the possibility of up to three lines of German sentries before crossing the border.

Two other escapees had found a part of the Ems that was only forty-five yards wide, with dense undergrowth on both banks in which they could hide. The two men crossed around midnight, evading the first line of patrols on the near bank. Two miles further on, they were almost surprised by another sentry and then, as they climbed over a wire fence, they touched an alarm wire that caused a bell to ring in a nearby cottage where a German patrol was based. The escapees flattened themselves to the ground as a guard raced past within five yards of them. Then they ran into the next field and lay flat again, while German soldiers with electric torches searched the area around the fence. They moved on soon afterwards, crossing a number of drainage ditches and eventually reached a thirty-foot dike, flanking a broad canal. They knew from their map that the far bank of the canal was definitely in Dutch territory. They swam across and walked on into freedom.

Before they could hope to emulate them, Gray, Blain and Kennard first had to cross Walchumer Moor, another vast expanse of marshland. Unable to detour around it, they were forced to drag themselves through it, sinking at each step into mire up to their calves. Even in the best of health it would have been an exhausting challenge; in their debilitated state it came close to finishing them, but somehow – perhaps driven by the thought that whatever they faced here on the moor was nothing to the hell on earth that would await them if they gave up and were returned to Niemeyer's tender care – they found the strength to struggle on. At last they saw a row of lights glimmering in the darkness ahead: the arc lamps illuminating the frontier. Suspended from posts some two hundred yards apart, the lights ran along the top of a dike raised fifteen feet or so above the surface of the surrounding marsh. A German sentry was patrolling on the near side of the border; there was no sign of any Dutch presence on the far side.

The three men huddled at the foot of the steeply sloping side of the dike, listening to the crunch of gravel as the sentry paced to and fro above them and timing the intervals between his returns. To their frustration the rain that had dogged them most of the way from Holzminden had now stopped, making the sentry much more likely to detect any noise they made as they tried to slip across the frontier. Nonetheless they decided to make a dash for it when the sentry was at the furthest point of his beat, but when Kennard tried to scale the steep bank, he could get no purchase on the wet grass and slipped and fell back among his comrades.

After the sentry again came and went, they eventually resolved to form a human ladder to climb the bank. Gray, the strongest, stood at the bottom with his back to the bank. He cupped his hands and helped Kennard up on to his shoulders. Blain, the slightest of the three, hauled himself over both of them until he was on Kennard's shoulders with his hands just inches from the bank top. At that moment the sentry returned and Blain froze, his hands no more than a few feet from the sentry's boots. By a miracle the sentry did not see them, and as he turned and paced away again, Blain dragged himself up on to the top of the dike, then turned round and reached down to help Kennard. Both men now reached down towards Gray, but try as he might, he could neither pass their bags up to them, nor reach their hands himself, and the sentry was returning. Blain and Kennard swung themselves back over the edge and hung by their fingertips as the sentry again passed by without seeing them.

As they dragged their exhausted bodies back on to the top of the dike, Gray had an inspiration. Looping the handles of two of their bags together, he threw them up to Kennard, who leaned far down the slope to reach them while Blain held his ankles. Kennard and Blain then gripped the first bag and hauled on it, while Gray, clutching the lower one, was half pulled as he half climbed up to join them. However, this had taken so long that the guard was now approaching once more and either their movements or the sound of their feet on the gravel as they made for the other side of the dike provoked him to shout a warning.

As one, the three men dived over the other side, tumbled down the slope and then began running into the marsh, floundering through the mud as they heard the crack and whine of a rifle shot behind them. The guard fired twice more but failed to hit them and by then the darkness had swallowed them. After that, there was only the diminishing sound of more shouts and curses, which seemed to confirm that they had now crossed the frontier. They embraced each other, standing in the middle of the marsh, then moved on towards the distant lights of a Dutch village, shining from the darkness ahead of them.

Colonel Rathborne had made his own escape in rather grander style. A fluent German speaker with plenty of German marks in his pocket, a pair of spectacles to give him a professorial air and a convincing set of civilian clothes, he had crossed the Dutch frontier several days ahead of the next three, Bousfield, Bennett and Leggatt. Having wriggled through the tunnel, wearing his pyjamas over his civilian clothes to protect them, he discarded the pyjamas, dusted himself down and strolled south-eastwards – the opposite direction to the one he would have been expected to take. When he reached the town of Göttingen, almost fifty miles away, he went to the railway station and bought a ticket for Aachen by way of Cassel and Frankfurt. He was helped by the surprising laxity of security precautions on the German railways for, though there were roaming ticket inspectors and itinerant policemen, there was no organized system for checking the identity documents of travellers.

Rathborne had only one anxious moment – in a town where he was changing trains. Having many hours to wait for his connection and supremely confident in his German vocabulary and accent, he walked into town from the station to buy a collar to improve his disguise. However, when the shop assistant asked him, 'What size?' he realized that his knowledge of German did not extend to the system of sizing collars and was forced to beat a hasty and rather undignified retreat without the collar.

When he reached Aachen, he was less than three miles from the Dutch border and he made his way safely across after dark, five days after escaping from Holzminden. To rub salt into Niemeyer's wounds, he sent the commandant a 'Wish you were here' telegram from the Netherlands: 'HAVING LOVELY TIME STOP IF I EVER FIND YOU IN LONDON WILL BREAK YOUR NECK STOP'.

It is surprising that even though confident in German as Gray and Rathborne were, they should have been able to escape detection by native German speakers altogether. The reason might have lain in the fact that the German Empire was a large and diverse new nation, formed less than fifty years before from previously autonomous kingdoms, grand duchies, duchies, principalities and free Hanseatic cities. Few Germans travelled far within their own borders and men from, say, Schleswig might never have encountered a native of Württemburg, so it is conceivable that an Englishman speaking tolerable German might have sounded no more alien to them than a native from a distant part of Germany.

In all, ten men – Gray, Blain, Kennard, Bennett and Bousfield of the thirteen-man working party, and Rathborne, Purves, Tullis, Campbell-Martin and Wilmer Leggatt of the others – had made successful home runs. Colonel Rathborne had been the first of the Great Escapees to reach Holland, arriving on the night of 28–29 July 1918, just five days after the break-out. Lieutenants Bousfield and Bennett came next, on the night of 1–2 August, closely followed by Captain Edward Wilmer Leggatt, who also reached Losser in the Netherlands that night. Gray, Blain and Kennard arrived on the night of 4–5 August and the following night, Stanley Purves, John Keil Tullis and an officer called Campbell-Martin also arrived at the Rijks quarantine camp. All of the successful escapees returned to England on 15–16 August 1918, just over three weeks after escaping from Holzminden. In both the numbers who had escaped from the camp and those who had crossed the border safely, it was the greatest escape in the whole of the First World War, though all the successful men probably shared Cecil Blain's one regret that 'I was not in the camp the next day to see Herr Hauptmann Niemeyer's face when the roll was called – I expect it was a wonderful show!'

As a reward for their refusal to accept captivity and their repeated attempts to escape, which were eventually crowned with success, Gray was promoted to major and Blain and Kennard to captain. All three were also decorated. Blain was awarded the Air Force Cross and Gray and Kennard who, although pilots, were still on the roll of their former regiments, the Military Cross. They received their decorations in a ceremony at Buckingham Palace, and King George V then invited them to dine with him at Windsor Castle and tell him more about their exploits. On 16 December 1919 Lieutenant Colonel Charles Edward Henry

Rathborne was awarded a bar to his DSO 'for gallantry in escaping from captivity whilst a prisoner of war'.

After their return to Britain, the testimony of the ten escapees about their experiences in Holzminden, coupled with a coded letter sent by Captain Tollemache from the camp, convinced officials of the Prisoners of War Department and the Army Council that 'something very drastic will have to be done' about Hauptmann Karl Niemeyer. They proposed 'to demand the immediate dismissal of the camp commandant', who was already considered to be 'rendered unfit for any care of PoWs' following the 'outrages at Ströhen' under his command, when guards had repeatedly bayoneted defenceless prisoners.

The other nineteen escapees were eventually recaptured, many of them having been spotted by civilians. Much of the German population could be mobilized to help track down escaped prisoners, and if a suspicious character was noticed, it was quite common for local schoolchildren to be given a day's holiday so that they could help to search likely hiding places. The last men through the tunnel, Captain Frank Sharpe and Bernard Luscombe, later 'a rubicund parson', but then just a rubicund lieutenant, were the first to be caught, while trying to pass through a village about fifteen miles downstream from the camp, after two days and two nights on the run. While they were being searched on their return to Holzminden, Niemeyer revenged himself on them by ripping their clothes to shreds and picking Sharpe's gold watch to pieces with his pocket knife. Then they were packed off to the cells.

A Canadian officer, Captain Clifford Robertson, was recaptured on the seventh day, as was Lieutenant Neil MacLeod, a twenty-five-year-old New Zealander from Wakapuaka, who had been the eleventh man through the tunnel. He was caught in a small wood near Osnabrück by a German soldier home on leave and out for an afternoon walk with his dog and gun. Lieutenant Walter Butler, the first man out, was among four men retaken on the tenth day. 'It was terribly hot and I suffered frightfully from thirst,' he later said. 'One day I drank from a stream, the water of which must have been foul, because soon after I felt ill. I told my two companions to go on while I rested and that evening I set off again. While I was walking through a village, I saw a bicycle and took it. I pedalled in the dead of night through a dense forest without being able to see what was on the road in front of me. Suddenly I bumped into something, fell off the bicycle and passed out. When I woke up, I found two rifles pointing at me and I was taken by two soldiers to the nearest police station.'

Captain William Langren and Lieutenants Frederick Mardock and Colin Lawrence were all apprehended near the River Ems. Another escapee wandered around Germany for a fortnight before eventually being caught by an old shepherd, but among the unluckiest was Second Lieutenant A. T. Shipwright, the man who had made an earlier unsuccessful escape attempt inside a rolled-up carpet. This time he was recaptured just a couple of hundred yards from the Dutch border. Lieutenant Robert Paddison, who had 'tried to escape many times but never got right away', was also seized right on the Dutch border. The other recaptured escapees were Captain Philip Smith, who was within three miles of the border when he was apprehended, Major John Morrogh and Lieutenants Thomas Burrill, Douglas Birch, Peter Lyon, Arthur Morris, David Wainwright, Frederick Illingworth and Andrew Clouston.

All the recaptured men were returned to Holzminden, where they were kept in solitary confinement on bread and water for from four to eight weeks. 'Put into cells in which they had no light on all night, they were allowed practically none of their personal necessaries owing to the fear that they might be used for tunnelling. Large wooden screens were put up in front of the windows, which had the effect of keeping out all light.' Even after their release from solitary confinement they faced a court martial and continued to be harassed, punished and returned to the cells on the slightest provocation. For example, Lieutenant Andrew Clouston was released from solitary confinement on 26 August 1918, but four days later he was sent back to the cells for smoking during *Appel*. He was one of scores of prisoners who were doing so at the time, but Clouston was the only one singled out.

All the recaptured escapees were court-martialled on 27 September 1918, charged with mutiny and 'conspiring to destroy Imperial Government property'. They were allowed to have a lawyer to defend them and a representative of the Netherlands ambassador in Berlin also attended the trial as an observer. The indictment listed nineteen defendants, citing their age, birthplace, religion and pre-war occupation, though in giving their details, at least some of the prisoners still had enough spirit not to miss the opportunity of indulging in yet another leg-pull at German expense. Arthur Morris might or might not have been a diamond trader before the war, but the thirty-one-year-old Australian Peter Lyon certainly hadn't been a pensioner. Those charged were listed as:

1. Oberleutnant Thomas Burrill, 32, shepherd/stockman.
2. Leutnant Douglas Birch, 20, unemployed.
3. Oberleutnant Peter Lyon, 31, pensioner.
4. Leutnant Arthur Morris, 34, diamond trader.
5. Leutnant Robert Paddison, 20, student.
6. Leutnant Clifford Robertson, 32, unknown trade.
7. Leutnant David Wainwright, 24, active [regular army] officer.
8. Hauptmann William Langren, 21, active [regular army] officer.
9. Oberleutnant Walter Butler, 25, rentier.
10. Hauptmann Philip Smith, 22, student.
11. Major John Morrogh, 34, active [regular army] officer.
12. Oberleutnant Colin Lawrence, 27, active [regular army] officer.
13. Leutnant Frederick Mardock, 22, engineer.
14. Hauptmann Neil McLeod, 25, active [regular army] officer.

15. Leutnant Frederick Illingworth, 27, active [regular army] officer.

16. Oberleutnant Andrew Clouston, 19, grammar-school pupil.

17. Hauptmann Frank Sharpe, 22, unknown trade.

18. Oberleutnant Bernard Luscombe, 28, student.

19. Leutnant Alan Shipwright, 21, volunteer soldier.

The verdict of the court martial, delivered with all due gravity, stated that:

The accused who are charged with breaching Section 122, 2 of the Criminal Code of the Reich have been interned in Holzminden Detention Centre for Officers. In the interest of public security their freedom of movement has been taken away from them by the authorized governing bodies. They have thus become prisoners in accordance with Section 122, 2 of the Criminal Code of the Reich.

The accused admit to having escaped from their camp in Holzminden on the night of July 23/24 1918. According to their statements and that of Sergeant Lehr, made under oath, other English prisoners of war managed to escape with them, among those a Lieutenant Colonel. In agreement with Sergeant Lehr's statement, their escape route can only have been through a tunnel that was discovered after the escape. As can be deduced from Sergeant Lehr's statement and the map on Sheet 10 of the official note enclosed in this file, its starting point was at an alcove concealed by wooden panelling under a staircase in a basement of a building serving as accommodation. From this point it led underneath the foundation wall of the building, passed under the courtyard and the surrounding wall, up to 8.5 metres deep. Then it rose gradually and ended in a bean field. The prisoners accommodated in the upper rooms – who were able to move freely between rooms in the building – reached the aforementioned staircase alcove by breaking through the air vent leading to the basement. The wood panelling concealing the staircase alcove contained a door that was unidentifiable from the outside and made up of loose wooden boards. It could be opened by means of a mechanism applied to the ceiling. Behind the timber wall, there were stacked bags made of all kinds of materials which were obviously meant to hold the soil excavated from the tunnel. Furthermore, a bellows was found that had a tubular construction attached to it and apparently served the sole purpose of supplying air to the people working in the tunnel. Moreover, there were coal shovels, [empty food] tins and similar items suitable for the excavation of a tunnel.

After statements from:

a) the majority of the accused that they were oblivious to the development and making of the tunnel

b) the accused Lyon, Luscombe, and Mardock that they would refuse to make any statements

c) the accused Birch that he had acted under orders

Major Morrogh as spokesperson for all of the accused declared: The escape had not been arranged and everyone had acted independently from the others. It was a matter that had been ordered, namely by the Lieutenant Colonel mentioned above. The order said to assemble at a certain point in time. Each one had a particular order of their own and had acted upon it.

This, however, does not exclude the assumption of a rebellion according to the aforementioned article of the law. A rebellion is defined as an aggregation of several people for a concerted illegitimate act. According to common interpretation of international law, military authority of an imprisoned officer over his charges is in abeyance and that military authority is exercised only by entities determined by the German Reich.

In case this principle had not been made known to the prisoners at the time of imprisonment – something that can hardly be assumed in this case – it will have become obvious to them by means of the actual conditions after imprisonment, as they were naturally aware of the characteristics of a rebellion, the aggregation of several people for the act carried out, and accordingly aware that they formed part of an aggregation of several people with the aim of a concerted illegitimate act.

This awareness, however, did not detain them from partaking in this act until its successful completion. This participation would also have been a given if other people than the accused and their associates who fled at the same time had carried out the works at the tunnel and the access to the same. In any case, everybody involved in the escape knew of the plan and offered their assistance to a certain extent, passively or actively, inasmuch as taking on their superiors' orders and choosing to make them their intentions. This suffices to constitute complicity.

It is therefore established that the accused as prisoners at Holzminden staged a rebellion and joined forces to carry out the escape on the night of July 23/24 1918, which constitutes an offence in accordance with Section 122, 2 of the Criminal Code of the Reich. Therefore they had to be penalized.

Considering that, from their point of view and from the point of view of international law, the accused did not carry out anything that could be classed as seditious, it did not seem appropriate to exceed the minimum penalty as stated in the quoted article of the law. The severity of the admitted minimum penalty however does hit them deservedly hard, even if it is considered that when Section 122, 2 of the Criminal Code of the Reich was established, it was probably not thought to extend it to prisoners of war, too, as whoever enters into war captivity accepts the given condition of this war captivity. These conditions are determined by the requirements of the German Reich, and – more so than for example the insular location of Great Britain – the central location of the German Reich that facilitates the escape of prisoners of war, and subsequent treason requires fierce intervention against delicts like the ones here present.

Duly convicted, the escapees were all sentenced to six months' imprisonment, but by this time the Armistice was imminent and the sentence was never enforced. Niemeyer's censors stifled any mention of the Great Escape in letters home from the remaining prisoners at Holzminden. A letter from Flight Lieutenant Leslie Nixon to his mother on 5 August 1918, twelve days after the escape, had a large section blacked out, which almost certainly referred to it. Nixon had enlisted as soon as war was declared in August 1914 when he was still under sixteen. His true age was discovered a few days later and he was discharged from the Army, but he re-enlisted in the Artists' Rifles in 1916. He transferred to the Royal Flying Corps a few months later and was posted to 3 Squadron in France, but was shot down on 5 December 1917 and sent to Holzminden. He had been one of the many frustrated men who were due to go through the tunnel when it became blocked.

His close comrade Lieutenant Leonard Pearson also missed out, then decided to take up the offer of internment in the Netherlands. On 14 October Pearson wrote to Nixon's mother from there, the first uncensored letter she had received from or about her son.

It was our great ambition to escape together and had not a certain tunnel fallen in before our turn came, we should have succeeded almost for certain. These opportunities come unexpectedly and therefore it is very necessary to be well-equipped as soon as possible. He [Nixon] begged me to ask you to do your utmost to help him in every way within your power and to get expert help to send the things out. Happily I was able to leave him most of the things he wanted, but he might lose those at any time in a second. What he still lacks are civilian clothes or German uniform: those can be sent out in khaki uniform, between the outside cloth and the lining. By far the most useful thing that you could possibly send out to him would be German money, very well concealed by an expert, in 20, 50 and 100 mark notes. At present he lacks a good frontier map, the scale should be two miles to the inch if not larger. In the food line, chocolate is absolutely invaluable, good thick blocks of it, preferably nut chocolate. Things like dates, compressed fruit tablets and pieces of biltong (a kind of dried meat) are also very useful and necessary.

As Leslie and I are such great friends, I hope you will also allow me to instruct Cox & Co [his bank] to send you twenty pounds to help with the work. All these things cost a lot of money and I'm about to mention a few more: a luminous compass, a four miles to the inch map right up to the frontier, and very strong *insulated* wire clippers will perhaps complete the catalogue. It is naturally very important that he should be warned some time before how and when to expect them.

In his letters home, Nixon had been careful not to distress his mother by revealing how grim conditions were at Holzminden, but Pearson showed no such tact, concluding his letter to her:

Very likely Leslie's letters have given you quite a wrong
impression about prisoners' camps in Germany, as
naturally he would not like to make you unhappy about
him and of course the truth about them would be
suppressed by the censors. Honestly they are very bad
indeed and of the six camps I have been to in Germany,
Holzminden is the worst, with the very, <u>very</u> worst
commandant. On the slightest excuse he stops the issue of
parcels and tins and closes the bathroom too, as he knows
that annoys an Englishman more than anything else. Living
on Hun rations means practical starvation, so in other
words, he starved us whenever he liked.

Many of those left at Holzminden after the 'Great Escape'
remained desperate to break out. The wiry New Zealander,
Captain Edgar H. Garland, whose own hopes had been
frustrated when the tunnel collapsed, made six subsequent
attempts to get away and at one point spent three weeks
hiding in a ventilator on the roof of a building. The new
tunnel that had been begun in the disused lavatory in the
cellars was also progressing fast and, according to Wilfred
Shaw, a number of men succeeded in escaping through it in
the very last days of the war. Shaw himself had been due to
leave via the tunnel, but 'it was taken in alphabetical order
... People from A to R did get out.' However, the man in
front of Shaw in the queue, the much persecuted airman
William Leefe Robinson, became claustrophobic as he tried
to make his way through, 'got the wind up and started yelling

and Gerry woke up and dug it up and dug 'em out. That was the end of the tunnel.' Shaw's account is uncorroborated by any other prisoner at Holzminden but unless it was a complete work of fiction – and there seems no reason why he would have invented the story – it is possible that Leefe Robinson's status as a Victoria Cross-winning hero, and his tragically early death soon after the war ended, persuaded his other comrades to say nothing about his embarrassing panic in the tunnel and leave his legend untainted.

Even at the best of times Leefe Robinson had never been the most robust physical specimen, and his maltreatment and prolonged incarceration in the damp, dark basement punishment cells at Holzminden had destroyed his health. Within a fortnight of returning home to England at the end of the war, 'this courageous young man who gave London its most dramatic war spectacle [by being the first pilot to shoot down a Zeppelin] made no spectacular exit himself. He died in bed on December 31, 1918.' Leefe Robinson had fallen victim to the influenza pandemic that was sweeping the world, but his former comrades all believed that 'his undermined constitution was undoubtedly the real cause of his death'.

CHAPTER 11

A HANNOVERIAN GENTLEMAN

The Disappearance of Niemeyer

'Goodbye to the Worst Camp in Germany' – A newspaper report on the liberation of Holzminden prisoners after the Armistice.

IN THE CLOSING stages of the war, as the inevitability of an Allied victory became apparent to all, Hauptmann Niemeyer and his underlings moderated their excesses towards the prisoners, no doubt in the hope of favourable treatment by the victors. One prisoner noted that 'the attitude of the Commandant altered enormously towards the end of the war when he could see Germany was being beaten', and as the Armistice approached, the prisoners noticed a distinct change in the attitude of all their captors. 'They had changed from a bullying to a fawning community.' In 'the strangest and most undignified contrast to the swaggering bully who had ruled this roost so long', Niemeyer removed the picture of the Kaiser from his office wall, ceased his choleric tours of the camp and met the new camp adjutant, Brian Manning, almost daily to offer fresh concessions. Having heard that some camp commanders would be tried for war crimes, Niemeyer was reported to have asked some British officers if it were true and if he were likely to be tried. When told that it was 'more than possible', he looked extremely frightened and claimed that he had 'always done all he could for the officers and that if there had been any unpleasant orders, they came from above'.

When the Armistice came into force on 11 November 1918, all the prisoners in the punishment cells were immediately released. Among them was the Canadian airman Lieutenant Hector Dougall, who had been enduring the solitary confinement imposed after his latest escape attempt. In 'a satisfying act of defiance' in retaliation for the lack of medical treatment, the withholding of Red Cross parcels, and his repeated spells of solitary confinement as punishment for his numerous escape attempts, Dougall climbed to the top of the main camp building, 'liberated' the camp's enormous state flag – the German eagle – and took it home to Winnipeg, as a souvenir.

Even before the Armistice had been formally declared, Niemeyer could not 'do enough for the officers'. He took off his uniform, walked about the camp in civilian clothes and told the prisoners, 'You see, I am no longer a Prussian officer, but a Hannoverian gentleman.' On 13 November 1918, just two days after the Armistice, the 'Hannoverian gentleman' simply disappeared, though he then telephoned Holzminden from Hannover, told the guards to put the senior British officer on the line and then asked him 'if he could do anything for us! The SBO speedily told him what he thought of him.'

Niemeyer's flight might have been the result of British pressure on the German government. In response to a question in the House of Commons, Sir George Cave, the

Home Secretary, revealed that after complaints about 'the conduct of the general in command of the district and the commandants of the camps, it is understood that this officer [von Hanisch] has now been removed from his command and the German Government has been informed that unless the commandants at Holzminden and Clausthal [the Niemeyer twins] are in future excluded from contact with our prisoners of war, measures of reprisal will be adopted'.

Captain Jack Shaw wryly noted the changed attitude of the guards who still remained at Holzminden. They 'had assumed so entirely respectful an attitude that they stood to attention when we spoke to them!' After 11 November, some prisoners with hidden caches of German marks ventured out of the camp to nearby villages, hoping to buy wine and meat. There was virtually no food available in the towns, but farmers were better off and several prisoners were successful. Hector Dougall found that he could buy rabbit, sausage, duck and chicken from local farmers. Prisoners were also allowed to go into the town of Holzminden without a guard, 'but it was not advisable to go in small parties as the townspeople were none too friendly to us'. 'Some prisoners were able to move surreptitiously back and forth to the town, on the lookout for "grub" and hoping to see the arrival of the first British troops. But prudently, most prisoners decided their chances of getting shot were high if they tried to "hoof it" away through the countryside.'

In the chaos of post-war Germany, it took some considerable time to effect the release of all the British prisoners of war, and by the end of November, those still at Holzminden were becoming anxious about their fate. They had no reliable source of news but knew that, if no further agreement had been reached by the time the month-long Armistice expired on 11 December, the war would resume, 'and if we were not out of Germany by then, we should remain indefinitely'.

Back in Britain, *The Times* had led a chorus of concern for the fate of the thousands of British prisoners still in captivity at Holzminden and scores of other camps, and urged, 'Some energetic attempt should be made to reach and succour these men and evacuate them from the hands of the enemy as quickly as possible.' Yet in early December 1918 there were still four to five thousand prisoners at the officers' and internees' camps at Holzminden. 'Two to three hundred are released daily and sent away without money or clothes, sometimes without shoes.' The deprivation they had endured was written on every face. A Belgian who had spent two years in Holzminden 'said he was thirty-eight, though he looked sixty'.

With Germany unwilling or unable to feed the hundreds of thousands of Allied prisoners still on its soil, huge numbers were simply being released and left 'to struggle home as best they can, starving and clothed only in filthy rags'. Prompted by the British government, Sir Douglas Haig notified the German High Command that Britain would not tolerate 'British prisoners being made to walk, unfed and miserably clothed, long distances to the Allied lines. Should

Germany persist in her brutal action, Britain will be compelled to take this into account in any question of revictualling Germany or satisfying the requirements of the German population.'

The threats had little effect: German civilians and soldiers were also struggling to find food and many were suffering from malnutrition. Enlisted British PoWs fared particularly badly since, overworked on forced labour and underfed for months and years, their physical condition was usually much worse than the officers', and they rarely had money with which to buy food, if there was any to be had. There were accounts of many dying by the roadside as they struggled towards the British lines, and Haig sent convoys of ambulances and food trucks ahead of the advancing British troops, in the hope of meeting the released prisoners of war trying to make their way across Germany. Those they found were taken to reception centres, where they were fed, washed, medically examined, then issued with boots and clean clothing before being sent home.

The first British PoWs had reached Calais as early as 15 November 1918, but those at Holzminden were still in captivity as Christmas approached. Some prisoners, unwilling to wait any longer for British troops to reach them, made their own arrangements: 'We bribed our guard to let us out . . . We covered 80 kilometres (about 50 miles) in 36 hours.' As they walked towards the Dutch frontier, they saw for themselves the chaos and anarchy into which Germany was descending as Communists, Socialists, Spartacists and Bolshevik soldiers' and workers' councils fought among themselves for control of Germany's fledgling republic and battled against the right-wing Freikorps, which included many former soldiers: 'Everything in Germany is in confusion. The Soldiers' Councils establish themselves and then the returning soldiers kick them out and take control. Then there is a counter-move by the Councils and no one knows who controls them.' At one town they entered, the British PoWs asked the Soldiers' Council to give them somewhere to sleep. 'The civilians then refused and told us to clear out, but we bribed the sentry and he went in and cleared the Bolshevists out.'

On 9 December, a Lloyd's underwriter, whose son was imprisoned at Holzminden, cabled the Prisoners of War Department of the War Office, seeking reassurance about 'the present condition of affairs at Holzminden' and issuing a forceful reminder that 'It is now a month since the Armistice was signed and . . . conditions of health, food and treatment at this Camp have been abominable all the time.' The bland reply offered no information other than that 'Arrangements have been made to supply food from depots at Rotterdam, Berne and Copenhagen; these depots are in direct communication with the camps.' The underwriter urged them to cable Sir Walter Townley, the British minister at The Hague who had appointed a Repatriation Committee to speed the return of PoWs.

However, the remaining prisoners at Holzminden were

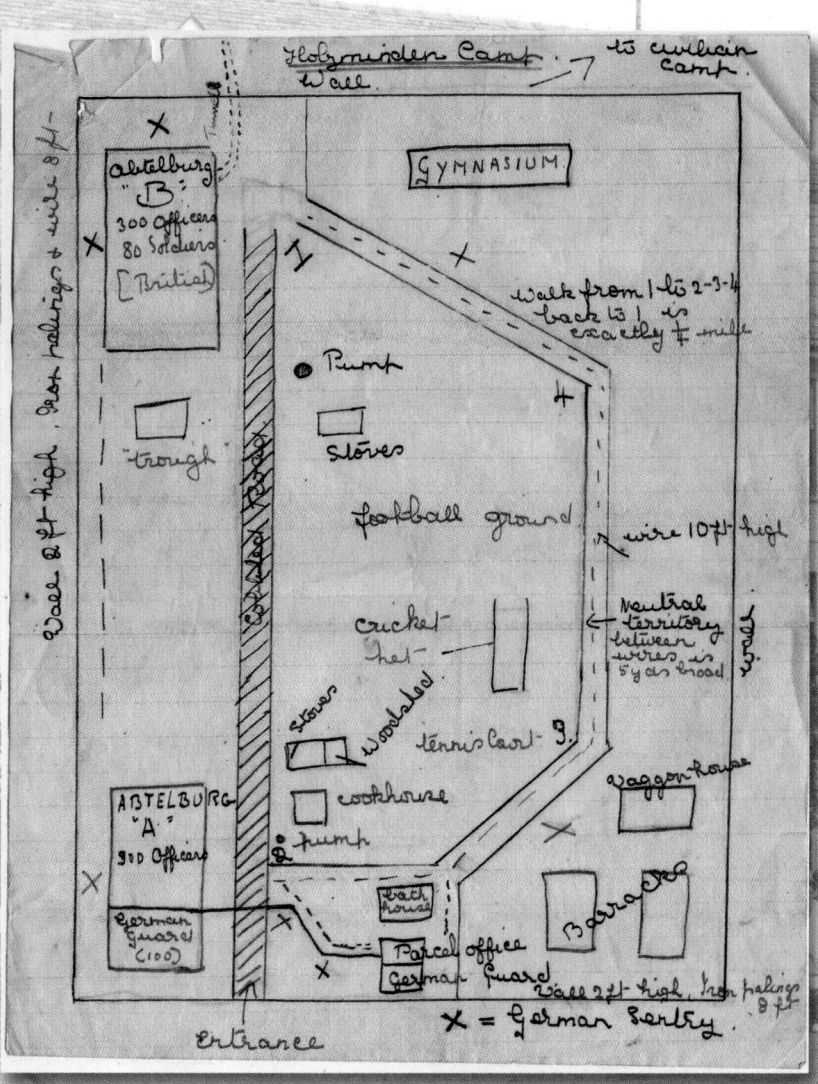

A sketch plan of Holzminden drawn by one of the escapees. The dotted lines at the top show the route of the escape tunnel.

Below: Escape equipment like wire-cutters was either stolen from civilian contractors working at the camp, obtained from bribable camp guards or shipped from England hidden inside food tins.

Below: A cross-section of the stairs leading down to the cellars in *Kaserne* B, where the punishment cells were housed. The entrance to the tunnel was reached by a hidden door in the barricade that the Germans had constructed to seal off the area under the stairs.

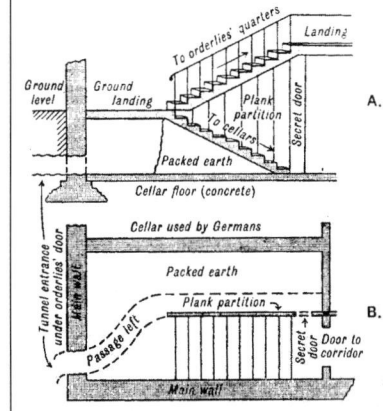

Above: The cramped entrance to the tunnel seen from inside the secret chamber behind the wooden barricade. The sacks on the right are full of earth and stones excavated from the tunnel.

Left: A camp guard presides over the exposed tunnel, after the escape in late July 1918. Niemeyer could not discover where the tunnel originated and only after he had forced British orderlies to excavate its entire length was the starting-point discovered, beneath the doorway visible over the guard's shoulder.

Below: Looking back along the exposed tunnel towards the end wall of *Kaserne* B from near the exit point in the crop-field. When complete, the tunnel, dug with knives, spoons and other primitive implements, was sixty yards long.

Prisoners improvised much of their escape equipment from the materials to hand. Captain Edward Wilmer Leggatt, one of the successful Holzminden escapees, believed that 'the hat is the most important item in a civilian disguise', and fashioned a Panama hat (**above left**) as part of his escape kit. The forage cap (**above right**) was made by Captain Jack Shaw, whose own hopes of escape through the tunnel were dashed when the roof caved in on the man in front of him.

Above: A pair of moccasins made by Edward Wilmer Leggatt, in the belief that they would make his footsteps quieter as he crept away from the escape tunnel.

Left: Stanley Purves' compass, made from a pair of magnetized needles suspended from a piece of thread, was so thin that he hid it in the paper wrapper for a Gillette razor blade (**above left**).

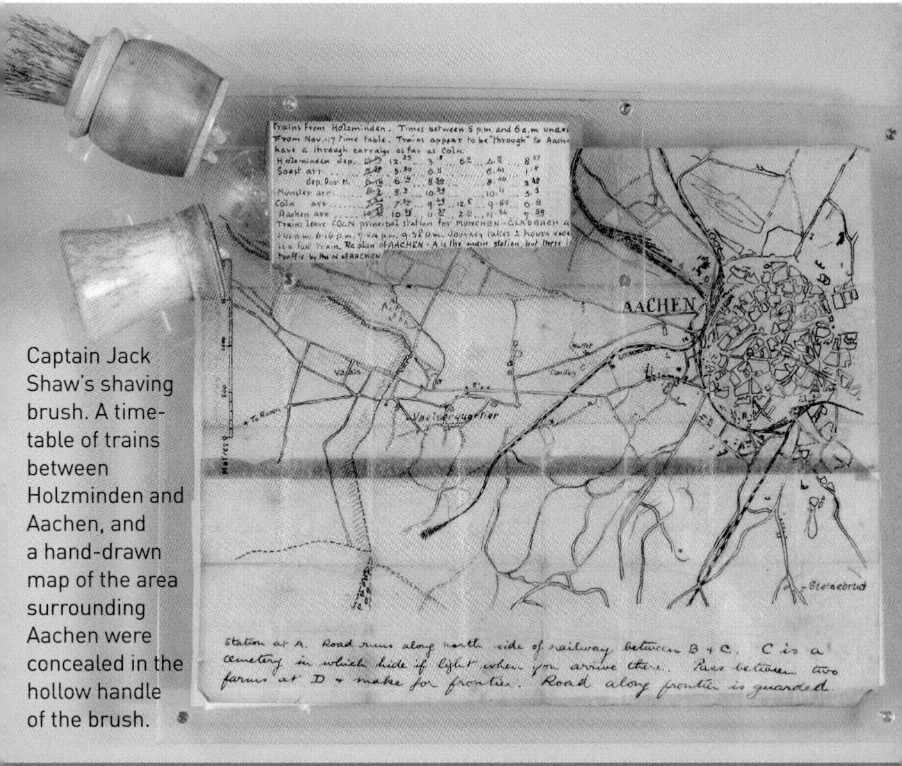

Captain Jack Shaw's shaving brush. A time-table of trains between Holzminden and Aachen, and a hand-drawn map of the area surrounding Aachen were concealed in the hollow handle of the brush.

Distance lends enchantment to the view... The last sight the successful escapees would have had of Holzminden after the break-out in July 1918.

Above: Free at last! Six of the Holzminden escapees photographed while recuperating in a quarantine camp after successfully crossing the Dutch border. From left: Captain David Gray, Captain Edward Wilmer Leggatt, Lieutenant Stanley Purves (sitting on the nurse's knee), Lieutenant Caspar Kennard (standing next to the Dutch guard), Lieutenant Cecil Blain and Captain John Tullis. The emaciated faces of Gray, Leggatt and Kennard in particular, show the hardships they had endured.

Farewell to Holzminden: wagons piled high with prisoners' belongings as they left the camp for the last time in December 1918. Anything they did not take with them was piled on the *Spielplatz* and set alight in a huge bonfire.

Above: 'A Peep into the Future: Scene at the dinner table when an ex-*gefangener* [prisoner-of-war] dines with his fiancée's people and gives expression to a little Holzminden slang.' A James Whale cartoon hinting at one of the pitfalls facing ex-PoWs readjusting to 'polite society'.

Above: Some of the Holzminden prisoners released after the Armistice, aboard the British India ship *Takada* taking them home across the North Sea.

A group of long-term prisoners at the Dutch border after their release as part of a prisoner exchange.

Above: The 20th Anniversary Dinner of the Holzminden escapees, with Colonel C. E. H. Rathborne presiding in the centre. The 'rubicund parson', Bernard Luscombe, is on the extreme right.

Below: Twenty years on. A group of Holzminden escapees reminisce over some of the artefacts brought to their anniversary dinner. The football was used in the nine-a-side matches at the camp – the largest number of men that could be accommodated on the cramped pitch on the *Spielplatz*. The tin of ox tongue contained compasses and other escape equipment.

chafing at their prolonged captivity and the next day, 10 December 1918, the senior British officer, who had commandeered Niemeyer's former office, telephoned the railway authorities at Cassel and demanded to know when a train would be sent to carry the Holzminden prisoners to the Dutch border. He reinforced his request by mentioning that the prisoners now had access to the camp armoury where they had 'counted nearly 450 rifles and certain boxes of ammunition which might, or might not, go off'. The railway authorities replied that, under the terms of the Armistice, all their rolling stock had to be handed over to the Allies. There was therefore none to spare to transfer the prisoners from Holzminden. 'Right you are,' the senior British officer replied. 'If you don't send a train by tomorrow night, we shall burn this place down and march off.' Within an hour he was notified that the requested train would be at Holzminden station at seven p.m. on 11 December.

At midday on their day of departure, the remaining prisoners at Holzminden 'had one glorious clearance', making a bonfire of everything movable in the camp, and few would have shed a tear if, in the process, the whole of the prison camp had also been burned to the ground. 'Not a thing of use to the Hun was left intact.'

'Tables, chairs, old clothing and everything we couldn't bring home were dragged outside into the "appel platz" for a fire ... In less than ten minutes a huge fire was crackling merrily. The idea grew and soon streams of officers were feeding the flames. The Huns, who were expecting to get all these articles as perquisites, were furious.' They called out the Fire Department to extinguish it, and tried to put it out with hosepipes, but the prisoners 'snatched their bayonets out of the scabbards and stabbed the pipe, and the fire went gaily on'.

'We cut their hoses to pieces,' one gleeful prisoner said. 'Everything smashed to pieces in the camp.' As the prisoners watched the blaze, they drank what was left of their carefully hoarded wine. Hector Dougall 'got beautifully drunk myself. So did most of the boys.' The people from the town thought the whole camp was on fire and came to stare through the railings. 'A weird sight we must have looked, dancing and leaping about.'

Before they left Holzminden for the last time, each prisoner was handed a pamphlet, *A Parting Word*, that had been prepared by the Republicans who had assumed power after the abdication of the Kaiser:

Gentlemen: The war is over. A little while, and you will see your native land again, your homes, your loved ones, your friends; you will once more take on your accustomed work. The fortune of war brought you as prisoners into our hands. You were freed, even against your will, from the fighting, from danger, from death. But the joys of peace could not be yours, for there was no peace. Now peace is coming, and peace means liberty. When you are already reunited with your families, thousands of our countrymen will still be pining in far-off prison camps, their hearts as hungry for home as yours.

You have suffered in confinement, as who would not? It was the fate of every prisoner in every prison camp throughout the world to eat his heart out with longing, to chafe against loss of liberty, to suffer from homesickness, brooding discouragement, blank despair. The days, the weeks, the weary years crept by and there was no end in sight. There were many discomforts, irritations, mis-understandings. Your situation has been a difficult one. Our own has been desperate, our country blockaded, our civil population and army suffering from want of proper sufficient food and materials, the enormous demands made upon our harassed land from every side. These and many other afflictions made it impossible to do all we would have liked to do. Under the circumstances we did our best to lessen the hardships of your lot, to ensure your comfort, to provide you with pastimes, enjoyment, mental and bodily recreation. It is not likely that you will ever know how difficult our circumstances have been.

We know that errors have been committed and that there have been hardships for which the former system has been to blame. There have been wrongs and evils on both sides. We hope that you will always think of that, and be just.

You entered the old empire of Germany. You leave a new Republic – the newest and, as we hope to make it, the freest land in the world. We are sorry that you saw so little of what we were proud of in the former Germany – our arts, our sciences, our model cities, our theatres, schools, industries, social institutions, as well as the beauties of our scenery and the real soul of our people, akin in so many things to your own.

But these things will remain part of the new Germany. Once the barriers of misunderstanding and artificial hatred have fallen, we hope that you will learn to know, in happier times, these grander features of a land whose unwilling guests you have been. A barbed wire enclosure is not the proper point of view from which to survey or judge a great nation.

The war has blinded all nations, but if a true and just peace will result in opening the eyes of the peoples to the fact that their interests are common – that no difference in flags, speech or nationality can alter the truth of the fraternity of all men – this war will not have been fought in vain. If the peoples at last realize that it is not each other who are their enemies, but the ruthless forces of imperialism and capitalism, of militarism of all sorts, of jingo-journalism that sows falsehood, hatred and suspicion, then this war will not have been fought in vain. Then peace will not be established in vain.

We hope that every one of you will go home carrying a message of goodwill, conciliation and enlightenment. Let all men in our new epoch go forth as missionaries of the new evangel, as interpreters between nation and nation.

The valiant dead who once fought against each other have long been sleeping as comrades side by side in the earth. May the living who once fought against each other labour as comrades side by side upon this self-same earth.

That is the message with which we bid you farewell.

It was a moving, carefully worded appeal to the nobler spirit of the British prisoners of war, but it was largely falling on deaf ears. As one commentator acerbically noted, most of the pamphlets were promptly 'put to the traditional use which soldiers the world over find for conveniently sized scraps of paper'.

That December evening, the British prisoners formed up for the last time in four companies on the *Spielplatz* and marched out of the camp four abreast. It was a pitch-dark night, lit only by the dancing flames of the still-blazing bonfire, which cast long shadows on to the wall as they filed out in a sombre silence. Apart from a small escort, most of the camp guards had made themselves scarce, lest any prisoners were tempted to exact impromptu reprisals before departing, but outside the camp the population of the town had lined the roads and 'watched with awe, envy and hate as we passed out of their sight for ever'.

The special train was already waiting at Holzminden station. The prisoners were 'packed in like sardines', though none complained about that, and they watched 'with great relief' as the train pulled out and they saw the dull red glow of the bonfire, still burning at the camp, grow fainter and fainter until it disappeared from sight altogether. The escort of camp guards with them included 'a certain NCO who had been marked down as a real rotter'. Some of the prisoners had sworn to be revenged on him and were planning to kidnap him if he was still on the train when it reached the Dutch border, but he frustrated them by getting off several stations before his comrades and so escaped his fate. Had he remained on the train, one prisoner said, 'I am afraid he would have had a very thin time indeed.'

After a three-hour halt at Münster, the prisoners travelled on towards the border with the Netherlands and, just before reaching it, they halted again for a few moments to pick up a 'bewhiskered and dirty' former Holzminden inmate, who was surprised to hear the war was over. 'He had escaped two months before and the Armistice had robbed him of a successful termination to his efforts!' At the frontier, they changed to a Dutch train. Until that moment, many had probably not allowed themselves to believe they were really free and homeward bound, but now a crowd of Dutch schoolchildren shouted a welcome to them as they crossed the border, and at once the ex-PoWs on the train 'just let ourselves go. Cheer after cheer went up from the whole train, hats being waved wildly out of the windows.'

They were 'given welcome and splendid rolls, butter and cheese' at Enschede and 'spent the night on straw in a mill there'. The next day they travelled on to Rotterdam where ships were waiting to take them home. More than four hundred men crowded on to the 105-berth 'British India boat "Takada"', and as soon as they got on board, they were all handed 'a small flag and a bar of chocolate'. To men who had endured years of black bread and gruel in which turnip skins were often the only ingredient, the food on board was 'a dream: bread and butter, tinned rabbit and bottles of stout at each meal'.

They cast anchor at midnight and steamed slowly through the night and the next day, taking a roundabout course to avoid uncleared minefields, then lying up off Hull the following night, before steaming up the Humber early the next morning. The homecoming ships passed through 'lines of torpedo boats and drifters, all of which gave us a grand howl on their whistles. It made one's back hair curl to hear this rousing welcome.' Admiral Beatty was there, 'waving his hat like a schoolboy', while the band played 'God Save the King'. As soon as the ship had tied up at the docks, a speech of welcome from the King was read to the prisoners by the lord mayor of Hull.

> The Queen joins me in welcoming you on your release from the miseries & hardships, which you have endured with so much patience and courage. During these many months of trial, the early rescue of our gallant Officers & Men from the cruelties of their captivity has been uppermost in our thoughts. We are thankful that this longed for day has arrived, & that back in the old Country you will be able once more to enjoy the happiness of a home & to see good days among those who anxiously look for your return. George R.I.

After the lord mayor had finished speaking, 'The whole

world seemed to be shouting and singing. Gangways were stretched over and we were soon in the arms of our own people again.' The former prisoners were all taken up the coast to Scarborough for a reception, 'being practically carried through the streets', and, said Captain Jack Shaw, 'England's fields had never seemed greener – to me at any rate.'

After their return to Britain, all of the former PoWs were asked to compile a report on the circumstances of their capture – partly to ensure that they had done all they could to avoid capture in the first place. They were also required to answer a questionnaire from the 'Government Committee on the Treatment by the Enemy of British Prisoners of War' and to provide a 'Statement of Extraordinary Experiences in German Internment Camps'. The questions included: 'Were you treated brutally yourself or did you see anyone else treated brutally?' and 'Did you see or hear of any order that the prisoners were to be subjected to any special punishment, collective or individual?'

A report drawing on the testimony of many of these former prisoners was produced in December 1918 by the Government Committee, chaired by Sir Robert Younger, a judge of the High Court. Younger observed that: 'It is not in the great events, including at least one case of homicide, which will receive special attention on some other occasion [i.e. during a war-crimes trial], that the true significance of the German horrors is to be found, but in the petty tyranny constantly exercised, the punishment of men for so-called offences, needless restrictions and the overbearing conduct of the German administration.'

The responses from former Holzminden inmates had built up a damning case against Hauptmann Karl Niemeyer, who had repeatedly breached the accords and conventions governing the treatment of prisoners of war and was on a British 'Black List'. In January 1919, largely as a result of Younger's report, the attorney general sent a cipher telegram to the foreign secretary, Arthur Balfour, while he was in Versailles for the Peace Conference, proposing that 'As part of the terms for enlargement of armistice, a condition be inserted requiring certain enemy officers who may from time to time be named, to be handed over and placed in safe custody with a view to their being dealt with for breaches of laws of war and humanity. The first set of such names will be transmitted within a few days.'

The name of Hauptmann Karl Niemeyer was among those transmitted and attempts were made to bring him to justice but 'Milwaukee Bill' had simply disappeared. Over the next four years there were occasional reported sightings of him and conflicting rumours about what had befallen him, but in 1923 a British newspaper carried a report claiming that Niemeyer had shot himself in a Hannover restaurant. Another source stated that he had committed suicide at his flat in Dresden. However, those reports remained unconfirmed and there were subsequent claims that Niemeyer and his twin brother, Heinrich, the commandant of

Clausthal prison camp, who was also wanted for war crimes, had both escaped justice by fleeing to South America.

Whatever his ultimate fate, Karl Niemeyer's epitaph might well be the conclusion drawn by Sir Robert Younger in the section of his 1918 report dealing with 'The Treatment by the Enemy of British Officers, Prisoners of War, under the 10th (Hannover) Army Corps': 'It is to this man's cruelty and injustice that the story of Holzminden must remain a tribute . . . its coarseness and cruelty; its intolerance and oppression; its injustice and dishonesty.'

The last word on the First Great Escape should not rest with Niemeyer. As one of the escapees, James Bennett, remarked, he and his comrades, despite labouring under extreme hardships and under the most appalling conditions, 'did the impossible with dumbfounding persistence and ingenuity'. Despite the barriers placed in their way and the constant surveillance of armed guards, they had 'proved one of the great truths: that you cannot keep really determined men locked up between four walls if they really mean to get out'.

EPILOGUE

The Holzminden Dining Club

24TH JULY, 1918

HOLZMINDEN TUNNEL

20th Anniversary Dinner

at Ye Olde Cheshire Cheese, Fleet Street, London

23RD JULY, 1938

The reunion dinner of the Holzminden escapees on the twentieth anniversary of the greatest escape of the First World War.

THE VOW OF lifelong friendship that Lieutenant James Bennett had made to Lieutenant Colin Lawrence when they were both prisoners in Holzminden had an unexpected consequence almost twenty years later, when Bennett saved Lawrence from prison by standing surety for him. Lawrence faced jail after being charged with malicious wounding after a drunken brawl, but Bennett, who had read of his old comrade's plight in the newspapers, attended the court hearing. Having told the magistrates that he was sure Lawrence would never harm anyone intentionally, he pleaded for leniency for him. 'Captain Lawrence and I faced death in the war when we were forced down in a seaplane, but fortunately, after several hours in the water, we were picked up by a German submarine ... [Lawrence] was captured twice in the war and was severely wounded in the head.' As a result of Bennett's plea, magistrates merely bound Lawrence over in the sum of fifty pounds for twelve months, and advised him to 'keep away from drink'. Bennett later revealed that his old comrade had now moved to a village two hundred miles away to start a new life. 'I cannot reveal where he is. He has gone there with his small child to forget this ordeal.'

None of the intrepid trio of Cecil Blain, David Gray and Caspar Kennard lived to enjoy a peaceful old age. Cecil Blain signed up for a further term of service in the renamed Royal Air Force – his brother suggested that part of his motivation might have been the hope of encountering the Niemeyer twins after the war and exacting his vengeance upon them. When the war ended, Blain became a test pilot, but in January 1919, he was killed in a crash while testing a Sopwith Dolphin at Martlesham Heath in Suffolk. Caspar Kennard returned to Argentina after the war, where he became the manager of an *estancia*, but he was killed in a shooting accident in 1935. David Gray remained a career soldier, joining the British Expeditionary Force fighting the Bolsheviks in Russia, then returning to India where, promoted to colonel, he became commanding officer of his old Indian Army regiment, the 48th Pioneers. On the outbreak of the Second World War, he resigned his commission, applied to join the RAF as a flight lieutenant and became a squadron leader before being compulsorily retired in 1942. His appetite for action undiminished, he immediately joined the Home Guard, but during his first weekend on duty, he was run over by a lorry and killed.

The first reunion of former Holzminden prisoners had been held at the Hotel Cecil in the Strand in December 1927, with C. E. H. Rathborne, DSO and Bar, now holding the rank of group captain, presiding. Sixty-one former prisoners attended, many of them men who had taken part in the Great Escape. The 'Holzminden Dining Club' was formed five years later, in 1932, with Captain R. W. Ainsworth as president, Brian Manning as honorary treasurer and Vernon Coombs as honorary secretary, its aim being 'to maintain the fellowship formed by Officer Prisoners of War during captivity'. The following year it was extended to former prisoners from other camps and was then renamed 'The Officer Prisoners of War Dining Club'; at its peak the membership reached eighty-one men.

A film entitled *Who Goes Next?*, directed by Maurice Elvey and starring Barry K. Barnes, a fictionalized retelling of the Great Escape from Holzminden, was released in March 1938 and later that year, on Saturday, 23 July 1938, the adviser to the film, Captain Jack Shaw, who was presented to the King after the war and was now the commandant of Buckinghamshire Police, was among twenty-five men who met in Ye Olde Cheshire Cheese in Fleet Street on the twentieth anniversary of the Great Escape. They brought with them photographs and souvenirs including some of the tools used to dig the tunnel, a tongue tin that had contained compasses and wire-cutters, 'a bully beef tin, with maps and compasses, which Captain Shaw of A House brought out of Germany with him', and the football they had used in the camp; it had been signed by other British officer prisoners and presented after the Armistice to Shaw, who had been the 'Honorary Secretary of the camp football competitions'. Once more C. E. H. Rathborne – by now promoted again, to air commodore – was in the chair, and eighteen of the twenty-nine escapees were there, along with seven guests: the orderlies who had helped them escape.

Five of the original escapees had died in the intervening years and the remainder were scattered around the globe, though 'everyone within 1,000 miles of London did come, and one or two from Malaya, India and New Zealand, who happened to be on leave, were also able to be present'. Andrew Clouston was not among them. He had become a commercial pilot after the war and settled in New York, though in 1937, with his co-pilot Mrs Kirkby-Green, he set a new record for the Croydon–Cape Town–Croydon flight, covering the round trip in seventy-seven hours and forty-nine minutes.

Stanley Purves sent a telegram. An engineer before the war, he had emigrated to Australia with his wife Sybil as soon as he was discharged, and pursued his trade by working on the construction of the Sydney Harbour Bridge before moving to Tasmania, where he became general manager of the Goliath Cement Works. Another escapee sent a telegram from his 4,500-acre orange farm in South Africa, and there were others from escapees and fellow prisoners who had settled in New York City, Toronto, Vancouver, Barbados, Hong Kong and New Guinea.

Those present at the reunion dinner included Lieutenant Churchill, who was now a civil servant in Malaya; Jack Shaw; Bernard Luscombe, now a parson in Norfolk; Second Lieutenant Reginald Gough, who had become headmaster and superintendent of the East Anglian School for Partially Sighted and Deaf Children; 'a man with an advertising business'; and a 'high official' of a company in the Far East. The orderlies included a taxi driver and a hospital attendant.

The menu for the dinner – 'Subject to alteration without notice and to the parcels room not being closed as a *strafe* [punishment]' – was: 'Potage Weser [River Soup – after the River Weser to the west of Holzminden that all the escapees had had to cross to reach the Netherlands]. Côtelettes de Porc Niemeyer. Pommes Nature (very). Sauerkraut. Pie Piper. And Ersatz kaffee.'

The biggest laugh of the evening greeted the arrival of a telegram from Milwaukee, Wisconsin. It read: 'GREETINGS STOP I KNOW DAMN ALL ABOUT YOU AND YOUR DINNER STOP CHARLES NIEMEYER STOP.' The originator was unknown, but was probably Andrew Clouston, or Lieutenant J. K. Bousfield who was now the general manager of the Asiatic Petroleum Company in Hong Kong.

The full guest list was: Air Commodore C. E. H. Rathborne; Major Hugh Durnford, the former adjutant at the camp who had become a fellow of King's College, Cambridge; Lieutenant Walter Butler; Lieutenant James Bennett; Captain Bernard Luscombe; Captain John Tullis; Colonel David Gray; Captain Edgar Garland; Captain Philip Smith; Captain Colin Lawrence; Captain Lee; Captain J. W. Johnson; Lieutenant W. F. N. Churchill; Lieutenant David Wainwright; Squadron Leader Alan Shipwright; Captain

Arthur Morris; Lieutenant Vernon Coombs; Captain Brian Manning; Captain William Langren; Captain Jack Shaw; Captain Waters; and the seven orderlies: G. E. Razey; F. E Sidwell; E. G. Harrison; Arthur Coleman; Ernest Collinson; L. W. Saunders; and T. E. Book.

Twenty years later, a dozen men, including Walter Butler, Brian Manning, Vernon Coombs, James Bennett, W. F. N. Churchill, John Tullis, William Langren, Philip Smith, Bernard Luscombe and G. E. Razey, attended what proved to be the last reunion of the Holzminden Great Escapees, though the last survivor, James Bennett, remained an active member of the Officer Prisoners of War Dining Club until 1977 when, then aged eighty-five, ill-health prevented him attending a dinner to commemorate the Golden Jubilee of the first reunion of the Holzminden Great Escapees. A dozen members of the Officer Prisoners of War Dining Club, also all over eighty, were present, but their advancing years meant that it was the last time they met.

The two *Kasernen* of Holzminden prison camp and the *Spielplatz* where *Appel* was called are still standing, just off Grimmenstein on the outskirts of Holzminden – though a third, more modern, building has been constructed between them. The old prison camp remains in military use as part of a base operated by the *Bundeswehr* (German Army). Once in open country, it has slowly been swallowed up by the outskirts of what is now the substantial industrial town of Holzminden.

EPILOGUE

The bean field where the tunnellers broke the surface is now a sports field encircled by an athletics track, but just beyond Liebigstrasse on the eastern perimeter of the base there are still allotments and fields of crops, just as there were when the First Great Escape was launched on the night of 23 July 1918.

ACKNOWLEDGEMENTS

My grateful thanks for their professionalism and enthusiasm to the staff of the Special Collections and Liddle Collection at the Brotherton Library, University of Leeds: Chris Sheppard, Richard Davies, Sharon Connell, Liza Giffen, Richard High, Katja Airaksinen, Kasia Drozdziak, Paul Whittle, Sian Prosser, Karen Mee, Tsendpurev Tsegmid, Jen Fox and Fiona Marshall.

My thanks also to the staff of: the Imperial War Museum's Manuscripts, Printed Books, Photographs, Sound and Exhibits Collections, and the Research Room; the National Archives at Kew; the British Library's Humanities, Rare Books and Map Rooms, the Newspaper Section at Colindale, and the British Library's out-station at Boston Spa; and the Australian War Memorial at Canberra.

I'm grateful to Christian Kuhrt for the translation of German documents, to Kevin, Carole and the staff at the Grove Bookshop, Ilkley, and to Adam Yates and Andrew Sharpe at Grove Rare Books, Bolton Abbey, for sourcing obscure titles for me.

My thanks as always to my agents Mark Lucas and Alice Saunders in London, Kim Witherspoon and David Forrer in New York, and the remarkable team at my publishers, Transworld: Bill Scott-Kerr, Larry Finlay, Marianne Velmans,

Emma Buckley, Helen Edwards, Richard Shailer, Polly Osborn, Sheila Lee, Phil Lord, Katrina Whone, Vivien Garrett and Hazel Orme.

Every effort has been made to contact copyright holders, but the author will be pleased to hear from the descendants or administrators of any copyright holders he has been unable to trace.

BIBLIOGRAPHY

DOCUMENTS

British Library
Maps
X.5292 Purves, Stanley, Escape map, Dassel to Bielefeld, Holzminden, Germany, 1918
X.5293 Purves, Stanley, Escape map of the Munster Region, Holzminden, Germany, 1918

Imperial War Museum
Documents
2170 Private Papers of A. Boyle
P 318 Private Papers of Group Captain L. G. Nixon
P 425 Private Papers of Major M. R. D. Pannett
P 430 Private Papers of Lieutenant G. W. Armstrong
P 438 Private Papers of Private R. Preston
67/392/1 Private Papers of Lieutenant F. N. Insoll
73/175/1 Private Papers of Captain Douglas Lyall Grant
73/181/1 Diary – unknown author
73/182/1 Private Papers of Lieutenant N. A. Birks
76/171/1 Private Papers of J. N. Dykes
76/206/1 Private Papers of Corporal A. Speight
79/12/1 Private Papers of Lieutenant Colonel N. MacLeod
80/32/2 Folder 10, Private Papers of Colonel Sir Geoffrey Christie-Miller, KCB DSO MC TD DL, Letter from Captain E. Christie-Miller, March 1918
82/35/1 Private Papers of Lieutenant Colonel A. E. Haig
83/11/1 Private Papers of Lieutenant W. C. Blain

86/62/1 Private Papers of Captain p. H. B. Lyon MC

87/62/1 Private Papers of Lieutenant Colonel R. J. Clarke

98/19/1 Private Papers of Captain J. S. Walter

Misc 15/316 *A Parting Word* – pamphlet containing a farewell message to prisoners of war.

Misc 153/2356 Anonymous Prisoner of War Journal 1917–19

Printed Books

K 90/2223 Collection of Newscuttings Relating to Major Jack William Shaw's Experiences as a Prisoner of War

K 90/2421 Whale, J., 'Our Life at Holzminden', in *Wide World Magazine*, July 1919, 314–19

Photographs

6008-01 Manning, B.

Q 69484 Holzminden PoW Camp; tunnel used to escape after it had been discovered and dug up, July 1918

Q 69485 View from Barracks Houses A and B, winter 1917/18

Q 69486 The larger Barracks House, B

Q 694847 Barracks House A

Q 694848 Hauptmann Niemeyer, commandant of Holzminden Camp

7902–06 Nixon, L. G.

HU 36567 Escape tunnel from Holzminden Prisoner of War Camp in Germany, July 1918, showing a German prison guard and camp inmates

8010–30 Armstrong, G. L. W. (Lt Col the Rev)

Q 111311–Q 111327 Views of the prisoner-of-war camps at Trier and Holzminden in Germany 1917–18

9403–03 Insoll, F. N.

HU 64562 Holzminden Prisoner-of-War Camp: Officers' Quarters

HU 94563 Holzminden Prisoner-of-War Camp: British prisoners leaving the camp

HU 64564 Holzminden Prisoner-of-War Camp: British prisoners boarding a train
HU 64565 Holzminden Prisoner-of-War Camp: British prisoners boarding a train

Sound
23157 Mapplebeck, Tom, Reel 2
6687 Hurd, Edward, Reel 3
9964 Coombs, Vernon C., Reels 2, 3, 4

Exhibits
EPH 809 Shaving brush, with concealed information, associated with Major J. W. Shaw
EPH 810 Tin of 'Armour Tongue' (and its escape-related contents) associated with Major J. W. Shaw
EPH 813 and 814 Conductor's batons used by Major J. W. Shaw during an escape attempt
EPH 816 Leather football associated with Major J. W. Shaw
EPH 828 Miniature brush and comb set associated with Major J. W. Shaw
EPH 3681 Escape equipment compass (and accessories) associated with Captain E. W. Leggatt
EPH 3682 Panama hat associated with Captain E. W. Leggatt
EPH 3683 Pair of moccasins associated with Captain E. W. Leggatt
EPH 3684 German battery-operated electric torch associated with Captain E. W. Leggatt

Liddle Collection, University of Leeds
ADD 001 David Russell Morrish papers
AIR 005 Joseph Martin Allen papers
AIR 344 Harold Wilfred (Homer) White papers
C-60 HAR Frederick William Harvey, *Comrades in Captivity*
GS 1449 W. R. Shaw papers
POW 002 Arthur Norman Barlow papers

POW 003 Norman A. Birks papers
POW 004 J. H. Birkinshaw papers
POW 016 V. C. Coombs papers
POW 029 Reginald Gough papers
POW 035 Holzminden Prisoner-of-War Camp
POW 036 Kenneth Hooper papers
POW 043 L. McNaught-Davis papers, 'Revelations From Behind Barbed Wire'
POW 046 Richard Milward papers
POW 049 Robert Paddison papers
POW 056 Recollections relating to PoWs and PoW camps
POW 072 Officer Prisoners of War Dining Club archive
RUH 20 Wallace Ellison papers

Sound
Tape 643 B. G. Austen recollections
Tape 688 J. Bennett recollections

National Archives
AIR 76/41 Blain, C. W.
FO 383/157 Germany: Prisoners: Reports on camps at Scheuen (Celle), Soltau, Holzminden, Magdeburg, Schloss Celle, Stadtvogtei (Berlin) and Cologne (Köln)
FO 383/158 Germany: Prisoners
FO 383/200 Germany: Prisoners
FO 383/201 Germany: Prisoners
FO 383/206 Germany: Prisoners
FO 383/210 Germany: Prisoners
FO 383/272 Germany: Prisoners, article from *Pall Mall Gazette*, 30 August 1917 on conditions for prisoners in labour camps. Transfer of British officer prisoners from Schwarmstedt to Holzminden Camp
FO 383/273 Germany: Prisoners, transfer of British officers from   Schwarmstedt to Holzminden
FO 383/274 Germany: Prisoners: Note Verbale, Berlin, 13

October 1917; Enquiry about the imprisonment of certain officers at Ströhen

FO 383/275 Germany: Prisoners: Reports of visits of inspection to the following internment camps: Holzminden; Extracts from statements by various British officers on conditions in camps under the jurisdiction of General von Hanisch of the Tenth Army Corps; Captain Tollemache: information in a coded letter on conditions at Holzminden Camp

FO 383/324 Germany (British Civilians)

FO 383/381 Germany: Prisoners

FO 383/390 Germany: Prisoners: Private A. G. Blake, No. 9649, 3rd Batt. Canadians

FO 383/398 Germany: Prisoners: Report on Treatment of British Prisoners of War in Germany; 2902 Statement by an officer prisoner, recently arrived in Switzerland, regarding Treatment of British Officers Interned in Germany; 2148 Report by Netherlands Legation, 4/12/17; 35477 Major A. E. Haig, Appendix K; 51790 report by Captain Christie-Miller

FO 383/399 Germany: Prisoners: Report on the Treatment by the Enemy of British Officers, Prisoners of War, under the 10th (Hannover) Army Corps; 'Niemeyer of Clausthal'; 'Niemeyer of Holzminden'; Colonel C. E. H. Rathborne; 108720 Appendix I

FO 383/400 Germany: Prisoners

FO 383/401 Germany: Prisoners

FO 383/414 Germany: Prisoners

FO 383/436 Germany: Prisoners

FO 383/440 Germany: Prisoners

FO 383/442 Germany: Prisoners: Letter requesting information on Lieutenant Leslie Holman, interned at Holzminden prisoner-of-war camp

FO 383/448 Russia: Prisoners

FO 383/467 Miscellaneous (General): Prisoners

FO 383/470 Constitution of the Committee on the Treatment by the Enemy of British Prisoners of War

FO 383/491 Germany: Prisoners: Response of Prussian Ministry of War to Allegations of Ill Treatment; Recommendation by Attorney General to Mr Balfour

FO 383/509 Germany: Prisoners: Lieutenant Andrew Clouston of Holzminden prisoner-of-war camp

HO 45/10763/270829 Committee on the Treatment by the Enemy of British Prisoners of War, 1914–19

WO 161/96/86, 970–972 Statement by Captain W. Loder Symonds

WO 161/96/89, 977–978 Statement by Second Lieutenant John Glover Hugo Frew

WO 161/96/114 Statement by Captain Edward Wilmer Leggatt

WO 161/96/118 Statement by Colonel C. E. H. Rathborne

WO 161/96/136, 1128–1134 Statement by Lieutenant F. J. Ortweiler

WO 161/97/39, 179–184 Statement by Surgeon Probationer Joe Alexander, Royal Naval Reserve

WO 161/97/45, 195–200 Statement by Captain Walter Reuben Wigmore Haight

Australian War Memorial
Canberra
PO2983.002 Photograph by John Richard Cash

RELAWM16875 Small escape compass used during escape from Holzminden PoW camp: Captain S. S. B. Purves, Royal Air Force

PERIODICALS

'Americans Beyond Treves', *The Times*, 4 December 1918, 8

Answers, 11 July 1938

'Beaten With Rifles', *Pall Mall Gazette*, 30 August 1917

'Britain to Punish German Fiends', *Daily Sketch*, 28 November 1918, 10

'British Prisoners', *The Times*, 24 October 1918, 3

'British Prisoners Dig Out', *New York Times*, 7 August 1918

'Candlelight Hero Recalls the Big Day', *Sunday Times*, 30 October 1977

Canfield, Kevin, 'James Whale: A New World of Gods and Monsters', in *Film Quarterly*, Vol. 58, No. 4, Summer 2005, 64–5

'Captain Jack Shaw of Marlow', *Bucks Free Press*, 5 June 1931

'Cologne Before the British Entry', *The Times*, 13 December 1918, 7

Cook, Tim, 'The Politics of Surrender: Canadian Soldiers and the Killing of Prisoners in the First World War', in *Journal of Military History*, Vol. 70, No. 3, 2006, 637–65

Coombs, V. C., 'Sixty Years On', in *RAF Quarterly*, Summer 1976

'Court Circular', *The Times*, 25 July 1938, 15

Davis, Gerald H., 'Prisoners of War and Communism: Review of Leidinger, Hannes; Moritz, Verena, Gefangenschaft, Revolution, Heimkehr: Die Bedeutung der Kriegsgefangenenproblematik für die Geschichte des Kommunismus in Mittel- und Osteuropa 1917–1920', in *HABSBURG, H-Net Reviews*, March 2004

Davis, Gerald H., 'Prisoners of War in Twentieth Century War Economies', in *Journal of Contemporary History*, Vol. 12, No. 4, October 1977, 623–34

'Food for Our Men in the Hands of the Huns', *Daily Sketch*, 22 November 1918, 2

'Foodless Prisoners: British Fiat to Germans', *Daily Sketch*, 21 November, 1918, 3

Frankfurter Zeitung, 31 December 1917

'German Cruelty', *Daily Sketch*, 29 November 1918, 10

'The German War Book: A Military Code', *New York Times*, 4 April 1915, BR125

'Goodbye to the Worst Camp in Germany', *Daily Sketch*, 13 January 1919, 6

'Haig to the Rescue', *Daily Sketch*, 23 November 1918, 3

'Heroes of the War's Greatest Escape', *News Chronicle*, 25 July 1938

'Holzminden Tunnel Reunion', *Sunday Express*, 8 May 1938

'"Human Moles" Who Bored their Way to Liberty', *Bucks Free Press*, 22 July 1938

'Huns and Our Prisoners', *Daily Mirror*, 25 October 1918, 2

'Huns' Last Crime the Greatest', *Daily Sketch*, 20 November 1918, 2

Illustrated Sporting & Dramatic News, 30 June 1917

Keeling, E. H., 'Prisoners and Parole', *The Times*, 22 May 1944, 5

MacArthur, R., *Occasional Review*, No. 1, 28 August 1918, Holzminden, Germany (PoW newspaper – only issue ever produced)

Mackenzie, S. P., 'Review of Richard B. Speed, Prisoners, Diplomats and the Great War', in *International History Review*, Vol. 13, No. 1, February 1991, 178–80

'Memories of Their Tunnel Escape', *Evening News*, 2 May 1938

'Notes', *Nature*, Vol. 98, 26 October 1916, 152–6

'Obituary, Air Commodore C. E. H. Rathborne', *The Times*, 29 December 1943, 6

'Over the Wire', London Diary, *The Times*, 2 April 1980, 16

'Personality Parade', *Daily Mirror*, 19 May 1938, 14

Phillimore, George G., 'Some Suggestions for a Draft Code for the Treatment of Prisoners of War', in *Transactions of the Grotius Society*, Vol. 6, 1920, 25–34

Phillimore, George G., and Bellot, Hugh H. L., 'Treatment of Prisoners of War', in *Transactions of the Grotius Society*, Vol. 5, 1919, 47–64

'Prison Commander's Fear', *New York Times*, 15 December 1918

'Prisoners at Holzminden', *The Times*, 13 March 1918, 5

'Saved War Comrade from Gaol', *Daily Mirror*, 13 January 1937, 2

'Search for British Prisoners', *The Times*, 16 January 1919, 7

Spoerer, Mark, 'The Mortality of Allied Prisoners of War and

Belgian Civilian Deportees in German Custody during the First World War', in *Population Studies*, Vol. 60, No. 2, July 2006, 121–36

Strauss, Frederick, 'The Food Problem in the German War Economy', in *Quarterly Journal of Economics*, Vol. 55, No. 3, May 1941, 364–412

Sunday Dispatch, 24 July 1938

Sunday Express, 24 July 1938

Sunday Graphic and Sunday News, 24 July 1938

'Tell of Tyranny in Prison Camps', *New York Times*, 6 December 1918

'The Torture of British Prisoners', *Daily Sketch*, 27 November 1918, 11

'375,000 Austrians Have Died in Siberia', *New York Times*, 28 January 1920, 19

'Torture of Our Officers', *The Times*, 5 December 1918, 9

'Tortured in German Salt and Coal Mines', *Daily Sketch*, 19 November 1918, 3

'The Tunnel to Freedom', *Daily Sketch*, 18 December 1918, 1

'2 Hun Brutes Who Must Be Tried', *Daily Sketch*, 5 December 1918

Vance, Jonathan F., 'The War behind the Wire: The Battle to Escape from a German Prison Camp', in *Journal of Contemporary History*, Vol. 28, No. 4, October 1993, 675–93

Whale, Lieutenant James, 'Our Life at Holzminden', in *Wide World Magazine*, July 1919, 314–19

BOOKS

Ackerley, Captain J. R., 'The Grim Game of Escape', in *Tunnelling to Freedom*, Dover Publications, Mineola, New York, 2004

Armstrong, H. C., *Escape!*, New York, 1935

Bass, Gary Jonathan, *Stay the Hand of Vengeance: The Politics of*

War Crimes Tribunals, Princeton University Press, Princeton, New Jersey, 2002

Bills, Leslie William, *A Medal for Life: The Biography of Captain William Leefe Robinson, VC*, Spellmount, Tunbridge Wells, 1990

Boden, Anthony, *F. W. Harvey: Soldier, Poet*, Sutton Publishing, Stroud, 1998

Caunter, John Alan Lyde, *13 Days: The Chronicle of an Escape from a German Prison*, London, 1918

Clarke, A. H. F., *To Kiel in the German Raider Wolf and After*, Colombo, 1920

Dennett, Carl P., *Prisoners of the Great War: Authoritative Statement of Conditions in the Prison Camps of Germany*, Boston, 1919

Durnford, Hugh, *The Tunnellers of Holzminden*, Cambridge University Press, Cambridge, 1920

Ellis, John, *Eye Deep in Hell: Trench Warfare in World War I*, Penguin, London, 2002

Escapers All: Being the Personal Narratives of Fifteen Escapers from War-Time Prison Camps, 1914–1918, London, 1932

Ferguson, Niall, *The Pity of War*, Basic Books, New York, 1999

Garrett, Richard, *P.O.W.: The Uncivil Face of War*, David & Charles, Newton Abbot, 1981

Georgiades, p. A., *Rapport-Mémoire de M. p. A. Georgiades*, Paris, 1919

Grinnell-Milne, Duncan, *An Escaper's Log*, London, 1926

Grosser Generalstab (Morgan, John Hartman, ed./trans.), *War Book of the German General Staff*, Stackpole Books, Mechanicsburg, Pennsylvania, 2005

Hansard, 5 February 1918, London, 1918

Harding, Geoffrey, *Escape Fever*, London, 1932

Hardy, J. L., *I Escape!*, Bodley Head, London, 1927

Harrison, M. C. C., and Cartwright, H. A., *Within Four Walls*, Penguin, Harmondsworth, 1940

Harvey, F. W., *Comrades in Captivity*, London, 1920

BIBLIOGRAPHY

Hervey, H. E., *Cage-Birds*, London, 1940

Herwig, Holger H., *The First World War: Germany and Austria-Hungary, 1914–18*, Hodder Arnold, London, 1997

Hinz, Uta, *Gefangen im Grossen Krieg: Kriegsgefangenschaft in Deutschland* [Captured in the Great War: War Captivity in Germany], 1914–1921, Klartext, Essen, 2006

Horrocks, Sir Brian, *A Full Life*, Fontana, London, 1962

Jackson, Robert, *The Prisoners: 1914–18*, Routledge, London, 1989

Ludendorff, Erich, *My War Memories*, New York, 1920

Lyon, Bryce, and Lyon, Mary (eds), *The Journal de Guerre of Henri Pirenne*, North-Holland Publishing, New York, 1976

Moynihan, Michael (ed.), *Black Bread and Barbed Wire*, Leo Cooper, London, 1978

Reports by the Joint War Committee and the Joint War Finance Committee of the British Red Cross Society and the Order of St John of Jerusalem on Voluntary Aid Rendered to the Sick and Wounded at Home and Abroad and to British Prisoners of War, 1914–1919, HMSO, London, 1921

Rimell, Ray, *The Airship VC: The Life of Captain William Leefe Robinson*, Aston Publishing, Bourne End, 1989

Spaight, James M., *Air Power and War Rights*, Longmans Green, London, 1947

Speed, Richard B., *Prisoners, Diplomats and the Great War: A Study in the Diplomacy of Captivity*, Greenwood Press, New York, 1990

Thorn, John C., *Three Years a Prisoner in Germany*, Vancouver, 1919

Vance, Jonathan F. (ed.), *Encyclopedia of Prisoners of War and Internment*, ABC–CLIO, Santa Barbara, California, 2000

War Office, *Statistics of the Military Effort of the British Empire during the Great War, 1914–1920*, London, 1922

Warburton, Ernest, *Behind Boche Bars*, London, ND

Waugh, Alec, *The Prisoners of Mainz*, London, 1919

Whitehouse, Arch, *The Years of the Sky Kings*, Award Books, New York, 1964

Winchester, Barry, *Beyond the Tumult*, Allison & Busby, London, 1971

Wingfield, Lawrence A., 'Hazards of Escape', in *Escapers All: Being the Personal Narratives of Fifteen Escapers from War-Time Prison Camps, 1914–1918*, London, 1932

1899 Convention for the Pacific Settlement of International Disputes, The Hague, 1899

1907 Convention for the Pacific Settlement of International Disputes, The Hague 1907

WEBSITES

Letter from Major M. R. Chidson regarding exploits of Lieutenant H.W. Medlicott in Germany, www.medlicott.eu/HEM_files/7_HWMedlicott. html

The Avalon Project: Laws of War: Laws and Customs of War on Land (Hague II); 29 July 1899 http://avalon.law.yale.edu/19th_century/hague 02.asp#art4

The Avalon Project: Laws of War: Laws and Customs of War on Land (Hague IV); 18 October 1907 http://avalon.law.yale.edu/20th_century/ hague04.asp

Essay on Prisoners www.iwmcollections.org.uk/prisoners/essay.php

www.royal.gov.uk/ImagesandBroadcasts/TheQueenandtechnol ogy.aspx

www.h-net.org/reviews/showrev.php?id=8975

www.worcestershireregiment.com/wr.php?main=inc/vc_w_l_ robinson_ page8

http://inthefootsteps.org.uk/Articles/1914- 18GreatWar/Holzminden Tunnellers.htm

http://1914-1918.invisionzone.com/forums/index.php? showtopic=104463

BIBLIOGRAPHY

http://brendadougallmerriman.blogspot.com/2008/11/
  remembrance.html
http://cas.awm.gov.au/item/RELAWM16875/
www.redcross.org.uk/About-us/Who-we-are/History-and-
  origin

NOTES

1. NO MERCY WILL BE SHOWN

p. 20 'Head counts': Gerald H. Davis, 'Prisoners of War in Twentieth Century War Economies', p. 626.

p. 20 'Between 7', '1.8 million': ibid., pp. 623, 629.

p. 20 '*Ad hoc* transfer': Gerald H. Davis, 'Prisoners of War and Communism'.

p. 20 '92,000': Niall Ferguson, *The Pity of War*, pp. 368–9.

p. 20 '191,652': Essay on Prisoners, http://www.iwmcollections. org.uk/prisoners/essay.php

p. 21 'Practically all': S. p. Mackenzie, 'Review of Richard B. Speed, Prisoners, Diplomats and the Great War', p. 179.

p. 22 'In view of': George G. Phillimore and Hugh H. L. Bellot, 'Treatment of Prisoners of War', pp. 60–1.

p. 22 'Sixty million': Gerald H. Davis, 'Prisoners of War in Twentieth Century War Economies', p. 626.

p. 23 'By 1916': Mark Spoerer, 'The Mortality of Allied Prisoners of War . . .' p. 123.

p. 23 'Purposeful and regular': Gerald H. Davis, 'Prisoners of War in Twentieth Century War Economies', p. 626.

p. 23 'Utilize their labour': 1899 Convention for the Pacific Settlement of International Disputes, quoted in Phillimore and Bellot, 'Treatment of Prisoners of War', pp. 47–9, 55.

p. 24 'Interpretations of': Gerald H. Davis, 'Prisoners of War in Twentieth Century War Economies', p. 627.

p. 24 'Vested interests': ibid.

p. 24 'The tariff': 1899 Convention for the Pacific Settlement of International Disputes, quoted in Phillimore and Bellot, 'Treatment of Prisoners of War', pp. 47–9, 55.

p. 24–5 'nine hundred thousand': Davis, 'Prisoners of War in Twentieth Century War Economies', pp. 628–9.

p. 25 'Utmost importance': Erich Ludendorff, *My War Memories*, p. 336.

p. 25 'An act of grace', 'Strict rule': Phillimore and Bellot, 'Treatment of Prisoners of War', pp. 47–8.

p. 26 'In the power': 1899 Convention for the Pacific Settlement of International Disputes, quoted in ibid., pp. 47–9.

p. 26 'Article 4' etc.: http://avalon.law.yale.edu/20th_century/hague04.asp

p. 29 '*Kriegsbrauch*': Grosser Generalstab, *War Book of the German General Staff*, pp. 21–2.

p. 30 'As soon as': Richard Garrett, *P.O.W.*, p. 96.

p. 30 'The German Government': NA FO 383/274 Note Verbale, Berlin, 13 October 1917.

p. 31 'Dr Josef Goebbels': Garrett, *P.O.W.*, p. 96.

p. 32 'The moment of greatest': *cf.* for example, Tim Cook, 'The politics of surrender', pp. 637–65.

p. 32 'No man in this': General Harper, quoted in John Ellis, *Eye Deep in Hell*, p. 78.

p. 32 'It is not reasonable': Phillimore and Bellot, 'Treatment of Prisoners of War', p. 48.

p. 33 'Between the place': J. L Hardy, *I Escape!*, p. xi.

p. 33 'It was not an uncommon': IWM 83/11/1 Papers of

Lieutenant W. C. Blain, p. 1.

p. 33 'Shockingly high': cf. Ferguson, *Pity of War*, pp. 368–9.

p. 34 'Fifty-two per thousand': Gary Bass, *Stay the Hand of Vengeance*, p. 107.

p. 34 'UK civilian death rate': War Office, *Statistics of the Military Effort of the British Empire*.

p. 34 '11,978': Mark Spoerer, 'The Mortality of Allied Prisoners of War . . .' pp. 125–9.

p. 34 'Such statistics': '375,000 Austrians Have Died in Siberia', *New York Times*, 28 January 1920, p. 19.

p. 35 'We were surprised': Garrett, *P.O.W.*, p. 94.

p. 35 'At least a thousand': Robert Jackson, *The Prisoners 1914–18*, pp. 53–4.

p. 36 'Should I consider': Garrett, *P.O.W.*, p. 94.

p. 36 'No guard is sent': IWM 73/175/1 Papers of Captain Douglas Lyall Grant.

p. 36 'Having gleaned': Hardy, *I Escape!*, p. 119.

p. 37 'With a little cardboard': M. C. C. Harrison, and H. A. Cartwright, *Within Four Walls*, p. 171.

p. 38 'Died from starvation': 'Britain to Punish German Fiends', *Daily Sketch*, 28 November 1918.

p. 38 'As thick as': '2 Hun Brutes Who Must Be Tried', *Daily Sketch*, 5 December 1918.

p. 39 'When I got back home': Liddle GS 1449 W. R. Shaw papers.

p. 39 'A Prussian of': Geoffrey Harding, *Escape Fever*, p. 77.

2. THE GERMAN BLACK HOLE

p. 43 'A most lovely': NA FO 383/399 Germany: Prisoners: Report on the Treatment by the Enemy of British Officers, Prisoners of War, under the 10th (Hannover) Army Corps.

p. 44 'Up to seven hundred': IWM 98/19/1 Papers of Captain J. S. Walter.

p. 45 'Neutral ground': IWM P425 Papers of Major M. R. D. Pannett.

p. 45 'Dogs trained to attack': NA FO 383/399 Report on the Treatment by the Enemy of British Officers, Prisoners of War, under the 10th (Hannover) Army Corps.

p. 45 'From the top': Letter from Major M. R. Chidson regarding exploits of Lieutenant H. W. Medlicott in Germany, http://www.medlicott.eu/ HEM_files/7_HWMedlicott.html

p. 46 'Considerable thickness': Liddle POW 029 Reginald Gough papers.

p. 46 'Brilliantly illuminated': A. H. F. Clarke, *To Kiel in the German Raider Wolf and After*, p. 138.

p. 46 'Far bank': Liddle POW 046 Richard Milward papers.

p. 46 'The country is': IWM 73/175/1 Papers of Captain Douglas Lyall Grant.

p. 47 'Red roofs': IWM P318 Watercolour, in Papers of Group Captain L. G. Nixon.

p. 48 'Twenty-two feet': NA WO 161/96/114 Statement by Captain Edward Wilmer Leggatt.

p. 48 'A washstand': IWM 73/175/1 Papers of Captain Douglas Lyall Grant.

p. 48 'Abominable': NA WO 161/96/136, Lieutenant F. J. Ortweiler, pp. 1131–3.

p. 48 'Use of hay': NA FO 383/399 Report on the Treatment by the Enemy of British Officers, Prisoners of War, under the 10th (Hannover) Army Corps.

p. 48 'The pillows': NA FO 383/398 Germany: Prisoners: Report on Treatment of British Prisoners of War in Germany.

p. 48 'Intervals that exceeded two': NA FO 383/399 Report on the Treatment by the Enemy of British Officers, Prisoners of War, under the 10th (Hannover) Army Corps.

p. 48 'Blankets were never': NA WO 161/96/136, Lieutenant F. J. Ortweiler, pp. 1131–3.

p. 48 'A big, bare barn': Liddle POW 043 L. McNaught-Davis papers, 'Revelations From Behind Barbed Wire', p. 47.

p. 49 'Will be shot at': IWM 73/175/1 Papers of Captain Douglas Lyall Grant.

p. 49 'Their duties': *Sunday Express*, 8 May 1938.

p. 49 'Resembling a badly-cut': Clarke, *To Kiel*, p. 139.

p. 49 'KG': Richard Garrett, *P.O.W.*, p. 104.

p. 49 'Old pieces of coloured': Liddle Tape 688 J. Bennett recollections.

p. 50 'Within easy reach', 'Tidying and dusting': IWM 76/171/1 Papers of J. N. Dykes.

p. 51 'Via Dolorosa': Michael Moynihan (ed.), *Black Bread and Barbed Wire*, p. x.

pp. 51 'So far as I was concerned', 'Making these autocratic': IWM 76/171/1 Papers of J. N. Dykes.

p. 52 'Death rates': NA FO 383/390 Germany: Prisoners: Private A. G. Blake, No. 9649, 3rd Batt. Canadians.

p. 52 'Our treatment': IWM 80/32/2 Folder 10, Letter from Edward Christie-Miller.

p. 52 'When we fall down': 'Beaten With Rifles', *Pall Mall Gazette*, 30 August 1917.

p. 52 'Private Barry': IWM 80/32/2 Folder 10, Letter from Edward Christie-Miller.

p. 53 'Lashed to a furnace': NA FO 383/390 Private A. G. Blake.

p. 53 'Beaten to death': IWM Misc 153/2356 Anonymous Prisoner of War Journal 1917–19.

p. 53 'Their condition': IWM 73/181/1 Diary – Unknown Author.

p. 53 'The orderlies': IWM 76/171/1 Papers of J. N. Dykes.

p. 54 'Buckets at night': NA FO 383/275 Reports of visits of inspection to the following internment camps: Holzminden.

p. 54 'Served out on the floor': NA FO 383/399 Report on the Treatment by the Enemy of British Officers, Prisoners of War, under the 10th (Hannover) Army Corps.

p. 54 'Teeming with rats': James Whale, 'Our Life at Holzminden', p. 316.

p. 54 'Utterly impregnable': *Sunday Express*, 8 May 1938.

p. 54 'Most closely guarded and escape-proof': Liddle Tape 688 J. Bennett recollections.

p. 54 'Hellminden': Anthony Boden, *F. W. Harvey: Soldier, Poet*, p. 204.

p. 54 'German black hole': 'Goodbye to the Worst Camp in Germany', *Daily Sketch*, 13 January 1919, p. 6.

p. 54 'This hole': IWM P430 Papers of Lieutenant G. W. Armstrong.

p. 54 'Dangerous cases': Liddle Tape 688 J. Bennett recollections.

p. 55 'Twenty separate': *Sunday Express*, 8 May 1938.

3. MILWAUKEE BILL

p. 59 '560', Liddle POW 036, Box 1, Major A. E. Haig, 'Report on Treatment in Germany', in Kenneth Hooper papers.

p. 59 'It was rather stupid': IWM 67/392/1 Papers of Lieutenant F. N. Insoll.

p. 60 'Quite comfortable', 'Caused the Hun', 'Subsequently we rejoined': IWM 73/175/1 Papers of Captain Douglas Lyall Grant.

p. 61 'Bury your notes': Hugh Durnford, *The Tunnellers of Holzminden*, p. 17.

p. 61 'German marks', 'Who spoke good': Liddle POW 043 'Revelations From Behind Barbed Wire', p. 45.

p. 61 'Whether this was': IWM 73/175/1 Papers of Captain Douglas Lyall Grant.

p. 62 'A band of Landworms': Ernest Warburton, *Behind Boche Bars*, p. 100.

p. 62 'The hidden treasure': IWM 73/175/1 Papers of Captain Douglas Lyall Grant.

p. 62 'Two thousand marks': Durnford, *The Tunnellers*, p. 17.

p. 62 'Presumably after': Liddle POW 002, Box 1, Arthur Norman Barlow papers.

p. 62 'Managed to pull': IWM 73/175/1 Papers of Captain Douglas Lyall Grant.

p. 63 'Handed a metal': Geoffrey Harding, *Escape Fever*, p. 78.

p. 63 'Henceforth by this': Liddle POW 043, 'Revelations', p. 45.

p. 63 'A civilian cap': John C. Thorn, *Three Years a Prisoner in Germany,* p. 42.

p. 63 'Removed the heel': IWM K90/2223 Collection of Newscuttings Relating to Major Jack William Shaw's Experiences as a Prisoner of War.

p. 63 'Neat sailer': *Illustrated Sporting & Dramatic News,* 30 June 1917.

p. 63 'Prominent oarsman': *Bucks Free Press,* 5 June 1931.

p. 63 'Gifted amateur musician': IWM 813 and 814 Conductor's batons used by Major J. W. Shaw.

p. 64 'Contains the names': Liddle GS 1449 W. R. Shaw papers.

pp. 64–5 'Dragged out', 'The English are sending', 'Best of luck', 'Wasn't very pleased': ibid.

p. 65 'Twenty-two men', 'A battered trunk': IWM Sound Archive 23157 Mapplebeck, Tom, Reel 2.

p. 66 'A friendly, if over-familiar', 'So now, yentlemen': Durnford, *The Tunnellers,* pp. 37, 19.

p. 66 '*Ersatz* coffee': Liddle ADD 001 David Russell Morrish papers.

p. 66 'The burnt malt': IWM P438, Papers of Private R. Preston.

p. 66 'The genial Karl': Durnford, *The Tunnellers,* p. 20.

p. 67 'These are not': ibid.

p. 67 'From half to': Sir Brian Horrocks, *A Full Life,* p. 21.

p. 67 'Sat comfortably': NA FO 383/399 Germany: Prisoners: Report on the Treatment by the Enemy of British Officers, Prisoners of War, under the 10th (Hannover) Army Corps.

p. 68 'Eight days', solitary': Harding, *Escape Fever,* pp. 87–8.

p. 68 'An unreasonable': NA FO 383/399 Report on the Treatment by the Enemy of British Officers, Appendix I.

p. 68 'The Pig of Hannover': 'Tell of Tyranny in Prison Camp', *New York Times,* 6 December 1918.

p. 68 'Specially bitter': NA FO 383/399 Report on the Treatment by the Enemy of British Officers, 'Niemeyer of Clausthal'.

p. 68 'Reputation as a strafer': NA FO 383/398 Report on Treatment of British Prisoners of War in Germany.

p. 68–9 'There were no Allied': IWM 73/175/1 Papers of Captain Douglas Lyall Grant.

p. 69 'A reign of terror': NA FO 383/398, 2902 Statement by an officer prisoner, recently arrived in Switzerland, regarding Treatment of British Officers Interned in Germany.

p. 69 'An organized system': NA FO 383/399 Report on the Treatment by the Enemy of British Officers.

p. 70 'The Terrible Twins': Barry Winchester, *Beyond the Tumult*, p. 65.

p. 70 'Three such cruel': NA FO 383/399 Report on the Treatment by the Enemy of British Officers, 'Niemeyer of Clausthal'.

p. 70 'Whether from accident': ibid.

p. 70 'Shriek, quivering': NA FO 383/398 Report on Treatment of British Prisoners of War in Germany.

p. 71 'Dogs and pig-dogs': NA FO 383/399 Report on the Treatment by the Enemy of British Officers.

p. 71 'I am hoping': 'Tell of Tyranny', *New York Times*, 6 December 1918.

p. 71 'Were at a perpetual': Liddle POW 003 Norman A. Birks papers.

p. 71 'Whenever he addressed': Durnford, *The Tunnellers*, p. 25.

p. 72 'You dare to': NA HO 45/10763/270829 Committee on the Treatment by the Enemy of British Prisoners of War.

p. 72 'England is not Germany': Durnford, *The Tunnellers*, pp. 26–7.

p. 72 'The worst feature': Letter to Miss Morrison from Lieutenant F. Robinson, The Royal Fusiliers, 18 April 1918, IWM 87/62/1 Papers of Lieutenant Colonel R. J. Clarke.

p. 72 'A kindly old': Durnford, *The Tunnellers*, p. 18.

p. 72 'All right, but': IWM 73/175/1 Papers of Captain Douglas Lyall Grant.

p. 72 'Put things right': NA HO 45/10763/270829 Committee on the Treatment by the Enemy of British Prisoners of War; and NA FO 383/399 Report on the Treatment by the Enemy of British

Officers, 'Niemeyer of Holzminden'.

p. 73 'Two good pals': IWM P430 Papers of Lieutenant G. W. Armstrong.

p. 73 'The redoubtable': Liddle POW 043, 'Revelations', p. 45.

p. 73 'Fierce moustaches': Liddle Tape 688 J. Bennett recollections.

p. 73 'The greatest exponent': Harding, *Escape Fever*, pp. 87–8.

p. 73 'Five brothers': Liddle POW 002, Box 1, Arthur Norman Barlow papers.

p. 73 'Milwaukee Bill': *Sunday Express*, 8 May 1938.

p. 73 'Billiard marker': NA FO 383/399 Report on the Treatment by the Enemy of British Officers, Colonel C. E. H. Rathborne.

p. 73 'A good deal of': Ray Rimell, *The Airship VC*, p. 91.

p. 73 'I give you three': F. W. Harvey, *Comrades in Captivity*, p. 225.

p. 73 'Cost price': Durnford, *The Tunnellers*, p. 37.

p. 74 'German embassy staff': NA FO 383/399 Report on the Treatment by the Enemy of British Officers, 'Niemeyer of Holzminden'.

p. 74 'He had told this': Thorn, *Three Years a Prisoner*, p. 41.

p. 74 'One week of': IWM K90/2223 Newscuttings Relating to Major Jack William Shaw.

p. 75 'Noted for his ferocity': *Sunday Express*, 8 May 1938.

p. 75 'The famous Niemeyer': IWM 80/32/2 Folder 10, Letter from Edward Christie-Miller.

p. 75 'That notorious': Lieutenant E. H. Garland, quoted in Richard Garrett, *P.O.W.*, p. 111.

p. 75 'Was clever': *Sunday Express*, 8 May 1938.

p. 75 'Stalk around': Thorn, *Three Years a Prisoner*, p. 42.

p. 75 'The personification of': '2 Hun Brutes Who Must Be Tried', *Daily Sketch*, 5 December 1918.

p. 75 'Rejoiced in': NA FO 383/398 Report on Treatment of British Prisoners of War in Germany.

p. 75 'Swagger up': NA FO 383/399 Report on the Treatment by the Enemy of British Officers, 'Niemeyer of Holzminden'.

p. 75 'Loathe the sight': Durnford, *The Tunnellers*, p. 69.

p. 75 'Take drugs': IWM 67/392/1 Papers of Lieutenant F. N. Insoll.

p. 76 'Source of considerable': Durnford, *The Tunnellers*, p. 38.

p. 76 'A morass': NA FO 383/399 Report on the Treatment by the Enemy of British Officers, 'Niemeyer of Holzminden'.

p. 76 'in time to order': '2 Hun Brutes Who Must Be Tried', *Daily Sketch*, 5 December 1918.

p. 76 'Most of the British': Harding, *Escape Fever*, pp. 89–90.

p. 76 'A particularly popular': ibid.

p. 77 'Summoning a patrol': NA FO 383/399 Report on the Treatment by the Enemy of British Officers.

p. 77 'To use their arms': NA FO 383/274 Enquiry about the imprisonment of certain officers at Ströhen.

p. 77 'Evidently we did not': Harding, *Escape Fever*, pp. 89–90.

p. 77 'The sentry charged': NA FO 383/274 Ströhen.

p. 77 'Just back from': NA FO 383/399 Report on the Treatment by the Enemy of British Officers.

p. 77 'Bayoneting was a common': NA FO 383/398 Report on Treatment of British Prisoners of War in Germany.

p. 77 'Captain Knight': NA FO 383/399 Report on the Treatment by the Enemy of British Officers.

p. 78 'If water was good': NA FO 383/274 Ströhen.

p. 78 'Got no further', 'Spent every penny': Harding, *Escape Fever*, pp. 87–8.

p. 79 'From what we hear': NA FO 383/275 Extracts from statements by various British officers on conditions in camps under the jurisdiction of General von Hanisch of the Tenth Army Corps.

p. 80 'Holy terror': *Sunday Express*, 8 May 1938.

p. 80 'Storming up and down', 'Usually resulted': Durnford, *The Tunnellers*, pp. 32–3

p. 80 'He tried to intimidate': Thorn, *Three Years a Prisoner*, p. 42.

p. 80 'Thundered and damned': *Sunday Express*, 8 May 1938.

p. 80 'Literally trembling': Liddle Tape 688 J. Bennett recollections.

p. 80 'The Germans all hated': IWM Sound Archive 9964 Coombs, Vernon C., Reel 3.

p. 80 'Disgraceful': IWM 82/35/1 Papers of Lieutenant Colonel A. E. Haig.

p. 80 'Protected throughout': NA FO 383/399 Report on the Treatment by the Enemy of British Officers, 'Niemeyer of Holzminden'.

p. 81 'Insolence and discourtesy': ibid.

p. 81 'The truth is not': IWM 82/35/1 Papers of Lieutenant Colonel A. E. Haig.

p. 81 'He had been unpleasant': NA HO 45/10763/270829 Committee on the Treatment by the Enemy of British Prisoners of War; and NA FO 383/399 Report on the Treatment by the Enemy of British Officers, 'Niemeyer of Holzminden'.

p. 81 'Crashed through': NA FO 383/398 Report on Treatment of British Prisoners of War in Germany, Appendix C; and NA FO 383/399, Report on the Treatment by the Enemy of British Officers.

p. 81 'Luckily he missed': Liddle POW 029 Reginald Gough papers.

pp. 81–2 'Very few of us', 'He started off fairly': Harding, *Escape Fever*, pp. 84–6.

4. SOLITARY CONFINEMENT

p. 85 'It is the duty', 'Cardinal offence', 'Not readily accepted': NA FO 383/399 Germany: Prisoners: Report on the Treatment by the Enemy of British Officers, Prisoners of War, under the 10th (Hannover) Army Corps.

p. 86 'Those who break out': E. H. Keeling, 'Prisoners and Parole', in *The Times*, 22 May 1944, p. 5.

p. 86 'Loyally observed', 'Cumulative sentences': NA FO 383/399 Report on the Treatment by the Enemy of British Officers.

p. 87 'Only to maintain': ibid.

p. 87 'Bread and water': Richard Garrett, *P.O.W.*, p. 102.

p. 87 'Under the worst', 'Sometimes without exercise': IWM 73/175/1 Papers of Captain Douglas Lyall Grant.

p. 88 'I herewith give': Liddle POW 003 Norman A. Birks papers, parole card annotated 'Holzminden, 13 May 1918'.

p. 88 'Any attempt', 'He was pretty certain': Hugh Durnford, *The Tunnellers of Holzminden*, pp. 29–30. An ell was a now obsolete unit of measurement, corresponding to the length of a man's arm.

p. 89 'Continual war': Geoffrey Harding, *Escape Fever*, p. 84.

p. 89 '7 November': NA WO 161/97/45, MO 46 Statement by Captain Walter Reuben Wigmore Haight.

p. 90 'British regiments have': Harding, *Escape Fever*, pp. 91–3.

p. 90 'Most courteously': NA FO 383/398, Report on Treatment of British Prisoners of War, 2148 Report by Netherlands Legation, 4/12/17.

p. 91 'Exorbitant rates', 'Certainly not less': NA FO 383/398 Germany: Prisoners: Report on Treatment of British Prisoners of War in Germany, Appendix C.

p. 91 'Informed by the camp': NA FO 383/398 Report on Treatment of British Prisoners of War, 2148 Report by Netherlands Legation, 4/12/17.

p. 91 'The Canteen made no': NA FO 383/275 Reports of visits of inspection to the following internment camps: Holzminden.

p. 91 'In the light of': NA FO 383/399 Report on the Treatment by the Enemy of British Officers.

p. 91 'In a strict military': ibid.

p. 92 'Immense compared': NA FO 383/398 Report on Treatment of British Prisoners of War in Germany, 35477 Major A. E. Haig, Appendix K.

p. 92 '*Kontobuch*', 'To a very large amount': NA WO 161/96/118 Statement by Colonel C. E. H. Rathbone.

p. 92 'Neglected to rub': Ernest Warburton, *Behind Boche Bars*, pp. 100–1.

p. 93 'Damning price lists': Durnford, *The Tunnellers*, p. 70.

p. 93 'Robbery and extortion': IWM 82/35/1 Papers of Lieutenant Colonel A. E. Haig.

p. 93 'This might offer': NA FO 383/398 Report on Treatment of British Prisoners of War, 51790 Report by Captain Christie-Miller.

p. 93 'I do not consider': NA WO 161/96/118 Statement by Colonel C. E. H. Rathborne.

p. 94 'The ordinary three': ibid.

p. 94 'I was more interested': Liddle POW 003 Norman A. Birks papers.

p. 94 'An innocuous stare': Durnford, *The Tunnellers*, p. 32.

p. 94 'For looking out of', 'The latest dodge': IWM 73/175/1 Papers of Captain Douglas Lyall Grant.

p. 94 'Twenty-seven days': NA FO 383/399 Report on the Treatment by the Enemy of British Officers, 108720 Appendix I.

p. 95 'No prisoner objected': ibid.

p. 95 'An old sea skipper': James Whale, 'Our Life at Holzminden', p. 316.

p. 96 'Very like being at school': IWM 73/175/1 Papers of Captain Douglas Lyall Grant.

p. 97 '13 May 1918': Liddle POW 003 Norman A. Birks papers.

p. 97 'The English Richthofen': NA FO 383/399 Report on the Treatment by the Enemy of British Officers.

p. 97 'To avenge the death', 'The Boche harried': Ray Rimell, *The Airship VC*, p. 93.

p. 97 'Pet escapees': NA FO 383/398 Report on Treatment of British Prisoners of War.

p. 97 'Small sentences': NA WO 161/96/136, Lieutenant F. J. Ortweiler, pp. 1131–3.

p. 97 'So restricted', 'He was very much': V. C. Coombs, 'Sixty Years On', in *RAF Quarterly*, Summer 1996; IWM Sound Archive 9964 Coombs, Vernon C., Reel 3; and Liddle POW 016 V. C. Coombs papers.

NOTES

p. 98 'An Inspector General': Durnford, *The Tunnellers*, pp. 155–6.

p. 98 'Whipped to the point': T. Gran, *Under British Flag*, p. 168, quoted in Rimell, *Airship VC*, p. 94.

p. 98 'Captain Robinson': NA FO 383/491 Response of Prussian Ministry of War to Allegations of Ill Treatment, pp. 235–6.

p. 98 'Algernon Bird': http://1914-1918.invisionzone.com/forums/ index.php?showtopic=104463

p. 99 'Private George Dellar', 'I told him I wanted': IWM 82/35/1 Papers of Lieutenant Colonel A. E. Haig; and NA FO 383/398, Report on Treatment of British Prisoners of War, Appendix C.

p. 99 'Taking their cue': NA FO 383/399 Report on the Treatment by the Enemy of British Officers, Colonel C. E. H. Rathborne.

p. 99 'Kicked downstairs': 'German Brutality to Prisoners', *The Times*, 4 December 1918, p. 8.

p. 100 'E. L. Edwards': *Sunday Express*, 8 May 1938.

p. 100 'A further eighteen months': IWM P430 Papers of Lieutenant G. W. Armstrong.

p. 100 'A very disrespectful': Liddle POW 016 V. C. Coombs papers.

p. 100 'They were pointing': IWM Sound Archive 9964 Coombs, Vernon C., Reel 3.

p. 100 'Loose a volley': Liddle Tape 688 J. Bennett recollections.

p. 100 'There were people': Liddle POW 004 J. H. Birkinshaw papers.

p. 101 'Slight improvement': NA FO 383/399 Report on the Treatment by the Enemy of British Officers, Colonel C. E. H. Rathborne; and WO 161/96/118 Statement by Colonel C. E. H. Rathborne.

p. 101 'Take their tone', 'An absolute worm': NA FO 383/399 Report on the Treatment by the Enemy of British Officers, Colonel C. E. H. Rathborne.

p. 101 'Swinging the lead': Durnford, *The Tunnellers*, p. 21.

p. 101 'Most offensive': NA FO 383/399 Report on the Treatment by the Enemy of British Officers, Colonel C. E. H. Rathborne.

p. 102 'Nothing less than': IWM 73/175/1 Papers of Captain Douglas Lyall Grant.

p. 102 'Flagrant and shameful', 'The higher the price': NA FO 383/399 Report on the Treatment by the Enemy of British Officers.

p. 102 'Undoubtedly encouraged': IWM 82/35/1 Papers of Lieutenant Colonel A. E. Haig.

p. 103 'One of the greatest nuisances': NA WO 161/96/118 Statement by Colonel C. E. H. Rathborne.

p. 103 'Boots or shoes and tobacco': Liddle ADD 001 David Russell Morrish papers.

p. 103 'Lacking some of': IWM 79/12/1 Papers of Lieutenant Colonel N. MacLeod.

p. 103 'It was fairly common': NA FO 383/399 Report on the Treatment by the Enemy of British Officers, Colonel C. E. H. Rathborne.

p. 103 'It was never possible': IWM K90/2223 Collection of Newscuttings Relating to Major Jack William Shaw's Experiences as a Prisoner of War.

p. 103 'Square Eyes': Durnford, *The Tunnellers*, p. 22.

p. 105 Descriptions of the camp food: Liddle POW 036 Box 1, Major A. E. Haig, 'Report on Treatment in Germany', in Kenneth Hooper papers; John C Thorn, *Three Years a Prisoner in Germany*, pp. 43–59; NA FO 383/399 Report on the Treatment by the Enemy of British Officers, Prisoners of War; IWM Sound Archive 9964 Coombs, Vernon C., Reel 2; Durnford, *The Tunnellers*, p. 43; IWM 83/11/1 Papers of Lieutenant W. C. Blain, p. 1–2; *Sunday Express*, 8 May 1938; Liddle POW 029 Reginald Gough papers; F. W. Harvey, *Comrades in Captivity*, p. 241; IWM 67/392/1 Papers of Lieutenant F. N. Insoll; Garrett, *P.O.W.*, pp. 108–16; Robert Jackson, *The Prisoners 1914–18*, p. 25.

pp. 73–4 'Very unfavourably', 'At a ruinous rate': Durnford, *The Tunnellers*, pp. 44–6.

p. 106 'At least four hundred': NA WO 161/96/136, Lieutenant F. J. Ortweiler, pp. 1131–3.

p. 106 'All officers who complain': Liddle ADD 001 David Russell Morrish papers.

p. 107 'The turnip winter': Mark Spoerer, 'The Mortality of Allied Prisoners of War', pp. 121–36.

p. 107 'Chronic shortages': Frederick Strauss, 'The Food Problem in the German War Economy', p. 387.

p. 108 'A complaint was made': Liddle ADD 001 David Russell Morrish papers.

p. 108 'Fruit and Cream': IWM 73/175/1 Papers of Captain Douglas Lyall Grant.

p. 108 'One such vendor': Garrett, *P.O.W.*, p. 110.

p. 109 'It seemed that the road': M. C. C. Harrison and H. A. Cartwright, *Within Four Walls*, p. 170.

p. 109 'Two machine guns': IWM 73/175/1 Papers of Captain Douglas Lyall Grant.

p. 110 'It was just over': ibid.

p. 111 'Produced a menu': Liddle AIR 005 Joseph Martin Allen papers.

p. 112 'Assumed a pale-green': IWM 73/175/1 Papers of Captain Douglas Lyall Grant.

p. 112 'Our parcels kept us': IWM K90/2223 Newscuttings Relating to Major Jack William Shaw.

p. 112 'People formed Messes': IWM Sound Archive 9964 Coombs, Vernon C., Reel 2.

p. 113 'Deputy commissioner': Carl p. Dennett, *Prisoners of the Great War*, quoted in Michael Moynihan (ed.), *Black Bread and Barbed Wire*, p. xv.

p. 116 'Standard card': Jackson, *The Prisoner*, pp. 62–5.

p. 117 'Lady Evelyn': ibid., p. 68.

p. 117 'Very many things': Liddle AIR 344 Harold Wilfred (Homer) White papers.

p. 117 'Some parcels sent from': Garrett, *P.O.W.*, p. 97.

p. 118 'Billiard tables': Holger H. Herwig, *The First World War*, p. 354.

p. 118 'Thurloe Place', 'All of it tasted': Jackson, *The Prisoners*, pp. 62–6.

p. 118 'Two million parcels': Jackson, *The Prisoners*, p. 64.

p. 119 'The British Science Guild', *Nature*, Vol. 98, 26 October 1916, pp. 152–6.

p. 120 'Twenty Red Cross workers': Garrett, *P.O.W.*, pp. 98–9.

p. 120 'Constant complaints': IWM 82/35/1 Papers of Lieutenant Colonel A. E. Haig.

p. 120 'Four out of five parcels': *Sunday Express*, 8 May 1938.

p. 121 'A German division': Garrett, *P.O.W.*, p. 98.

p. 121 'Lieutenant Burrows': NA FO 383/398 Report on Treatment of British Prisoners of War, Appendix D.

p. 121 'Considerable leakage': Durnford, *The Tunnellers*, pp. 41–2.

p. 122 'Stabbed several times': Liddle POW 029 Reginald Gough papers.

p. 122 'Slash them to pieces': IWM Sound Archive 9964 Coombs, Vernon C., Reel 2.

p. 122 'They were very badly fed': NA FO 383/399 Report on the Treatment by the Enemy of British Officers, Colonel C. E. H. Rathborne.

p. 122 'Hack to mincemeat': Durnford, *The Tunnellers*, pp. 40–1.

p. 122 'Not a tin': NA FO 383/399 Report on the Treatment by the Enemy of British Officers.

p. 123 'Used promiscuously': NA FO 383/398 Report on Treatment of British Prisoners of War.

p. 123 'Privates who were': Liddle POW 043 L. McNaught-Davis papers, 'Revelations From Behind Barbed Wire', p. 47.

p. 123 'Sugar, jam': NA FO 383/399 Report on the Treatment by the Enemy of British Officers.

p. 123 'Cigarettes were': NA WO 161/96/136, Lieutenant F. J. Ortweiler, pp. 1131–3.

p. 123 'Watching a German': A. J. Evans, *The Escaping Club*, p. 73.

p. 123 'One of my tins': IWM K90/2223 Newscuttings Relating to Major Jack William Shaw.

p. 124 'Common box', 'Nothing edible': Durnford, *The Tunnellers*, p. 23.

p. 124 'Closed at nightfall': Liddle POW 046 Richard Milward papers.

p. 124 'If at all': NA FO 383/398 Report on Treatment of British Prisoners of War.

p. 124 'The only time': IWM 82/35/1 Papers of Lieutenant Colonel A. E. Haig.

p. 125 'Impromptu ice rink': *cf.* illustration in Durnford, *The Tunnellers*, pp. 31–2.

p. 125 'There has been': IWM 82/35/1 Papers of Lieutenant Colonel A. E. Haig.

p. 125 'Great care': IWM 76/171/1 Papers of J. N. Dykes.

p. 125 'Little appetite': IWM 73/175/1 Papers of Captain Douglas Lyall Grant.

p. 125 'Pay through the nose': IWM 73/175/1 Papers of Captain Douglas Lyall Grant.

p. 125 'Reckoned to charge': NA WO 161/97/45, MO 46 Statement by Captain Walter Reuben Wigmore Haight.

p. 125 'Fifty-five thousand marks': NA FO 383/399 Report on the Treatment by the Enemy of British Officers.

p. 126 'Capacious pockets': Durnford, *The Tunnellers*, p. 44.

p. 126 'That must have been': Liddle POW 029 Reginald Gough papers.

p. 126 'Fourth class bread': Liddle ADD 001 David Russell Morrish papers.

p. 126 'When hard', 'It was only when': Liddle POW 029 Reginald Gough papers.

p. 127 'Poor chaps', 'Made a rush': ibid.

p. 127 'When a more suitable': Harvey, *Comrades in Captivity*, p. 227.

p. 128 'Officers washing': NA FO 383/399 Report on the Treatment by the Enemy of British Officers.

p. 128 'The loathsome state': Harvey, *Comrades in Captivity*, p. 227.

p. 128 'The so-called': IWM 73/175/1 Papers of Captain Douglas Lyall Grant.

p. 128 'The few drops': James Whale, 'Our Life at Holzminden', p. 316.

5. BARBED-WIRE FEVER

p. 131 'Barbed-wire fever': Gerald H. Davis, 'Prisoners of War and Communism'.

p. 131 'Although bulletins': IWM Sound Archive 9964 Coombs, Vernon C., Reel 3.

p. 132 'Our hosts are': IWM 73/175/1 Papers of Captain Douglas Lyall Grant.

p. 132 'Through German spectacles', 'Russian peace news': ibid. Papers of Captain Douglas Lyall Grant.

p. 133 'The purposelessness': Anthony Boden, *F. W. Harvey: Soldier, Poet,* p. 200.

p. 133 'The silent battles': Michael Moynihan (ed.), *Black Bread and Barbed Wire,* p. x.

p. 133 'Little cliques': IWM Sound Archive 9964 Coombs, Vernon C., Reel 3.

p. 133 'Certainly there were': Liddle POW 016 V. C. Coombs papers.

p. 133 'One quite often': IWM P318 Papers of Group Captain L. G. Nixon.

p. 133 'In future': IWM 73/175/1 Papers of Captain Douglas Lyall Grant.

p. 134 'Always a prominent': F. W. Harvey, *Comrades in Captivity,* pp. 228–9.

p. 134 'He didn't care': IWM 73/175/1 Papers of Captain Douglas Lyall Grant.

pp. 134–5 'You stood': Harvey, *Comrades in Captivity,* pp. 228–9.

p. 135 'Recited Molière': 'Over the Wire', London Diary, *The Times,* 2 April 1980, p. 16.

p. 135 'But there is no', 'The teams consisted': IWM 73/175/1 Papers of Captain Douglas Lyall Grant.

p. 135 'A race meeting': IWM Sound Archive 9964 Coombs, Vernon C., Reel 3.

p. 135 'So far as they': IWM EPH 816 Leather football associated with the First World War experiences of Major J. W. Shaw.

pp. 135–6 'Arc light was accidentally broken': IWM 82/35/1 Papers of Lieutenant Colonel A. E. Haig.

p. 136 'Proved a good way': Liddle POW 029 Reginald Gough papers.

p. 136 'To allow oneself': IWM 73/175/1 Papers of Captain Douglas Lyall Grant.

p. 136 'Five thousand books': *Occasional Review*, 28 August 1918.

p. 136 'He wasn't a reverend': Liddle POW 016 V. C. Coombs papers.

p. 136 'There was one man': IWM Sound Archive 9964 Coombs, Vernon C., Reel 3.

p. 137 'To put it bluntly': IWM 73/175/1 Papers of Captain Douglas Lyall Grant.

p. 137 'There was nothing': Hugh Durnford, *The Tunnellers of Holzminden*, p. 57.

p. 137 'Gaiety Theatre': Liddle POW 016 V. C. Coombs papers.

p. 137 '*Home John*': *Occasional Review*, 28 August 1918; and IWM Sound Archive 9964 Coombs, Vernon C., Reel 3.

p. 137 'Unlike other pantomimes': IWM 73/175/1 Papers of Captain Douglas Lyall Grant.

p. 137 'They used to laugh': IWM Sound Archive 9964 Coombs, Vernon C., Reel 3.

p. 137 'Must have looked': Liddle POW 016 V. C. Coombs papers.

p. 139 'The attitude of': Harvey, *Comrades in Captivity*, p. 238.

p. 139 'For which he could': Kevin Canfield, 'James Whale: A New World of Gods and Monsters', in *Film Quarterly*, Summer 2005, p. 64.

p. 140 'Intoxicating': http://www.pictureshowman.com/articles_personalities_whale.cfm

p. 140 '*Journey's End*': http://www.worldwar1.com/tgws/smtw 0706.htm

p. 140 'The free discussion': *Occasional Review*, 28 August 1918.

p. 140 'A pioneer', 'Acquired a reading', 'Read the Old Testament': Liddle AIR 344 Harold Wilfred (Homer) White papers.

p. 141 'Prisoners do quaint': Liddle ADD 001 David Russell Morrish papers.

p. 141 'Making illicit': Liddle POW 003 Norman A. Birks papers.

p. 141 'I used to talk', 'One was made to feel': J. L. Hardy, *I Escape!*, pp. 3, 100.

p. 142 'Not only did I not': J. R. Ackerley, *The Grim Game of Escape*, p. 9.

p. 142 'The much vaunted', 'Our government': IWM 73/175/1 Papers of Captain Douglas Lyall Grant.

pp. 142–3 'Sinecure', 'Near-endless': ibid.

p. 143 'An extraordinarily stout': ibid.

p. 143 'The order that': IWM Sound Archive 23157 Mapplebeck, Tom, Reel 2; *cf* also Richard Garrett, *P.O.W.*, p. 117.

p. 144 'Shaking his fist': Sir Brian Horrocks, *A Full Life*, p. 21.

p. 144 'I am Niemeyer': Liddle POW 002, Box 1, Arthur Norman Barlow papers.

p. 144 'You damn well': *Sunday Express*, 8 May 1938.

p. 144 'Generally recognized': Liddle POW 043 L. McNaught-Davis papers, 'Revelations From Behind Barbed Wire', p. 67.

p. 145 'Then the fun': Liddle POW 029 Reginald Gough papers.

p. 146 'This splash': John C. Thorn, *Three Years a Prisoner in Germany*, pp. 43–59.

p. 146 'Solidly nailed': M. C. C. Harrison and H. A. Cartwright, *Within Four Walls*, p. 172.

p. 147 'It took exactly': Thorn, *Three Years a Prisoner*, pp. 43–59.

p. 147 'Using red quilting', 'Tommy's cooker': ibid.

p. 148 'It is remarkable': Lawrence A. Wingfield, 'Hazards of Escape', p. 296.

p. 148 'A *Canadischer*': Thorn, *Three Years a Prisoner*, pp. 43–59.

p. 148 'Passed the commandant': ibid.

p. 149 'Signal of three shots': Liddle POW 029 Reginald Gough papers.

p. 150 'Did not take much': Ernest Warburton, *Behind Boche Bars*, p. 98.

pp. 151–2 'Called in the local': ibid.

p. 152 'We wondered', 'in a private garden': Thorn, *Three Years a Prisoner*, pp. 43–59.

p. 154 'Every turn': ibid.

pp. 154–5 'No doubt': ibid.

p. 156 'The continual sound': ibid.

p. 157 'Two dirty looking': ibid.

p. 158 'It would have shocked', 'Imagine our feelings': ibid.

p. 159 'Made as usual', 'I could picture': ibid.

pp. 159–60 'Had no idea': Horrocks, *A Full Life*, p. 21.

p. 160 'The sentry taking them': IWM 73/175/1 Papers of Captain Douglas Lyall Grant.

p. 160 'A pyjama jacket': Horrocks, *A Full Life*, p. 22.

p. 160 'Taken the elementary': ibid.

p. 161 'Some did not even': *Sunday Express*, 8 May 1938.

p. 161 '*Guten Tag*': Thorn, *Three Years a Prisoner*, pp. 43–59.

p. 162 'What we would give': ibid.

p. 163 'Lieutenant Riley', 'Three others': Liddle POW 043 'Revelations';, p. 68.

pp. 163–4 'In my best German': Thorn, *Three Years a Prisoner*, pp. 43–59.

p. 164 'A tunic', 'At six o'clock': ibid.

6. INVETERATE ESCAPEES

p. 167 'Nearly went crazy': IWM K90/2223 Collection of Newscuttings Relating to Major Jack William Shaw's Experiences as a Prisoner of War.

p. 167 'Within three weeks': *Sunday Express*, 8 May 1938.

p. 167 'The ground-floor windows': Liddle POW 016 V. C. Coombs papers.

p. 168 'You see, yentlemen': Barry Winchester, *Beyond the Tumult*, pp. 109–10.

p. 168 'When a sentry': Hugh Durnford, *The Tunnellers of Holzminden*, pp. 53–4.

p. 168 'His own men as well': NA WO 161/96/86, 0227 Statement by Captain W. Loder Symonds.

p. 169 'The Letter Boy', 'The Electric Light Boy': Durnford, *The Tunnellers*, pp. 81–4.

p. 170 'Obliging canteen attendant': ibid.

p. 170 'Kurt Grau': Winchester, *Beyond the Tumult*, p. 126.

p. 170 'Quite good but not too': IWM 73/175/1 Papers of Captain Douglas Lyall Grant.

p. 170 'For the purpose of': Winchester, *Beyond the Tumult*, pp. 111–12.

p. 170 'An almost legendary': Letter from Major M. R. Chidson regarding exploits of Lieutenant H. W. Medlicott in Germany, http://www.medlicott.eu/HEM_files/7_HWMedlicott.html

pp. 171–2 'Dressed in old', 'Dented the crown': ibid.

p. 172 'Assisted in hoisting', 'Displayed great staying': IWM 73/175/1 Papers of Captain Douglas Lyall Grant.

p. 173 'Not a single officer': NA WO 161/97/39, MO 40 Statement by Surgeon Probationer Joe Alexander.

p. 173 'Many bullets': NA FO 383/399 Germany: Prisoners: Report on the Treatment by the Enemy of British Officers, Prisoners of War, under the 10th (Hannover) Army Corps.

p. 173 'No one was hit': IWM 73/175/1 Private Papers of Captain Douglas Lyall Grant.

p. 173 'Tragic footnote': Durnford, *The Tunnellers*, pp. 60–1.

p. 174 'So skilfully': ibid., pp. 65–7.

p. 175 'Set to in real': IWM K90/2223 Newscuttings Relating to Major Jack William Shaw.

p. 175 'Laundry basket': Liddle POW 029 Reginald Gough papers.

p. 175 'A. T. Shipwright': 'Heroes of the War's Greatest Escape', *News Chronicle*, 25 July 1938.

p. 175 'That unpleasant fatigue': Durnford, *The Tunnellers*, pp. 67–8.

p. 176 'Things were so rushed': Liddle POW 029 Reginald Gough papers.

p. 176 'A most bitter': Liddle POW 043 L. McNaught-Davis papers, 'Revelations From Behind Barbed Wire', p. 69.

p. 176 'I was given', 'All my boys': Liddle POW 002 Arthur Norman Barlow papers.

p. 176 'Attending some function': Liddle POW 029 Reginald Gough papers.

p. 177 'Imitating his': F. W. Harvey, *Comrades in Captivity*, p. 226.

p. 177 'There was always some plot': Liddle Tape 688 J. Bennett recollections.

p. 177 'Wild ideas': IWM Sound Archive 9964 Coombs, Vernon C., Reel 3.

p. 177 'Improvised umbrella': Durnford, *The Tunnellers*, p. 67.

p. 177 'The spars of deck chairs', 'The speed with which': Liddle POW 029 Reginald Gough papers.

p. 178 'Slippery board': Liddle POW 043, 'Revelations', pp. 51, 68.

p. 178 'Twenty feet lower': IWM Sound Archive 9964 Coombs, Vernon C., Reel 3.

p. 178 'If properly supported', 'There would, of course': IWM K90/2223 Newscuttings Relating to Major Jack William Shaw.

p. 179 'Three weeks below': ibid.

p. 179 'The third escaper': Liddle POW 043, 'Revelations', pp. 68–9.

p. 179 'Called to the sentry': 'German Brutality to Prisoners', *The Times*, 4 December 1918, p. 8.

p. 180 'He had reckoned without': Harvey, *Comrades in Captivity*, p. 236.

p. 180 'A boycott': Durnford, *The Tunnellers*, pp. 64–5.

pp. 180–1 'Quite certain': IWM Sound Archive 9964 Coombs, Vernon C., Reel 3.

p. 181 'Had wind of': NA FO 383/398 Germany: Prisoners:

Report on Treatment of British Prisoners of War in Germany.

p. 181 'Supporting himself': NA WO 161/96/136 Lieutenant F. J. Ortweiler, pp. 1131–3.

p. 181 'Aiming at the groundline': IWM 73/175/1 Papers of Captain Douglas Lyall Grant.

p. 181 'There was no need whatever': NA FO 383/398 Report on Treatment of British Prisoners of War.

p. 181 'The efforts crystallized': Liddle Tape 688 J. Bennett recollections.

p. 181 'The brainchild': Robert Jackson, *The Prisoners 1914–18*, p. 94.

p. 181 'Lieutenant Ellis': Liddle POW 046 Richard Milward papers.

p. 182 'The Poles': Liddle GS 1449 W. R. Shaw papers.

p. 182 'After each tunnel': IWM 83/11/1 Papers of Lieutenant W. C. Blain, p. 14.

p. 182 'Anyone trying it': Liddle Tape 688 J. Bennett recollections.

p. 183 'Knew most of the orderlies': *Sunday Express*, 8 May 1938.

p. 184 'Which the Huns': Liddle POW 029 Reginald Gough papers.

p. 184 'Never inspected': *Sunday Express*, 8 May 1938.

p. 185 'A real schamozzle': Liddle Tape 688 J. Bennett recollections.

p. 185 'To save his own skin': *Sunday Express*, 8 May 1938.

p. 185 'Slavish devotion': Durnford, *The Tunnellers*, p. 74.

p. 187 'To the irritation': IWM P425 Papers of Major M. R. D. Pannett.

pp. 188–9 'No tunneller ever': Liddle Tape 688 J. Bennett recollections.

p. 189 'Really didn't know': IWM Sound Archive 9964 Coombs, Vernon C., Reel 3.

7. THE RAT-HOLE

p. 193 'The hours during': '"Human Moles"' *Bucks Free Press*, 22 July 1938.

p. 193 'Morning inspections': IWM P425 Papers of Major M. R. D. Pannett.

p. 194 'Whatever suitable': V. C. Coombs, 'Sixty Years On', in *RAF Quarterly*, Summer 1976.

p. 194 'Kitchen knives': *Sunday Dispatch*, 24 July 1938.

p. 194 'Penknives, spoons': 'Candlelight Hero Recalls the Big Day', *Sunday Times*, 30 October 1977.

p. 194 'Sharpened tin': 'Captain' Jack Shaw of Marlow', *Bucks Free Press*, 5 June 1931.

p. 194 'No patent gadgets': IWM 83/11/1 Papers of Lieutenant W. C. Blain, p. 14.

pp. 194–5 'Ten months in the Fatherland': M. C. C. Harrison and H. A. Cartwright, *Within Four Walls*, p. 170.

p. 195 'Sulphuric acid': *Sunday Express*, 8 May 1938.

p. 195 'Merely a rat-hole': Liddle POW 029 Reginald Gough papers.

p. 195 'Sixteen inches': Liddle Tape 688 J. Bennett recollections.

p. 195 'About as wide': IWM 83/11/1 Papers of Lieutenant W. C. Blain, p. 14.

p. 196 'Mattress-cases': *Sunday Graphic and Sunday News*, 24 July 1938.

p. 196 'Bags made of old': IWM K90/2223 Collection of Newscuttings Relating to Major Jack William Shaw's Experiences as a Prisoner of War.

p. 196 'We carried it': 'Candlelight Hero Recalls the Big Day', *Sunday Times*, 30 October 1977.

p. 198 'Come out now': Hugh Durnford, *The Tunnellers of Holzminden*, pp. 97–8.

p. 199 'Christmas dinner': Liddle POW 004 J. H. Birkinshaw papers.

p. 200 'Good cheer': Liddle POW 003 Norman A. Birks papers.

pp. 150–1 'The worst I ever': Liddle POW 043 L. McNaught-Davis papers, 'Revelations From Behind Barbed Wire', p. 52.

p. 200 'Showed our appreciation': IWM 73/175/1 Papers of Captain Douglas Lyall Grant.

p. 201 'One of the originators', 'It wouldn't be necessary', 'More or less': Liddle Tape 643 B. G. Austen recollections.

p. 202 'Stationed almost directly': IWM P425 Papers of Major M. R. D. Pannett.

p. 203 'A hundred thousand prisoners': War Office, *Statistics of the Military Effort of the British Empire*, quoted in Mark Spoerer, 'The Mortality of Allied Prisoners of War . . .', p. 127.

p. 203 'Arrived looking like': IWM 73/175/1 Papers of Captain Douglas Lyall Grant.

p. 204 'Rather than wait': IWM P425 Papers of Major M. R. D. Pannett.

p. 204 'A form of neurasthenia': Carl p. Dennett, quoted in Michael Moynihan (ed.), *Black Bread and Barbed Wire*, p. xvi.

p. 205 'Employed on any front': George G. Phillimore and Hugh H. L. Bellot, 'Treatment of Prisoners of War', pp. 51–3.

p. 205 'Unless they desire', 'Operates indiscriminately': ibid., pp. 55–6, 51–3.

p. 206 'Holland looked': John C. Thorn, *Three Years a Prisoner in Germany*, p. 86.

p. 206 'The first party': Liddle POW 043, 'Revelations', p. 54.

p. 206 'Rathborne had previously': NA WO 161/96/118 Statement by Colonel C. E. H. Rathborne.

pp. 206–7 'Any demonstration': IWM 82/35/1 Papers of Lieutenant Colonel A. E. Haig.

p. 207 'After a final': IWM 73/175/1 Papers of Captain Douglas Lyall Grant.

p. 207 'Many clashes': Thorn, *Three Years a Prisoner*, p. 90.

p. 208 'Presumably because': 'Candlelight Hero Recalls the Big Day', *Sunday Times*, 30 October 1977.

p. 209 'Learning the cattle': Barry Winchester, *Beyond the Tumult*, p. 12.

p. 209 'Munshi', 'Brecklen Kamp': ibid., pp. 126, 110, 104–5.

p. 210 'Hearing the thud': Durnford, *The Tunnellers*, p. 95.

p. 210 'Not so finely': IWM 83/11/1 Papers of Lieutenant W. C. Blain, pp. 14–15.

p. 211 'Their daily routine': IWM P425 papers of Major M. R. D. Pannett.

p. 212 'Towards the end': ibid., p. 15.

p. 213 'The most agonizing': 'Candlelight Hero Recalls the Big Day', *Sunday Times*, 30 October 1977.

p. 214 'Sucked air', 'Suffocating work': ibid.

p. 214 'There were many rats': IWM 83/11/1 Papers of Lieutenant W. C. Blain, p. 15.

8. THE BLACK BOOK

p. 217 'They might share': *Frankfurter Zeitung*, 31 December 1917.

pp. 217–8 'Placed officer prisoners': Hansard, 5 February 1918.

p. 218 'Ramsgate, Margate': James M. Spaight, *Air Power and War Rights*, p. 220.

p. 218 'Niemeyer ordered': IWM P425 Papers of Major M. R. D. Pannett.

p. 218 'An extra letter': Hugh Durnford, *The Tunnellers of Holzminden*, pp. 106–7.

p. 219 'Eight days': ibid., pp. 108–9.

p. 220 'Heated arguments': IWM 83/11/1 Papers of Lieutenant W. C. Blain, p. 15.

p. 221 'With infinite care': *Answers*, 11 June 1938.

p. 221 'Only the thinnest': IWM K90/2223 Collection of Newscuttings Relating to Major Jack William Shaw's Experiences as a Prisoner of War.

p. 221 'Removable panel': ' "Human Moles" ', *Bucks Free Press*, 22 July 1938.

p. 222 'Vigorous exercise': IWM 73/175/1 Papers of Captain Douglas Lyall Grant.

p. 222 'Keeping their strength': IWM Sound Archive 9964 Coombs, Vernon C., Reel 3.

p. 222 'At least they seemed': Liddle POW 029 Reginald Gough papers.

p. 222 'In honour bound': Durnford, *The Tunnellers*, p. 128.

p. 223 'Perfectly justified': Liddle POW 029 Reginald Gough papers.

p. 223 'All Germans': Liddle POW 002, Box 1, Arthur Norman Barlow papers.

p. 223 'The Germans while': John C. Thorn, *Three Years a Prisoner in Germany*, pp. 43–59.

p. 223 'The lid of a round': IWM 83/11/1 Papers of Lieutenant W. C. Blain, p. 6.

p. 223 'We got a German': IWM Sound Archive 23157 Mapplebeck, Tom, Reel 2.

p. 223 'A pickle jar': Liddle POW 003 Norman A. Birks papers.

p. 224 'A group of Canadian': Thorn, *Three Years a Prisoner*, p. 78; Australian War Memorial RELAWM16875, Small compass used during escape from Holzminden PoW camp, Captain S. S. B. Purves, Royal Air Force.

p. 224 'The hat is': IWM EPH 3682 Panama hat.

p. 225 'Attached to his braces': IWM EPH 3681 Compass and accessories.

p. 225 'Battery-operated': IWM EPH 3684 German battery-operated electric torch associated with Captain E. W. Leggatt.

p. 225 'An inveterate escapee': NA WO 161/96/114 Statement by Captain Edward Wilmer Leggatt.

p. 225 'A miniature brush': IWM EPH 828 Miniature brush and comb set associated with Major J. W. Shaw.

p. 225 'People used to': IWM Sound Archive 9964 Coombs, Vernon C., Reel 3.

p. 225 'Usually returned': Barry Winchester, *Beyond the Tumult*, p. 98.

p. 226 'The amount of illegal': Liddle POW 002, Box 1, Arthur Norman Barlow papers.

p. 226 'An enormous pair': IWM 83/11/1 Papers of Lieutenant W. C. Blain, p. 3.

pp. 226–7 'Escape material': IWM Sound Archive 23157 Mapplebeck, Tom, Reel 2.

p. 228 'Some bloke', 'Old Gerry': Liddle GS 1449 W. R. Shaw papers.

p. 228 'Lawyers, businessmen': Liddle POW 002, Box 1, Arthur Norman Barlow papers.

p. 228 'One of the guiding', 'Left his bed', 'In walked three': IWM K90/2223 Newscuttings Relating to Major Jack William Shaw.

p. 230 'There were always': Liddle POW 016 V. C. Coombs papers.

p. 230 'There is nothing better': J. L. Hardy, *I Escape!*, p. 58.

p. 230 'When bent over': IWM K90/2223 Newscuttings Relating to Major Jack William Shaw.

p. 230 'A pair of wire-cutters': Hardy, *I Escape!*, p. 172.

p. 230 'They could dye cloth': IWM Sound Archive 9964 Coombs, Vernon C., Reel 3.

p. 230 'Older officers': Liddle ADD 001 David Russell Morrish papers.

p. 231 'Terribly ingenious': IWM Sound Archive 9964 Coombs, Vernon C., Reel 3.

p. 231 'There was not a more': Durnford, *The Tunnellers*, pp. 85–6.

p. 231 'As full of moving': F. W. Harvey, *Comrades in Captivity*, pp. 230–1.

p. 232 'Discovering underneath': IWM K90/2223 Newscuttings Relating to Major Jack William Shaw.

p. 232 'Several contraband': Liddle POW 029 Reginald Gough papers.

pp. 232–3 'On this plank': Hardy, *I Escape!*, p. 10.

p. 233 'Black Book': IWM 82/35/1 Papers of Lieutenant Colonel A. E. Haig.

p. 234 'Lemon juice': Lawrence A. Wingfield, 'Hazards of Escape', p. 297.

p. 234 'If a capital': Liddle POW 003 Norman A. Birks papers.

p. 234 'Invisible writing': IWM 83/11/1 Papers of Lieutenant W. C. Blain, p. 3.

p. 235 'Pascal's Crème': Barry Winchester, *Beyond the Tumult*, pp. 39–40.

p. 235 'Nip off with': Liddle POW 029 Reginald Gough papers.

p. 236 'Transparent Pears' soap': Wingfield, 'Hazards of Escape', p. 298.

p. 236 'A cake of decent': Liddle POW 029 Reginald Gough papers.

p. 236 'The great mole': 'Captain Jack Shaw of Marlow', *Bucks Free Press*, 5 June 1931.

p. 236 'Norman Insoll': IWM 67/392/1 Papers of Lieutenant F. N. Insoll.

p. 236 'An illuminated': Liddle POW 049 Robert Paddison papers.

p. 237 'Magnapole Cream': IWM 67/392/1 Papers of Lieutenant F. N. Insoll.

p. 237 'I should like': *Sunday Express*, 8 May 1938.

p. 238 'The officer noticed': Liddle Tape 688 J. Bennett recollections.

p. 238 'After that about 14': Liddle POW 029 Reginald Gough papers.

p. 238 'A very minute': IWM EPH 809 Shaving brush, with concealed information, relating to Major J. W. Shaw.

p. 239 'Halford's Curry': IWM K90/2223 Newscuttings Relating to Major Jack William Shaw.

p. 239 'Armour Tongue': IWM EPH 810 Tin of 'Armour Tongue' (and its escape-related contents).

p. 239 'Ruthlessly made': NA FO 383/399 Germany: Prisoners: Report on the Treatment by the Enemy of British Officers, Prisoners of War, under the 10th (Hannover) Army Corps.

p. 240 'A small dynamo', 'So neatly': Liddle POW 029 Reginald Gough papers.

p. 241 'A real thriller', 'Scrapping like any', 'All but empty': ibid.

p. 241 '26 January': Liddle POW 043 L. McNaught-Davis papers, 'Revelations From Behind Barbed Wire', p. 53.

NOTES

p. 242 'Quaint little spectacled': Durnford, *The Tunnellers*, p. 114.

p. 242 'We took it as': Geoffrey Harding, *Escape Fever*, pp. 95–6.

p. 242 'Soldiers poured': Liddle POW 043, 'Revelations', p. 53.

p. 242 'It was far from': IWM 73/175/1 Papers of Captain Douglas Lyall Grant.

p. 242 'A right royal': Liddle POW 043, 'Revelations', pp. 53–4.

p. 242 'Under their noses': Liddle Tape 688 J. Bennett recollections.

p. 242 'Full of zeal': Durnford, *The Tunnellers*, p. 114.

p. 243 'Not equal to': Harding, *Escape Fever*, pp. 95–6.

p. 243 'Obtained heaps': Liddle POW 043, 'Revelations', p. 53.

p. 243 'A dummy beam': *Sunday Express*, 8 May 1938; and Liddle Tape 688 J. Bennett recollections.

p. 244 'Frenzied argument', 'As if he had scored': Durnford, *The Tunnellers*, pp. 115–16.

p. 244 'We used wine': IWM 73/175/1 Papers of Captain Douglas Lyall Grant.

p. 245 'An amusing climax': Durnford, *The Tunnellers*, pp. 116–17.

p. 245 'An umbrella': ibid., p. 114.

p. 245 'German Sherlock': Robert Jackson, *The Prisoners 1914–18*, p. 98.

p. 245 'Lost his hat': Liddle POW 043, 'Revelations', p. 53.

p. 245 'Detachable starched', 'Even examined': *Answers*, 11 June 1938, in IWM K90/2223 Newscuttings Relating to Major Jack William Shaw.

p. 245 'Mardock pinched', 'They couldn't find': Liddle Tape 688 J. Bennett recollections.

p. 246 'So we were not': Liddle POW 043, 'Revelations', p. 53.

p. 246 'For the past few': IWM 73/175/1 Papers of Captain Douglas Lyall Grant.

9. ZERO DAY

p. 249 'These officers walking': Hugh Durnford, *The Tunnellers of Holzminden*, p. 105.

p. 250 'Are you in the tunnel': ibid., p. 104.

p. 252 'Mostly old men': NA FO 383/399 Germany: Prisoners: Report on the Treatment by the Enemy of British Officers, Prisoners of War, under the 10th (Hannover) Army Corps.

p. 252 'Old bathman': ibid., Colonel C. E. H. Rathborne.

p. 252 'A fine little sport': F. W. Harvey, *Comrades in Captivity*, pp. 237–8.

p. 252–3 'A most seductive': Durnford, *The Tunnellers*, pp. 87–8, 120–1.

p. 255 'Came the great day': Liddle Tape 688 J. Bennett recollections.

pp. 255–6 'Bit of white rag': IWM K90/2223 Collection of Newscuttings Relating to Major Jack William Shaw's Experiences as a Prisoner of War.

p. 256 'The little flag': Liddle Tape 688 J. Bennett recollections.

p. 256 'Four yards from': IWM P425 Papers of Major M. R. D. Pannett.

p. 256 'Looking in that direction': IWM K90/2223 Newscuttings Relating to Major Jack William Shaw.

p. 257 'Well, gentlemen': Harvey, *Comrades in Captivity*, p. 240.

p. 257 'Already resident': IWM P425 Papers of Major M. R. D. Pannett.

p. 258 'Unusual distinction': 'Saved War Comrade From Gaol', *Daily Mirror*, 18 January 1937, p. 2.

p. 258 'Who was somewhat': Durnford, *The Tunnellers*, p. 127.

p. 259 'More risks': ibid.

p. 260 'Escape Committee': IWM Sound Archive 23157 Mapplebeck, Tom, Reel 2.

p. 260 'Unnecessary heartburning': IWM P425 Papers of Major M. R. D. Pannett.

p. 260 'Politely but firmly': Durnford, *The Tunnellers*, pp. 129–30.

p. 261 'The only people': the camp adjutant, Hugh Durnford, credited himself with the role of rousing the escapers; other versions of the story say it was a Major Dannatt.

p. 261 'About five foot nine': Liddle Tape 688 J. Bennett recollections.

p. 262 'Break-out man': NA FO 383/509 Lieutenant Andrew Clouston of Holzminden prisoner-of-war camp.

p. 262 'A big, coarse-featured': Liddle POW 002, Box 1, Arthur Norman Barlow papers.

p. 262 'Along the hole': Walter Butler, quoted in Durnford, *The Tunnellers*, pp. 159–61.

p. 263 'The night air': Liddle Tape 688 J. Bennett recollections.

p. 263 'He was fast asleep': *Evening Standard*, 24 July 1938.

p. 265 'Figures with big bags': IWM 83/11/1 Papers of Lieutenant W. C. Blain.

p. 266 'Blain banged his head': Barry Winchester, *Beyond the Tumult*, pp. 156–8.

p. 267 'The last man': Liddle POW 029 Reginald Gough papers.

p. 268 'According to Caspar Kennard': Winchester, *Beyond the Tumult*, pp. 171–2.

p. 268 'He was stopped': Durnford, *The Tunnellers*, p. 134.

p. 269 'Morrogh had told the orderlies': IWM P 318 Papers of Group Captain L. G. Nixon.

p. 269 'On Lee': IWM K90/2223 Newscuttings Relating to Major Jack William Shaw.

p. 269 'Thirty-first in the queue': IWM EPH 813 and EPH 814 Conductor's batons used by Major J. W. Shaw.

p. 269 'Groans, curses': IWM P425 Papers of Major M. R. D. Pannett.

p. 271 'Tumble to': ibid.

p. 272 'Since he also believed': *Sunday Express*, 24 July 1938.

p. 272 'How many?': Durnford, *The Tunnellers*, p. 139.

p. 272 'Twenty-six men missing': IWM P425 Papers of Major M. R. D. Pannett.

p. 272 'Jaw dropped': Durnford, *The Tunnellers*, p. 139.

p. 272 'Thoroughly deflated': IWM Sound Archive 9964 Coombs, Vernon C., Reel 3.

p. 272 'For a second': Liddle POW 029 Reginald Gough papers.

p. 273 'Safety of Camp', 'The bullet shattered': IWM 82/35/1 Papers of Lieutenant Colonel A. E. Haig.

p. 273 'One fellow was slightly': IWM K90/2223 Newscuttings Relating to Major Jack William Shaw.

p. 273 'Known as Bobbie': Harvey, *Comrades in Captivity*, p. 230.

p. 273 'By coincidence': Durnford, *The Tunnellers*, pp. 162–3.

p. 274 'Rapping his stick': NA FO 383/398 Report on Treatment of British Prisoners of War in Germany.

p. 274 'Much strafing': NA WO 161/96/136 Lieutenant F. J. Ortweiler, pp. 1131–3.

p. 274 'Broadly permitted': 'Candlelight Hero Recalls the Big Day', *Sunday Times*, 30 October 1977.

p. 274 'A lot of shooting': Liddle POW 003 Norman A. Birks papers.

p. 274 'Under the approving', 'A large piece of black bread': Durnford, *The Tunnellers*, pp. 150–1.

p. 275 'A great log': IWM 67/392/1 Papers of Lieutenant F. N. Insoll.

p. 275 'Came up and fired': Richard Garrett, *P.O.W.*, pp. 108–16.

p. 275 'Rather given to taking': IWM 73/175/1 Papers of Captain Douglas Lyall Grant.

p. 275 'Out of bounds': Durnford, *The Tunnellers*, p. 141.

p. 275 'Got very nasty': IWM Sound Archive 9964 Coombs, Vernon C., Reel 3.

p. 276 'Sausages, Meat': IWM P425 Papers of Major M. R. D. Pannett.

p. 276 'Reprisals Niemeyer had ordered': MacArthur, R., *Occasional Review*, 28 August 1918.

p. 276 'Forbidden to congregate': IWM Sound Archive 9964

Coombs, Vernon C., Reel 3.

p. 276 'Disturbed three times': Durnford, *The Tunnellers*, p. 155.

p. 276 'Endeavoured to get': Liddle POW 029 Reginald Gough papers.

pp. 276–7 'They sent a boy': IWM 67/392/1 Papers of Lieutenant F. N. Insoll.

p. 277 'All he could advise': Liddle POW 029 Reginald Gough papers.

p. 277 'Even though Niemeyer': *Sunday Express*, 8 May 1938.

p. 277 'Cross-questioned': Liddle Tape 688 J. Bennett recollections.

p. 278 'About 1,000': Garrett, *P.O.W.*, p. 126.

p. 278 'Also fell prey': Durnford, *The Tunnellers*, pp. 145–6.

p. 278 'Begun a new one': IWM K90/2223 Newscuttings Relating to Major Jack William Shaw.

p. 278 'A disused lavatory': Liddle GS 1449 W. R. Shaw papers.

p. 278 'Difficult prisoner', 'Staged a diversion': Diary of Hector Fraser Dougall, quoted in http://brendadougallmerriman. blogspot.com/2008/11/remembrance.html

10. DEAD OR ALIVE

p. 283 'Dead or alive': *Sunday Express*, 8 May 1938; and Liddle Tape 688 J. Bennett recollections.

p. 283 'Some pepper': M. C. C. Harrison and H. A. Cartwright, *Within Four Walls*, p. 172.

p. 284 'They found potatoes': John C. Thorn, *Three Years a Prisoner in Germany*, pp. 43–59.

p. 285 'Milk in a can': Harrison and Cartwright, *Within Four Walls*, p. 177.

p. 285 'It is believed': IWM 79/12/1 Papers of Lieutenant Colonel N. MacLeod, newspaper clipping.

p. 285 'With buttons', 'All hell': 'Candlelight Hero Recalls the Big Day': *Sunday Times*, 30 October 1977.

p. 286 'We were always afraid': Liddle Tape 688 J. Bennett recollections.

p. 286 'Almost fainting': *Sunday Express*, 8 May 1938.

p. 286 'An old Cambridge': Hugh Durnford, *The Tunnellers of Holzminden*, p. 162.

p. 286 'Travelling only': 'Candlelight Hero', *Sunday Times*, 30 October 1977.

p. 287 'Knew there was someone': Liddle Tape 688 J. Bennett recollections.

p. 287 'Dead beat': *Sunday Express*, 8 May 1938.

p. 287 'Two beautiful': BL X5292 and X5293 Stanley Purves, Two Maps for the Escape from Holzminden.

p. 287 'Partly to obstruct': IWM K90/2223 Collection of Newscuttings Relating to Major Jack William Shaw's Experiences as a Prisoner of War.

p. 288 Australian War Memorial PO2983.002 Photograph by John Richard Cash.

p. 288 'Asylum at Vechta': Barry Winchester, *Beyond the Tumult*, pp. 140–2.

p. 289 'We hereby certify': ibid.

p. 290 'Crude raft', 'Caley's Marching Chocolate': ibid., pp. 160–3.

pp. 290–7 For a fuller account of Gray, Blain and Kennard's escape, see ibid., pp. 173–86.

p. 294 'Two other escapees': Harrison and Cartwright, *Within Four Walls*, p. 177.

p. 297 'Göttingen': Durnford, *The Tunnellers*, p. 143.

p. 298 'What size?': V. C. Coombs, 'Sixty Years On', in *RAF Quarterly*, Summer 1996; and IWM Sound Archive 9964 Coombs, Vernon C., Reel 3.

p. 298 'Telegram': IWM 79/12/1 Papers of Lieutenant Colonel N. MacLeod. p. 229 '28–29 July': NA FO 383/399 Germany: Prisoners: Report on the Treatment by the Enemy of British Officers, Prisoners of War, under the 10th (Hannover) Army Corps.

p. 299 '1–2 August': 'Candlelight Hero', *Sunday Times*,

30 October 1977.

p. 299 '15–16 August': IWM EPH 3682 Captain Edward Wilmer Leggatt, Panama hat.

p. 299 'August 15 and 16', 'I was not in the camp': IWM 83/11/1 Papers of Lieutenant W. C. Blain, pp. 15–16.

p. 299 'A ceremony at': Winchester, *Beyond the Tumult*, p. 188.

p. 300 'For gallantry': Obituary, *The Times*, 29 December 1943, p. 6; http://inthefootsteps.org.uk/Articles/1914-18GreatWar/HolzmindenTunnellers.htm

p. 300 'Something very drastic': NA FO 383/275 Captain Tollemache: information in a coded letter on conditions at Holzminden Camp.

p. 300 'Quite common': Liddle POW 003 Norman A. Birks papers.

p. 300 'A rubicund parson': *Evening Standard*, 24 July 1938.

p. 300 'Ripping their clothes': Durnford, *The Tunnellers*, p. 144.

p. 301 'Caught in a small wood': IWM 79/12/1 Papers of Lieutenant Colonel N. MacLeod.

p. 301 'It was terribly hot': 'Personality Parade', *Daily Mirror*, 19 May 1938.

p. 301 'Captain William': Durnford, *The Tunnellers*, pp. 144–5.

p. 301 'Caught by an old': *Sunday Express*, 24 July 1938.

p. 301 'Among the unluckiest': 'Heroes of the War's Greatest Escape', *News Chronicle*, 25 July 1938.

p. 301 'A couple of hundred': *Sunday Dispatch*, 24 July 1938.

p. 302 'Tried to escape': Liddle POW 049 Robert Paddison papers.

p. 302 'Put into cells': *Sunday Express*, 8 May 1938.

p. 302 'Four days later': NA FO 383/509 Lieutenant Andrew Clouston of Holzminden prisoner-of-war camp.

p. 302 'Conspiring to destroy': IWM 79/12/1 Papers of Lieutenant Colonel N. MacLeod.

pp. 303–4 'Those charged': court transcript, Liddle POW 049 Robert Paddison papers.

pp. 304–7 'The accused who are': ibid.

p. 307 'Duly convicted': *Sunday Express*, 8 May 1938.

p. 308 'A letter from': IWM P318 Papers of Group Captain L. G. Nixon.

p. 308–9 'It was our great': ibid.

p. 310 'Very likely': ibid.

p. 310 'Captain Edgar': *News Chronicle*, 25 July 1938.

p. 310 'Alphabetical order', 'Got the wind up': Liddle GS 1449 W. R. Shaw papers.

p. 311 'This courageous young': Arch Whitehouse, *The Years of the Sky Kings*, p. 27.

p. 311 'His undermined constitution': Liddle POW 029 Reginald Gough papers.

11. A HANNOVERIAN GENTLEMAN

p. 315 'The attitude of': IWM Sound Archive 9964 Coombs, Vernon C., Reel 3.

p. 315 'They had changed': Liddle POW 003 Norman A. Birks papers.

p. 315 'The strangest and most': Hugh Durnford, *The Tunnellers of Holzminden*, p. 159.

p. 315 'More than possible': V. C. Coombs, 'Sixty Years On', in *RAF Quarterly*, Summer 1996.

p. 316 'Always done all': 'Prison Commander's Fear', *New York Times*, 15 December 1918.

p. 316 'A satisfying act of defiance': Diary of Hector Fraser Dougall quoted in http://brendadougallmerriman.blogspot.com /2008/11/remembrance.html

p. 316 'Do enough for': 'Prison Commander's Fear', *New York Times*, 15 December 1918.

p. 316 'If he could do anything': IWM K90/2223 Collection of Newscuttings Relating to Major Jack William Shaw's Experiences as a Prisoner of War.

p. 317 'The conduct of': 'Huns and Our Prisoners', *Daily Mirror*, 25 October 1918.

p. 317 'Had assumed so entirely': IWM K90/2223 Newscuttings Relating to Major Jack William Shaw.

p. 317 'Rabbit, sausage': Diary of Hector Fraser Dougall quoted in op.cit.

p. 317 'But it was not advisable': Liddle POW 029 Reginald Gough papers.

p. 317 'Some prisoners were able': Diary of Hector Fraser Dougall, quoted in op.cit.

p. 318 'And if we were not': Liddle POW 029 Reginald Gough papers.

p. 318 'Some energetic attempt': 'German Brutality to Prisoners', *The Times*, 4 December 1918.

p. 318 'Two to three hundred': 'Cologne Before the British Entry', *The Times*, 13 December 1918, p. 7.

p. 318 'Struggle home': 'Huns' Last Crime the Greatest', *Daily Sketch*, 20 November 1918.

p. 318 'Being made to walk': 'Foodless Prisoners: British Fiat to Germans', *Daily Sketch*, 21 November 1918, p. 3.

p. 319 'Haig sent convoys': 'Haig to the Rescue', *Daily Sketch*, 23 November 1918, p. 23.

p. 320 'Everything in Germany': 'German Brutality', *The Times*, 4 December 1918, p. 8.

p. 320 'The present condition', 'Arrangements have been made': NA FO 383/442 Letter requesting information on Lieutenant Leslie Holman, interned at Holzminden prisoner-of-war camp.

p. 321 'Counted nearly 450', 'If you don't send': IWM K90/2223 Newscuttings Relating to Major Jack William Shaw.

p. 321 'Not a thing of use': Liddle POW 029 Reginald Gough papers.

p. 321 'Tables, chairs': James Whale, 'Our Life at Holzminden', p. 319.

p. 321 'Snatched their bayonets': Liddle POW 029 Reginald

Gough papers.

p. 322 'We cut their hoses', 'Got beautifully drunk': Diary of Hector Fraser Dougall quoted in op.cit.

p. 322–5 'A weird sight': Whale, 'Our Life at Holzminden', p. 319.

pp. 322–5 'Gentlemen: The war is over': IWM Misc 15/316 *A Parting Word*.

p. 325 'Put to the traditional': Robert Jackson, *The Prisoners 1914–18*, p. 153.

p. 325 'Watched with awe': Whale, 'Our Life at Holzminden', p. 319.

p. 325 'Packed in like sardines', 'A certain NCO', 'I am afraid': Liddle POW 029 Reginald Gough papers.

p. 326 'Bewhiskered': IWM K90/2223 Newscuttings Relating to Major Jack William Shaw.

p. 326 'Just let ourselves go': Whale, 'Our Life at Holzminden', p. 319.

p. 326 'Given welcome': IWM K90/2223 Newscuttings Relating to Major Jack William Shaw.

p. 326 'British India boat': IWM 76/206/1 Papers of Corporal A. Spaight.

p. 327 'Lines of torpedo boats': ibid.

p. 327 'The Queen joins me': http://www.royal.gov.uk/ Imagesand Broadcasts/TheQueenandtechnology.aspx

pp. 327–8 'The whole world': Whale, 'Our Life at Holzminden', p. 319.

p. 328 'Being practically': IWM K90/2223 Newscuttings Relating to Major Jack William Shaw.

p. 328 'Were you treated': Liddle POW 003 Norman A. Birks papers.

pp. 328–9 'It is not': NA HO 45/10763/270829 Committee on the Treatment by the Enemy of British Prisoners of War.

p. 329 'British "Black List"': Liddle POW 046 Richard Milward papers.

p. 329 'As part of the terms': NA FO 383/491 Recommendation by Attorney General to Mr Balfour.

p. 329 'Conflicting rumours', 'In 1923': Liddle POW 003 Norman A. Birks papers.

p. 330 'Fleeing to South America': IWM K90/2223 Newscuttings Relating to Major Jack William Shaw; and Richard Garrett, *P.O.W.*, p. 111.

p. 330 'It is to this man's cruelty': NA FO 383/399 Germany: Prisoners: Report on the Treatment by the Enemy of British Officers, Prisoners of War, under the 10th (Hannover) Army Corps.

p. 330 'Did the impossible', 'Proved one of the great truths': Liddle Tape 688 J. Bennett recollections.

EPILOGUE

p. 333 'Captain Lawrence and I', 'I cannot reveal': 'Saved War Comrade From Gaol', *Daily Mirror*, 13 January 1937, p. 2.

p. 334 'Killed in a crash', 'Shooting accident', ' Run over by a lorry': Barry Winchester, *Beyond the Tumult*, p. 189.

pp. 334–5 'Sixty-one former prisoners', 'To maintain the fellowship': V. C. Coombs, 'Sixty Years On', in *RAF Quarterly*, Summer 1996.

p. 335 'The Officer Prisoners': Liddle POW 016 V. C. Coombs papers.

p. 335 'A bully beef tin', 'Honorary Secretary': IWM 79/12/1 Papers of Lieutenant Colonel N. MacLeod.

p. 336 'Everyone within 1,000': ibid.

p. 336 'Croydon–Cape Town–Croydon': Liddle POW 002 Arthur Norman Barlow papers.

p. 336 'Goliath Cement Works': BL X.5292 and X.5293 Stanley Purves, Two Maps for the Escape from Holzminden.

p. 336 '4,500-acre orange farm': *Sunday Express*, 24 July 1938.

p. 336 'Lieutenant Churchill': *Sunday Dispatch*, 24 July 1938.

p. 336 'Bernard Luscombe': *The Times*, 24 February 1926.

p. 336 'Reginald Gough': Liddle POW 029 Reginald Gough papers.

NOTES

p. 337 'A man with an advertising', 'High official': *Sunday Express*, 24 July 1938.

p. 337 'Subject to alteration': IWM 79/12/1 Papers of Lieutenant Colonel N. MacLeod.

p. 337 'GREETINGS STOP': ibid.

p. 337 'Asiatic Petroleum Company': 'Memories of Their Tunnel Escape', *Evening News*, 2 May 1938.

pp. 337–8 'The full guest list': Court Circular, *The Times*, 25 July 1938; and IWM 79/12/1 Papers of Lieutenant Colonel N. MacLeod.

p. 338 'James Bennett': 'Candlelight Hero Recalls the Big Day', *Sunday Times*, 30 October 1977.

PICTURE ACKNOWLEDGEMENTS

Every effort has been made to seek out copyright holders. Those who have not been contacted are invited to get in touch with the publishers.

In the text:

17, 41, 57, 165, 191, 215: illustrations by C. E. B. Bernard from F. W. Harvey's *Comrades in Captivity*, 1920; 83, 129: by James Whale from *Wide World Magazine*, July 1919; 247: Tom Coulson at Encompass Graphics; 254: Tom Coulson at Encompass Graphics; 257: reproduced with the permission of Leeds University Library, Liddle Collection, POW 029 Gough; 281: from *Beyond the Tumult* by Barry Winchester, 1975; 313: *Daily Sketch* 18 December 1918; 331: Imperial War Museum/N. A. MacLeod 19/12/1

Picture sections

Photos are listed clockwise from top left.

First section

Occupants of *Kaserne* A at Holzminden: reproduced with the permission of Leeds University Library, Liddle Collection, AIR 005 J. M. Allen

Holzminden PoW Camp: Imperial War Museum/Q 69486;
cook-house: Imperial War Museum/P318 L. G. Nixon;
Hauptmann Karl Niemeyer: John Cash, Imperial War
Museum/MacLeod 79.12.1; illustration by James Whale from
Wide World Magazine, July 1919; 'A' House: Imperial War
Museum/ P318
L. G. Nixon

Camp money: courtesy Michael Melching; barrack-room
interior: Australian War Memorial/P05382_003; W. R. Shaw:
reproduced with the permission of Leeds University Library,
Liddle Collection, GS 1449 W. R. Shaw; prisoners' room:
Imperial War Museum /HU64562; prisoners'
bedroom: Imperial War Museum /L. G. Nixon 011222

Holzminden camp orchestra: reproduced with the permission
of Leeds University Library, Liddle Collection, POW 016 V. C.
Coombs; sports ground in winter: Imperial War
Museum/Q69485; playing hockey:
reproduced with the permission of Leeds University Library,
Liddle Collection, POW 003 N. A. Birks; football associated
with Major J. W. Shaw: Imperial War Museum/EPH 000816;
theatre group: reproduced
with the permission of Leeds University Library, Liddle
Collection,
POW 016 V. C. Coombs

'Aunty's home-made jam runs amok' by C. E. B. Bernard:
courtesy Adam Yates; 'You have der tins . . .': illustration by C. E.
B. Bernard from F. W. Harvey's *Comrades in Captivity*, 1920;
menu card, June 1918: reproduced with the permission of Leeds
University Library, Liddle Collection AIR 005 J. M. Allen; menu
card, Christmas 1917: reproduced with the permission of Leeds
University Library, Liddle Collection POW 004 J. H.
Birkinshaw; illustration by James Whale from *Wide World*

PICTURE ACKNOWLEDGEMENTS

Magazine, July 1919

Second section

Sketch plan: reproduced with the permission of Leeds University Library, Liddle Collection, ADD 001 D. R. Morrish

Two views of the tunnel after discovery: both John Cash, Imperial War Museum/N. A. MacLeod 79.12.1; section and plan of the stairs from *The Tunnellers of Holzminden* by G. Durnford, 1920; tunnel entrance: Imperial War Museum/N. A. MacLeod 79.12.1; wire cutters: Australian War Memorial/RELAWM01038 J. R. Cash

Panama hat associated with Captain. E. W. Leggatt; forage cap associated with Major J. W. Shaw; shaving brush with concealed information associated with Major J. W. Shaw; all Imperial War Museum/EPH3681; /EPH812; /EPH809; view of Holzminden: reproduced with the permission of Leeds University Library, Liddle Collection, POW 046 R. Millward; escape compass: Australian War Memorial/RELAWM16875; pair of moccasins: Imperial War Museum/EPH3683

Escapers in Holland from *Beyond the Tumult* by Barry Winchester, 1975; released prisoners on the *Takada*: reproduced with the permission of Leeds University Library, Liddle Collection, POW 003 N. A. Birks; 'A Peep into the Future' by C. E. B. Bernard: courtesy Adam Yates; group of exchanged prisoners in Holland: reproduced with the permission of Leeds University Library, Liddle Collection, POW 004 J. H. Birkinshaw; last prisoners leave Holzminden: Imperial War Museum/HU64562

Two views of the anniversary dinner: both Imperial War Museum/N. A. MacLeod 79.12.1

INDEX

INDEX

INDEX

INDEX

First Blitz

The Secret German Plan to Raze London to the Ground in 1918

By Neil Hanson

FAR FROM THE killing fields of France, a little-known battle was fought in the skies over London that nearly altered the course of the First World War, and with it the history of the twentieth century itself. The margin between survival and total destruction came down to less than one hour . . .

In four years, the Luftwaffe's England squadron had moved from crude canvas-and-wire light aircraft to four-engined giants as big as anything that flew in the Second World War. This, combined with the development of a revolutionary incendiary bomb, gave Germany the chance to raze London to the ground. It was a chance that they came within an ace of taking . . .

'The 1940s bombing raids over London have taken such a powerful grip upon our imagination that the existence of an earlier Blitz, in the First World War, will come to many readers as a complete surprise. Yet as Neil Hanson demonstrates in this gripping and well-researched book, it was in many ways more terrifying'

DAILY MAIL

'Clearly and engagingly written, his book puts more academic historians to shame by discovering a big subject, investigating it thoroughly and drawing bold but far-reaching conclusions from it'

SUNDAY TELEGRAPH

The Unknown Soldier
The Story of the Missing of the Great War

By Neil Hanson

'One of the best books I've read on the insanity of life in the trenches'
DAILY MAIL

OF ALL THE million British dead of the First World War, only one – the Unknown Soldier – was ever returned to his native land. An anonymous symbol of all those lost without trace in the carnage of the battlefields, he was laid to rest in Westminster Abbey amid an outpouring of grief that brought the whole nation to a standstill.

Drawing on largely unpublished letters and diaries, Neil Hanson has resurrected the lives and experiences of three unknown soldiers – a Briton, a German and an American. Every word is based on the testimony of those who fought, those who died and those who mourned at home; each life described in unforgettable detail.

Few books have ever shown the true and horrific reality of warfare, or told such a moving story of human life and loss. These rare insights into three soldiers' lives capture the Great War in all its profound tragedy.

'Stories to break the heart. An unforgettable picture of life in the hottest sectors of the Western Front'
NEW YORK TIMES

'Hanson, an excellent writer, skilfully blends an astonishing mine of information into an absorbing and moving narrative . . . fascinating'
LITERARY REVIEW

'Neil Hanson's prose (has) an almost unbearable poignancy . . . (and) all the sombre grandeur of the Beethoven funeral march'
SUNDAY TIMES

The Confident Hope of a Miracle

The True Story of the Spanish Armada

By Neil Hanson

'Continual destruction in the foretop, the pox above board, the plague between decks, hell in the forecastle and the devil at the helm.'

IT IS THE summer of 1588, and the fate and future of England hangs in the balance. Obsessed by the dream of reclaiming England for the Catholic Church, Philip II of Spain has assembled a huge fleet of castle-crowned galleons ripe for the task. Lying in wait in the Netherlands lies a battle-hardened Spanish army, ferocious professionals with a taste for rape, looting and atrocity.

Across the Channel the English are scraping together bands of barely trained men, many armed only with scythes, stakes or longbows. Great warning beacons stand all along the coast of England. Their only hope lies in the English Navy.

But Philip's Armada is doomed before it even leaves port. As soon as it engages with the English fleet, its shortcomings are clear in the face of superior tactics and firepower. Within hours, the mightiest fleet ever assembled is mercilessly harried into fleeing north, at the mercy of the elements and the dream of subduing the Protestant English lies in tatters.

A triumphant combination of historical detail and storytelling flair, *The Confident Hope of a Miracle* draws on undiscovered and little known personal papers and records to tell the epic story of the Spanish Armada in all its scope.

'The finest ever recreation of a monumental battle . . . Riveting stuff'
SUNDAY TIMES